THE KENNEDY FAMILY
and the Story of
Mental Retardation

THE KENNEDY FAMILY

and the Story of Mental Retardation

Edward Shorter

 Temple University Press
PHILADELPHIA

Temple University Press, Philadelphia 19122
Copyright © 2000 by Temple University
All rights reserved.
Published 2000
Printed in the United States of America

⊗The paper used in this publication meets the requirements of the American National
Standard for Information Sciences—Permanence of Paper for Printed Library Materials,
ANSI Z39.48–1984

Library of Congress Cataloging-in-Publication Data

Shorter, Edward, 1941–
    The Kennedy family and the story of mental retardation / Edward Shorter.
        p. cm.
    Includes bibliographical references and index.
    ISBN 1-56639-782-0 (alk. paper)—ISBN 1-56639-783-9 (pbk. : alk. paper)
        1. Mentally handicapped—Services for—United States.   2. Mental retardation—
United States.   3. Mental health promotion—United States.   4. Mental Health
Services—United States.   5. Kennedy family.   I. Title.

    HV3006.A4 s65 2000
    362.3'8'0973—dc21
                                                                                    00-020338

ISBN 13: 978-1-56639-783-4 (pbk : alk. paper)

050708P

In memory of Elizabeth Boggs

Contents

Preface

The history of mental retardation (MR) is massively important, and almost nobody knows anything about it. Approximately 2 percent of America's children are born with mental retardation. Prospective parents agonize about testing for Down Syndrome and other genetic diseases that may cause MR.

Today, people with mental retardation are at center stage of the large disabilities scene. Most people with MR live in group homes or are otherwise cared for in humane settings, unlike the grim institutions in which they once dwelled. Just as with issues of race, gender, and physical disabilities, a concerned nation has taken up the cause of mental retardation and vowed to give those with MR a chance to develop themselves as individuals. This didn't happen accidentally but, in large part, because of the focus on MR issues of one of this nation's best-known families.

Under the leadership of Eunice Kennedy Shriver, sister of John F. Kennedy, the Kennedys embraced MR in the same way other great families took on various special causes. The Macys and medical research come immediately to mind. The Kennedys never donated huge amounts of money, but they provided a more precious commodity that ultimately made a greater difference than money: leadership. By studying the Kennedys' resolve to apply their considerable political power to the cause of the mentally retarded, readers can learn a great deal about how one makes a difference.

Many people are sincerely concerned about social problems and dedicated to their resolution. Yet how, exactly, does one make a difference? This is not an easy question to answer.

This book shows how the Kennedys were able to translate concern and dedication into a concrete policy agenda, into social programs that would matter to the lives of millions of individuals. Eunice, her mother Rose, her brother Bobby, her husband Sarge—all were able to ensure that well-intentioned policies ended up with successful outcomes.

A word about how this book happened. I had a lucky accident. In the course of my previous research on the history of psychiatry, a quite separate study, I became aware of the untold history of mental retardation and of the role of the Kennedys in finding solutions. Through an act of considerable generosity (and taking a big chance that I wasn't looking for "dirt"), Eunice Kennedy Shriver and her husband Sargent Shriver threw open to me not only their personal and family records, held at the family foundation in Washington, D.C., but also the Kennedy papers in the John F. Kennedy Presidential Library in Boston, including the records of Joseph P. Kennedy, Sr. No historian has ever received such exceptional access to the Kennedy papers before. The very richness of this material detoured me from writing a general history of MR to writing an account of MR and the Kennedy family. The present book is thus more narrowly conceived than what I first had in mind. But the story is an extraordinary one.

One must, however, be careful about claiming too much. The Kennedys were not the only players in the campaign to prevent mental retardation and improve the lives of the mentally retarded. Academic scientists, social activists, and especially the parents' movement played key roles. It is indeed to Elizabeth Boggs, one of the most forceful of the parent-activists, that this book is dedicated. However, we don't have space in this volume for the entire history of efforts on behalf of the mentally retarded, and I have omitted the saga of the parents' early efforts as well as much of the later political infighting in which the parents' organization, the National Association for Retarded Children, was active.

I didn't know any of the Kennedys before starting this project, and I have seen none of them since (nor did they aid in any way in the preparation of the book). Therefore, this book is in no sense an autho- rized account. But as I plunged into the material, into the stories of old Joe Kennedy dealing with Cardinal Cushing in Boston, or young Eunice Kennedy's steely determination to dedicate her life to something other than tennis and bridge, I realized that these people really did make a difference. Eunice and her branch of the family had always been serious about dedicating themselves to public service, and mental retardation presented them with a chance to relieve one of the most ignored and desperate social problems facing the country in those years: the millions of children with MR who languished in foul institutions or were cooped up at home together with their desperate parents. There is a lot about the Kennedys in this book that will appeal to aficionados of the history of this great and tragic family. There is much in here about the lives of the mentally retarded and their brave parents for those whose hearts will rise at the telling of this saga. Putting the Kennedys and those with MR together in the same book is unconventional, but it's a story whose time has come.

SOME THANKS are in order. My good friend Michael Levine helped this manuscript to see the light of day in various ways. Erika Steffer and Susan Bélanger did splendid service as research assistants. Andrea Clark, the administrator of the History of Medicine Program at the University of Toronto, has to be thanked for providing a protective cover that let me spend time researching and writing. It is, I realize, tedious for readers to see in such acknowledgments mention of the interlibrary loan people of the author's university. Yet I could not let this opportunity pass without mentioning their dedicated work. For comments upon earlier drafts, I should like to thank Edward Berkowitz, Robert Cooke, Gerald Grob, and James Hilty. Anne Marie Shorter affectionately provided the author with comfort and sustenance throughout the writing of this book, and my gratitude to her is profound. Janet Francendese of Temple University Press has been most helpful. I am also terribly grateful for the fine editorial work of Yvonne Ramsey.

Toronto, Canada

THE KENNEDY FAMILY

and the Story of
Mental Retardation

Useless People

The Kennedy family targeted mental retardation with good cause. In the 1950s, the mentally retarded were among the most scorned, isolated, and neglected groups in American society. Mental retardation was viewed as a hopeless, shameful disease, and those afflicted with it were shunted from sight as soon as possible. "There is no cure, no hope, no future," said one author, summing up social attitudes. "If you are once a mental retardate, you remain one always."[1]

Mental retardation involves inadequate development of the brain in the womb or during childhood so that the person acquires subaverage intellectual functioning (below 70 IQ) and is unable to meet the stresses of daily life. MR affects about 2 percent of the U.S. population. Other developmental disabilities that strike in childhood, such as epilepsy or cerebral palsy (CP), also affect the brain—and may overlap with MR—yet they do not necessarily affect intelligence. There are many causes of MR. Some, such as Down Syndrome, are chromosomal in nature and involve the genetic material. Others are acquired in utero or in early childhood.[2] In up to half of all cases of MR, the actual cause is unknown. Yet, in the past, all converged to make the child an outcast, a social pariah, and that is the point of this chapter: that historically, people with MR were seen as useless, marginalized at the rim of society and deemed to be nothing more than burdens.

No agency of the federal government devoted itself to MR children, no foundation took up their cause, and the tiny voice of the nascent parents' movement barely made itself heard in the media and the corridors of power. Some parents would send their MR children off to institutions and then publish notices of their death in the local papers.[3] And when a child did die in these stinking MR asylums, he or she might be buried in an unmarked or numbered grave. This seemed fitting and proper for children thought to be lacking in their full humanity. Parents of retarded children could only welcome death for their afflicted offspring, said Pearl Buck, a Nobel prize winner and herself the mother of a retarded daughter.[4] That was in 1950.

If You Had a Mentally Retarded Child

If you had a mentally retarded child in 1950, what would you do? What choices were there?

The initial news was often shattering. As parents with mentally retarded children looked back, their reaction to the discovery of the baby's condition stood out with crystal clarity. Crozet Duplantier, sports editor of the *New Orleans States-Item,* recalled hearing in 1956 the news from his wife when their baby boy, their first son after two daughters, was about a year old. "I'll never forget the words," he recalled. "Chris is retarded," his wife said. "He's a mongoloid [a Down Syndrome child]."

Duplantier's world "stood still for a moment." He remembered the same feeling in his stomach as when he was machine-gunned by the Japanese on the beach at Guadalcanal. But unlike combat, he said, "This problem would not go away. I was weak, sick, near despair as I realized that my first son was going to be a child all his life."[5]

Mrs. X, a housewife in New Haven, Connecticut, first learned the news from her own mother, who had cared for the baby while Mrs. X was still convalescing from the delivery. Three weeks after the baby's birth Mrs. X's mother told her, "He is not a well child."

"Not a mongolian idiot!"

"Yes," her mother said.

Mrs. X "went into hysterics." "I couldn't wait to get to the hospital. I couldn't wait! They didn't want me to go and tried to stop me. . . ." Now she knew why her husband "didn't get too enthusiastic about all my plans and hopes for the baby those three weeks. I couldn't understand his reaction."[6]

When Grover Powers, head of pediatrics at Yale, broke the news to another New Haven couple whose child had not sat up after twelve months, the mother "ran down the stairs crying with the baby" while the husband paid Dr. Powers. When she got back into the car with the friends who had driven them to the doctor's office, she was crying so hard she couldn't "tell them what was the matter."[7]

After parents recovered from the initial shock of an MR diagnosis for their child, shame was the next emotion they had to confront. In the high-functioning days of mid-century America, there was something fundamentally shameful about low intelligence. A diagnosis of MR for one's child suggested that perhaps you yourself—as the parent—were at fault because bad blood coursed through your veins. Pearl Buck's baby Carol was born in China in 1921. Pearl Buck recalled how accepting the Chinese were of any infirmity, and if they noticed anything at all would just laugh with the baby. But then one day on the streets of Shanghai, Buck learned that not everyone was so kind. "Two young American women walked along the street, newcomers from my own country, I suppose by their smart garments. They stared at my child and when we had passed one of them said to the other, 'The kid is nuts.'" From that day on, Buck began to shield her daughter.[8]

Upon returning to the States, Buck realized in common with other parents of MR children that the embarrassment was collective. "Parents have been bewildered and ashamed when their child is backward, when he cannot learn in school, when perhaps he cannot even learn to talk. . . . Neighbors whisper that So-and-so's child is 'not right.'" The parents pretend, perhaps, that the child is only slow. "The shame of the parents infects all the children and sorrow spreads its blight."[9]

If you elected to keep your child at home in 1950 rather than in an institution, you might conceal the child from neighbors. "Until the 1950s," said Wolf Wolfensberger, an MR specialist at the University of Syracuse who was to become a leader of the anti-institutional movement, "parents of handicapped children were isolated," hiding their children away "in attics and closets and sheds and basements."[10] Neighbors might say, "I don't want my child playing with the retarded. It may rub off."[11]

Thus, many parents were literally trapped along with their MR children. As Mr. G. of Brooklyn, the parent of a retarded daughter, wrote to a sympathetic congressman, "One cannot wholly comprehend the enormity of this problem, until they or their loved ones have been pierced by [this] arrow. . . . For some reason or other my child has refused to go out of doors. As a result she has been confined to her home for nearly eight long years.

"As a result my wife and I have gradually become a part of her own secluded little world. Now we are both beginning to feel that the walls are gradually closing in on us."

Mr. G. included in his letter to this congressman a poem he had written about his daughter:

Forgotten and bewildered she craves for affection,
Always looking for kindness, love and protection.
Her room full of toys yet this child is so sad
Because her only companions are Mommy and Dad.

A doll in the corner and one on her chair
Sitting so quietly the loneliness to share.
The sun fills the room to brighten her day,
But the neighborhood children with her do not play.[12]

Like the G.'s, other parents would find themselves withdrawing from life, from former friends and acquaintances. Said one New Haven mother in the mid-1950s, "I stayed a little more in the park by myself. . . . Rarely did we get a call from our friends any more." She avoided other people with children. "There would be hard feelings."[13] One mother wrote to Eunice Kennedy Shriver, the member of the Kennedy family most dedicated to the cause of mental retardation, "Mrs. Shriver, my son is like the Christ Child. No one will take him in."[14]

So the task of raising the child would be solely on the parents' shoulders, and this vacuum of social isolation made it enormously difficult for parents to cope with their mentally retarded children. Aside from a community program in Minnesota going back to around 1920, there was virtually no local help to give a mother relief, no schooling for seriously retarded children. The philosophy of the day was, "Let the institution do it; it's their job."[15]

And so, in the pattern of the stay-at-home wife of the 1950s, mothers of MR children would stay at home, too. But unlike other mothers who had friends and community activities and for whom life seemed full, the mother of a special child had few options for socializing, for herself or her child. She would end up devoting her life to that child. Dale Evans, a country singer who was a movie star in her own right and wife of cowboy actor Roy Rogers, recalled the frantic struggle to get the baby to smile. This was in the early 1950s. The pediatrician kept asking her to make the child smile. "He said if a baby didn't smile until he was three months old, it meant that he was at least fifty per cent retarded in his mental growth." Dale "worked overtime" getting that baby to smile. She "had always been 'career minded.'" Even when she was a young girl she wanted to succeed, and succeed *big*, in show business, and for a long time she put that career before everything else in her life." But after Baby Robin arrived, in August 1950, "it didn't seem to mean so much to her, after all."[16]

For those materially less well situated than the Rogers family, MR meant an endless round of visiting doctors and waiting in clinics, hoping finally to get an exact diagnosis or some promise of therapy. The following example is one day in the quest of "Mrs. Brown," who lived in the Boston region, to establish what was the matter with her child: "We went to the clinic at 9 a.m. and it was 2 p.m. before we could get in to see the doctor. They wouldn't tell you when your name was coming up so you could go out for a sandwich. It was terribly disturbing because of all those screaming kids . . . all those deformed kids with their mothers changing and bottling them."

Then in walked one of "Dr. Black's" private patients. In two minutes she was seen.

"Oh boy," thought Mrs. Brown, "this is the way to go."[17] But one had to be relatively well-to-do to become a private patient of the few doctors knowledgeable about MR.

Yet the parents who looked back wanted their bravery, rather than their despair, emphasized. It was a matter of pride to them that they kept their heads above water, and with apparent effortlessness to the outside world. But how exhausting it was to *seem* to be a well-adjusted MR parent. Janet Bennett, herself the mother of a Down Syndrome child, remembered watching another mother in a shoe store as that mother's "mongoloid daughter marched up and down among the racks, humming, clapping her hands, talking to her image in the mirror. Every bone, muscle, and nerve in the mother's body was concentrated on the task of appearing composed, at ease, unembarrassed." It was not enough to be just the child's mother, said Bennett. "What was more important was the role of 'well-adjusted parent,' of conveying the message to an ever-observing public that she was managing, she was doing well; it was not getting her down." The mother presented to Bennett's practiced glance "a picture of someone very hard at work in service to a relentless awareness."[18] This relentless awareness was part of the cost of not putting the child in an institution.

It never stopped. Whether proud or humble, rich or poor, women who chose to keep their MR children at home endured a life of little else save caring for those afflicted children—as a report in 1974 by Marian Wright Edelman of the Children's Defense Fund put it—"all day, every day, for years, without outside support for [the children's] learning or their family's relief."[19]

What about putting the child in an institution? Although many mildly retarded children did stay at home, a significant number of those with severe retardation who reached adulthood did at some point in their lives find their way into an MR institution.[20] The institution towered over the MR scene in the first half of the twentieth century—a physician's first recourse, a last possibility for desperate parents.

Doctor's Orders

There were a few good institutions, such as the Vineland Training School in Vineland, New Jersey, where the numbers were small and the staff provided dedicated and caring service. Yet the vast majority of institutions for the mentally retarded were hell-holes. How could parents have consigned their children to such places?

The extraordinary policy of putting children in retardation warehouses far from home sprang mainly from the doctors. Thousands of parents were willing to contemplate saying goodbye forever to their small children—for that is what institutionalization truly entailed—only because their doctors were urging them to do so. Virtually all physicians immediately and insistently advised the parents to put the child away.

The experts of the day hammered this theme into medical audiences. At a 1947 meeting of the American Association on Mental Deficiency (AAMD)—the chief professional organization dealing with MR at the time—C. Anderson Aldrich, a pediatrician at the Mayo Clinic, called for "separation of Mongolian idiots from their mothers immediately after birth." He advised physicians to explain to the mother "that the child is not strong enough to be brought to her for a few days." Meanwhile, the father and relatives would be told that "no one is to blame" and the baby would be whisked away.[21]

Family doctors followed such advice unswervingly. When the doctor spotted "Mongoloid symptoms" in the three-week-old baby of Dale Evans and Roy Rogers, he told them to "put the baby in a 'home.'" It was what he always advised in situations like this: "They'd have to give the child up sometime, anyway, and it was easier to do it quickly, before the child became entrenched in their hearts." After the doctor left, Dale Evans was "so stunned she couldn't answer." Roy said no.[22]

In 1947, kindly old "Dr. Albert" of Bloomington, Indiana, told John and Lorraine Frank, whose baby was born with MR, "Once it is clear that a child is hopelessly subnormal, there isn't any question about the wisdom of institutionalizing the child." Even though Lorraine might not intend to, the Franks would harm the child by keeping him at home, said Dr. Frank, and they would harm themselves as well. After this conversation, John Frank decided to place his young lad in an institution: it would be best for all.[23]

One imagines the parents' helplessness in the face of their child's condition, and in their dependency upon the physician for advice. For many families, the crisis would come after the child's first seizure (or "fit" as such episodes were once called)—a bewildering and terrifying event. (MR children often suffer damage to their central nervous systems, which may cause convulsions.) John Murray was just leaving the house for work one day when his wife Emily called him back urgently. "John, come!"

"I rushed into Little John's room to find him on his back, a large puddle of vomit on the sheet, his eyes open and not seeing. His body twitched symmetrically—feet and legs, fingers and arms, even cheeks and eyebrows—and his voice box was emitting soft, regular grunts or groans." They took Little John to the hospital, where the doctor told them, "There's no hope at all."[24] Throughout their ordeal, the advice of all the doctors had been to put the child "away." The medical hammering was relentless.

Why were physicians in those days so gloomy when faced with mental retardation? It was partly a problem of ignorance. They had not studied MR in the medical school curriculum. As for clinical experience, the only place one could get it was in the horrible MR institutions. "The official way to train physicians in mental retardation," said Gunnar Dybwad, a psychologist who was one of the pioneers of the reform movement, "was to take them on a visit to the nearest state institution, where they were shown the worst clinical cases. Invariably some physicians went out and vomited because they couldn't take it. They took an oath never to look at one of those places again."[25] So that's how most physicians were introduced to MR—never again to return to the subject!

It is no surprise, therefore, that the vast majority of doctors believed mental retardation to be hopeless, its victims incapable of development and bereft of their essential humanity. The family could only benefit by being spared the presence of such a "vegetable."

Believing MR to be untreatable, physicians resented their own therapeutic helplessness. Parents who kept their children at home would present the doctor with a continual reminder of his own medical impotence. Though physicians did not say this aloud, it is clear that at a deeper psychological level some of them wanted the child out of sight because retardation was not within the compass of what they considered themselves to do well: diagnose and treat acute illness. As Sargent Shriver, Eunice Kennedy Shriver's husband, said of those days, "Doctors like to treat patients they can cure. If you deal with mental retardation, what the hell. . . ."[26]

Participating in the conversation with Shriver was Robert Cooke, the Shrivers' adviser and head of pediatrics at Johns Hopkins University in the late 1950s. Cooke added, "So few people went into mental retardation because there was no cure. Why does anybody want to go into a field where you can't cure the patient?"[27] Cooke himself did not share this attitude of therapeutic nihilism. (He taught that medicine must be "as concerned with care as cure.")[28] Yet only such thinking could explain the singular brusqueness and lack of feeling with which physicians often approached parents dependent upon them for advice.

Renowned MR specialist, "Dr. Graham," telling the Franks the prognosis of their son, said, "It is too bad that John Peter did not die at the time of that second severe seizure in Bloomington.

"If his case runs in the normal pattern, it will go something like this. He will be very slow in everything. . . . He will never be able to talk.

"Sometime between the ages of four and six, if he can run around, he may be impossible for your wife to manage. He may be hitting and biting."

An operation, said Dr. Graham, might arrest momentarily the lad's downward course, "and you may think thereafter that he is improving. But he won't be. If it doesn't happen before that, he will sooner or later get some kind of simple infection . . . and he will die. There is nothing left to hope for except that he will not be too miserable until that time comes."[29] What parent could not have emerged sobbing and despondent from such a brutal consultation?

Above all, blame fell upon the psychiatrists. Before the mid-1950s, it had been psychiatrists who chaired state mental health commissions (under whose ambit MR fell) and who often ran MR institutions. But the psychoanalytic movement, based upon Sigmund Freud's doctrines, grew explosively in the United States after the World War II, and it was under the influence of psychoanalysis that psychiatry washed its hands of MR. The analysts had breathtakingly erroneous notions of the causes of MR, believing mental retardation to be the result of faulty parent-child dynamics, of "refrigerator mothers" and the like. And the analysts certainly had little interest in the treatment of retarded children, believing them inaccessible to psychotherapy, the only kind of therapy that analysts were capable of providing.

In 1947, George S. Stevenson, the medical director of the National Committee for Mental Hygiene in New York, indicted his psycho-analytically-oriented colleagues for their abandonment of the mentally retarded. Unlike former times, when people like Dr. Walter Fernald, an enlightened institution director in Waltham, Massachusetts, sponsored community MR clinics, "Today . . . child guidance clinics do not want to accept the mentally deficient. 'You can't do psychotherapy with them.'" Stevenson noted that psychoanalysis had given "the coup de grace to the field of mental deficiency. Its spirit began to ebb."[30]

Yet having no one else to turn to, parents still sought out psychiatrists and, in the 1950s, would receive from them what was basically grief coun-seling rather than developmental advice about their mentally retarded child. At a meeting of MR professionals in 1956, Salvatore DiMichael, executive director of the National Association for Retarded Children, criticized physicians for redirecting their concerns from the child's development to the emotional dynamics of the marriage. Physicians were "ascrib[ing] parental behavior, no matter what it was, to the emotions of guilt and shame, as though one were dealing with parents in phases of abnormal behavior." In other words, doctors saw parents' efforts to improve the child's lot as evidence of psychopathology on the part of parents, who needed instead to passively accept their child's condition.[31] And passive acceptance meant the decision to institutionalize.

The Decision

Sooner or later families with MR children would have to confront the "all-or-nothing proposition," as disability scholar Stanley Herr put it. They would have to face either lifelong commitment of the child in a state institution or "the financial and social burdens of care alone."[32]

"But he is so tiny, and sweet, and so beautiful," said the Murrays to each other. "Is there to be nothing more?"[33] If the decision to institutionalize at the doctor's urging was not made during the child's infancy, institutionalization would sometimes occur later as the child, lacking school and neighborhood playmates, became restive in the confinement of the home. Elizabeth and Fitzhugh Boggs, two early activists in the parents' movement, felt they could no longer manage their profoundly retarded child David after he started, at age five or six, to move about on his own. He required constant supervision. "We built a fence three feet high around the house," Elizabeth Boggs said later. "He got to where he could climb that—and he didn't know to stay out of the road." He slept much less than his parents, "and he loved to make noises. It got to where Fitzhugh was falling asleep at work." The Boggs decided to place David, at the age of seven, in a private institution on the New Jersey shore. "When we came home from delivering him," said Elizabeth, "I broke down totally. It is a very difficult thing to be separated from your child. You feel a strong sense that you have failed."[34]

Pearl Buck described dropping her daughter off at the Vineland Training School. "In the afternoon of that day which was so dreadful in its passing the head asked me to come to the assembly hall." Buck, having spent many years in China, was asked to say a few words about her experiences with Chinese children. She stood on the platform "and saw before me hundreds of children's faces looking up at me. What heartache loomed behind each one, what years of pain, what tears, what frightful disappointment and despair! They were here for life, prisoners of their fate. And among them, one of them, my child must henceforth be."[35]

If Vineland was the Ritz of the institutional world, one can imagine the shock awaiting parents who brought their children to the overcrowded state institutions. "Your boy is now a ward of the state," the Reillys were told when they dropped their child, age ten, off at the facility at Medical Lake in Washington State. "If you are wise, you will go home, have other children and forget him." (Newland Reilly, a Spokane newspaperman, was so enraged at hearing this that he destroyed the later career of this superintendent.)[36]

Some parents chickened out. One mother, during the admission interview, was told that her son "would be placed in the 'worst building' with 140 residents, most substantially older than he. . . . She was told that she could not see her son until three months after his admission." The mother learned that "most of the residents in the dormitory were nude and many were abusive in their behavior. She learned that there were no chairs in the dormitory because the 'State' did not provide them. In answer to the question, 'Do the residents have anything to do?' the admitting physician replied, 'No.'" The mother thereupon withdrew her application, despite the family doctor's warning that she herself could no longer care for the child.[37]

Another family tried to postpone the day of reckoning by writing Senator Edward Kennedy. "Dear Senator Kennedy," said the mayor of a small coal town in West Virginia, "I am writing to you in behalf of Mr. and Mrs. Y. . . . They are the parents of a twenty-one-year-old mentally retarded son, William.

"For the past twenty-one years, William has received the best possible care. He has been treated as an equal by his family. The townspeople have also treated him as an equal and have gone out of their way to help him.

"Recently, William has become a problem to his family. His behavior has become aggressive towards others. His family doctor referred him to a state mental institution, but his family won't commit him because of the filthy conditions of the state institutions in this area." The family could not afford a private institution. Could Senator Kennedy help?[38]

Most heartrending of all were those parents who had not a clue about what awaited them when they traveled "Heartbreak Road"—as the road to the Southbury Training School in Connecticut was called—to drop their children off. "I took my friend Lois because I had to have someone," said a New Haven mother who was bringing her son to be admitted. "Daniel walked right away from me and went to pushing a chair across the floor. I remember going into the dayroom and seeing all those children. It was so barren. And all those naked kids running around. And my Daniel came up there all dressed up, long pants and a blazer. I had brought up fifty dollars worth of clothes and they had no clothes on. I burst out crying." The mother tried to take Daniel away. The matron seized her and physically ejected her.[39]

What kind of institutions were these?

Early Days

The world has not always been gentle with the mentally retarded. Martin Luther, the early-sixteenth-century Protestant reformer, advocated killing them. In the year 1540 in the town of Dessau, Luther had seen a twelve-year-old boy who "did nothing but gorge himself as much as four peasants or threshers. He ate, defecated and drooled and, if anyone tackled him, he screamed. If things didn't go well, he wept."

Luther believed the child to be a "changeling," a "mass of flesh" with no soul whom the Devil had corrupted. Luther told the Prince of Anhalt, "If I were the Prince, I should take this child to the Moldau River . . . and drown him." When the prince refused to follow this advice, Luther counseled that the local congregation pray "that the dear Lord take the Devil away." This was done, and the boy was dead within a year.[40]

In time, Western society abandoned the view that the retarded represented devilish changelings. But it did not abandon the notion that the retarded were lacking in a basic dimension of their humanity. The treatment that mentally retarded people in the 1800s received from their families and villages defies belief. When the mental health reformer Dorothy Dix toured Massachusetts in the early 1840s "as the advocate of helpless, forgotten, insane and idiotic men and women," she encountered conditions that shocked the members of the Massachusetts legislature:

Medford—"One idiotic subject chained, and one in a close stall for 17 years."

Bridgewater—"Three idiots; never removed from one room."

Cohasset—"One idiot, one insane; most miserable condition."[41]

Other sources give a less grim impression of the situation for those who were, at least, moderately retarded: they were not bound in chains or confined in narrow rooms but were allowed to exist in the community on the same terms as everyone else. Charles Dickens, in his novel *Little Dorrit* of the mid-1850s, allows the mentally retarded Maggy to sound slightly foolish and drop her potatoes carelessly, picking them up again along with "a great quantity of mud." But Maggy ran errands, earned her own living, and was not in essential matters much different from the mass of nonretarded working-class Londoners.[42] If Maggy fit smoothly into the surrounding world, it was because few working-class people of her day required much formal education. Stevedores, carters, and chimney sweeps, they worked in an industrial, urban society that was as yet scarcely literate, where intelligence was neither highly valued nor in demand among the laboring orders.

With the advent of universal primary education and the need for a skills-based rather than a brawn-based labor force, the situation began to change for the mentally retarded. Those who were not intellectually agile were devalued. Henry Goddard, one of the early psychologists specializing in MR, explained this crucial new feature in the lives of the retarded:

> While these children in an earlier and simpler form of life might be able to learn and do enough to make their way in the world . . . in these days of stricter competition, in these days of machinery requiring judgment for its management, in these days when the hundred and one occupations which used to be performed upon the farm are now performed in the shop and the larger part of farming and other industrial work is done by machinery, it requires a higher degree of intelligence than formerly and those children who are just a little below the line in mental ability are no longer able to take their part in the world.[43]

That was in 1911.

This opinion was not mere ranting on the part of a man who believed, as Goddard did, in genetic degeneration as the cause of retardation. In 1981, Elizabeth Boggs said that in the high-powered modern "economic and social marketplaces," mentally retarded people would find themselves left behind because they are less productive than their nonretarded counterparts: "They are deficient in competitive competence in a competitive culture."[44]

Those left behind in a competitive marketplace are by no means in a hopeless situation. They may still contribute and lead fulfilling lives, but they must be trained. And here lay the origins of the first institutions for the retarded in the United States. They began as training schools in the mid-nineteenth century.

In 1848, two boarding schools for children with MR were founded in Massachusetts. One was public, its funding approved by the legislature in May of that year; the school was to be directed by Samuel Howe and situated in Boston in a wing of a school for the blind. The other was private, founded by Hervey Wilbur in his own home in the town of Barre. (The private school at Barre existed into the twentieth century. The public school established its own quarters in South Boston as the Massachusetts School for the Feeble-Minded, then moved in 1893 to Waltham.)

In 1853, New York State followed, its legislature authorizing an MR training school in Syracuse with construction beginning the following year.[45] By the end of the 1850s, other training schools were created at Columbus, Ohio (1857), and Lakeville, Connecticut (1858). A private school that originated in 1852 in Germantown, Pennsylvania, first tried various locations and eventually settled in 1857 in Media, Pennsylvania. Initially called the Pennsylvania School for Feeble-Minded Children, it was later named Elwyn Training School after Alfred Elwyn, a prominent early supporter. The Elwyn school accepted a number of public-supported residents.[46]

Intellectually, the guiding spirit behind much of this innovation was a Frenchman, Edouard Seguin, who migrated to America in 1850 at the age of thirty-eight. Working with the mentally retarded in France, Seguin had discovered that if given sufficient coaching, they could make great progress. He devised an elaborate system of drills for MR children of all levels that included a healthy dose of physical exercise.[47] Seguin briefly joined the staff of the institution at Syracuse in 1854 and later established his own "Physiological School" at Orange, New Jersey. Thus, he functioned generally as the guiding light of early American MR educators.[48]

Animated by the desire to reform and improve, these early institutions resembled boarding schools more than asylums and treated their charges more like pupils than inmates, or "residents" as they came to be called. The boys and girls boarded only until age sixteen. They spent two-month summer vacations at home and often journeyed home as well on frequent visiting days. Admission and discharge were entirely voluntary, and there were no uniforms. The early institutions virtually all followed Seguin's views that the educational plan must be tailored to the special needs of each pupil.[49] Unlike the later custodial institutions, these early training schools had high discharge rates: between 1853 and 1870, the Elwyn school's was 50 percent.[50]

In the 1870s, however, quite a different note began to sound in the development of MR institutions. In 1871, the Elwyn Training School added a custodial department for mentally retarded people of all ages.[51] In 1878, the Syracuse school established at Newark, New York, a branch "for women who were too old for the Syracuse institution but were unsuitable for discharge." (This institution put particular emphasis on segregating women of "childbearing age.")[52] A fatal evolution was at work here. As the children taught by these training schools matured, their families were refusing to take them back. Having nowhere else to place them, the training schools had to keep them on as adults. Boarding schools for mentally retarded children were becoming custodial asylums where residents became inmates on a lifelong basis.[53]

From this hesitant trickle in the 1870s, the custodial movement turned into a torrent in the 1890s. Not only did many of the former training schools establish custodial wings, such as those at Lincoln, Illinois (1890), and Faribault, Minnesota (1894). The new MR institutions of the 1890s were supposed to serve simultaneously as schools and custodial asylums. Thus, the four hundred inmates at the Missouri Colony for the Feeble-Minded at Marshall, established in 1899, were all admitted under court order, meaning they were not to leave.[54] In 1894, a sixteen hundred-bed asylum opened at Rome, New York, "for the custodial care of the feeble-minded."[55]

In the years before World War I, many other large institutions opened. The population of such places rose by 340 percent between 1880 and 1905.[56] These MR asylums emphasized the lifelong confinement of mentally retarded people under court order rather than training them during adolescence for discharge to the community as adults. This was a very different proposition from the training schools of the mid-nineteenth century.

Genetic Alarm

Before the 1890s, MR institutions had emphasized the melioration of retardation and even, they hoped, its cure through education and training. This approach fit well with the generally liberal political philosophy that pervaded mid-nineteenth-century American society as a whole, with its preference for social improvement through self-betterment. After 1890, a sea change occurred. Writers on MR began to emphasize the permanence of mental retardation and to evoke the dangers that the mentally retarded posed for the surrounding social order. This approach went hand-in-glove with the doctrine of genetic alarm, which insisted that retardation was inherited as a dominant "Mendelian" characteristic, meaning that if one of your parents had it, you had a 50 percent chance of getting it, too.

Lurking in the background of this half-cocked genetics was a larger social philosophy called Social Darwinism, which held that in international politics only the strongest nations, and in the community only the strongest individuals, had the right to survive.[57] Indeed said the Social Darwinists, nature herself had preordained this triumph of the strong as a part of the process that Darwin had called natural selection. The mentally retarded unfortunately were weak. Useless people, they had no contribution to make to society and should simply be warehoused until weeded out by premature death.

The superintendents of MR institutions did not work these ideas out on their own. American society as a whole borrowed them in the years after 1880 from the Europeans: from psychiatrists, such as Benedict-Augustin Morel in France, who in 1857 argued that psychiatric illness resulted from intellectual and moral "degeneracy," a condition that was inherited and that became worse as it was passed from generation to generation. These notions also came from geneticists such as Sir Francis Galton, who in the late nineteenth century introduced the term "eugenics"—the improvement of "the inborn qualities of the race" by breeding in good characteristics and breeding out bad ones.[58]

As these ideas crossed the ocean, they landed in the world of mental retardation via two somewhat different channels: the institution supervisors, who already in the 1870s were speaking of protecting society from retarded degenerates; and a rather progressive group of psychologists who, although they did believe in "poisoned blood" and the like, also thought the mentally retarded capable of being educated (and who laid the groundwork of the special education movement).

It was no accident that the private institution at the Elwyn asylum village became the first to acquire a custodial department, for there Isaac Kerlin held court. Kerlin had come to Elwyn as an assistant physician in 1857, shortly thereafter becoming director and remaining in that position until his death in 1893. Beginning in the mid-1880s, Kerlin launched a sustained assault in print upon the mentally retarded, calling them, for example, in 1884 a "tremendous burden to the thrifty tax-payer, who must be protected from the rapacious social ills which deplete his own strength."[59] Even more influential was Walter Fernald, director of the Massachusetts School for the Feeble-Minded in Waltham. Although Fernald did much to further the anatomical understanding of MR and the sympathetic care of mentally retarded people, he was at heart a degenerationist.[60] In 1912 he said that "the only way to reduce the number of the feeble-minded is to prevent their birth. The perpetuation of defective family stocks should be inhibited." Indeed, Massachusetts had already begun such a policy. "This segregation carried on thoroughly for a generation would largely reduce the amount of feeble-mindedness."[61]

Kerlin and Fernald were powerful voices, advocating the systematic herding of all mentally retarded persons into giant institutions where they would remain: for women, until they had completed their childbearing years; for men—inherently dangerous and criminal—until death.

State laws started to become much more restrictive for the mentally retarded.[62] Parole from the Rome Asylum became highly curtailed. In 1918, New York State created a central registry of all mentally retarded persons to monitor their breeding and take charge of their defective offspring. With New York's new Mental Deficiency Law of 1919, paroles, furloughs, and voluntary committals came to an end. Institutions became places, as Stanley Herr put it, of "absolute incarceration."[63]

This rhetoric had a decidedly authoritarian flavor. In 1920, Helen Mac-Murchy (the inspector general of MR institutions in Ontario), speaking in tones that would not have been unfamiliar to the budding totalitarian movements in Europe, called the mentally retarded "permanent children [who] need permanent parents." "We must make a happy and permanent home for them during their lives," she said. "The only Permanent Parent is the State."[64]

How things had changed since the sunny 1850s! By 1914, people with mental retardation were viewed as prostitutes, criminals, and sexual libertines.[65] Not only were they viewed as a threat to property, they were seen as menaces to the gene pool. Lifelong incarceration of these subhuman brutes in isolated asylums, where their degraded sensibilities would be obtunded to the absence of amenities, was not only fitting but proper.

To these vicious doctrines the budding science of psychology brought its mite. In particular, Henry Goddard at Vineland propagated the view of mental retardation as a consequence of genetic degeneracy. It was Goddard who waved at American society the specter of the "Kallikak" family. Having founded Vineland's psychology laboratory in 1906, Goddard set out to study intensively the home backgrounds of many of the young patients.[66] As he sent investigators into the home of "Deborah Kallikak" (whose real name was Emma Wolverton), age seventeen in 1906, a veritable swamp of psychopathology was discovered. There were mentally retarded, crazed, alcoholic, and violent relatives all over the Kallikak family tree. It was, as one fellow investigator said, this "stream of degeneracy . . . gathering force with time" from the piney woods that had created the Deborah Kallikaks of this world.[67]

What was in fact wrong with Deborah Kallikak, if anything, is unclear.[68] But from Goddard's viewpoint, she and other "high-grade morons" were a menace to American society primarily for sexual reasons: they would go out and reproduce, polluting the racial stock with generations of future Kallikaks. As Goddard wrote in 1913, "To-day if this young woman were to leave the Institution, she would at once become a prey to the designs of evil men or evil women and would lead a life that would be vicious, immoral, and criminal, though because of her mentality she herself would not be responsible. There is nothing that she might not be led into, because she has no power of control, and all her instincts and appetites are in the direction that would lead to vice."[69]

The ideas of psychiatrists such as Kerlin and Fernald, and psychologists such as Goddard, had enormous resonance within American society in general and MR circles in particular. Although in the 1920s the genetic alarm had started to be seen as a false alarm within scientific circles, in the real world it did not subside, nor within medicine as practiced on the periphery. In 1927, Oliver Wendell Holmes thundered from the bench of the U.S. Supreme Court, upholding a sterilization law for the mentally retarded: "Three generations of idiots are enough."[70] New York social worker Stanley Davies admitted in 1930 that the "social indictment" of MR had been "grossly overdrawn." Nonetheless in an influential MR textbook he persisted in upholding the doctrine of "degenerate stock."[71] Even at liberal Southbury Training School in Connecticut, with its opening in 1940 presented as a beacon of progress in the MR world, superintendent Ernest Roselle could still say that his young charges were "of concern to society from the standpoint of eugenics, because most of them are reproductive."[72] Thus, inappropriate versions of genetic notions dawdled on into the mid-twentieth century.

But we must be careful not to throw the baby out with the bath water. Severe MR is in considerable measure a genetic condition. And part of what the degenerationists perceived turned out in fact to be true: some conditions did worsen as they passed from generation to generation. "Fragile X," a chromosomal condition shown in 1991 to be among the commonest causes of MR (10 percent of all cases), does in fact become more severe as it is passed on: the gene responsible for it evidently expands every time it is reproduced.[73] (Successive reproduction also seems to worsen several other neurological disorders, such as Huntington's disease and myotonic dystrophy, as defective genes are transmitted from generation to generation.) Thus, the eugenics school may have exaggerated heredity somewhat in the causation of MR, but it was not a complete exaggeration.

What the eugenists did instead was to misapply these hereditarian doctrines, first in a philosophical sense by assuming that people with a genetic condition affecting their intelligence were somehow subhuman, thus grossly overvaluing the importance of intelligence. Second, the genetic alarm movement made a factual error. By assuming that the mentally retarded were doomed to uselessness and unable to make a contribution to society, eugenists overlooked the extent to which the mentally retarded can be habilitated, encouraged to earn their own way, and live independently, enjoying life to the maximum—as indeed the rest of the population tries to do.

The Horror Period

The genetic alarm ushered in the horror period in the history of mental retardation. The institutions became unspeakable traps for forgotten people, living in a state of squalor and deprivation unmatched in modern American history. By 1960, the treatment of those with MR had become a national scandal. If ever a group has justly warranted the attention of a charitably-minded family such as the Kennedys, it was the mentally retarded.

It was not willful neglect or indifference that propelled the institutional system toward this abyss of subhuman treatment for the mentally retarded, for the asylum superintendents believed themselves to be honorable men. It was their shifting perceptions of the mission of the institutions they governed. If the hereditarian doctrine was in fact true, they said to themselves, could education and skill training really be so important? As Arthur Rogers, superintendent of the institution in Faribault, Minnesota, asked in 1898, "Does the Education of the Feeble-minded Pay?"[74] Around the turn of the century, Charles Bernstein, head of the Rome State Custodial Asylum, declared, "I firmly believe that no feeble-minded person should be taught to read and write. . . . I have seen any number of feeble-minded children, who, if they had not been taught to read and write, would have been happy in an institution. They are making their parents unhappy when they come to visit them. . . . We are sorry that we ever taught any of them to read and write, because they find what they are losing in the world and are constantly hankering after it, and it makes them miserable and their friends miserable, and they oftentimes run away and make the community miserable."[75] These are comparable to arguments opposing literacy for antebellum slaves.

With the shift toward custodialism, state facilities for the mentally retarded abandoned the notion of serving clients. State institutions existed to protect society. The head of the large MR asylum at Polk, Pennsylvania (which had prided itself on using Seguin's "educational methods" when it opened in 1897), said at the height of the genetic alarm period, "We must get away from the idea, and get the public away from the idea, that our institutions for the feeble-minded are institutions simply for the training of feeble-minded children." The most important objective was getting the "able feeble-minded woman" off the streets, so that she would not be able to reproduce.[76]

To get the mentally retarded off the streets, the number of state institutions rose from 8 in 1876, to 21 in 1900, to 84 in 1950, finally reaching a high point of 110 in 1960.[77] There were perhaps two hundred additional private residential homes and schools for the mentally retarded, of much smaller average size.[78] It is these public institutions that command our curiosity because of their flagship function, though at no time did they house more than 10 percent of all mentally retarded people.

What were these state institutions like?

New York television reporter Geraldo Rivera described his introduction to Willowbrook, a large institution on Staten Island:

When Dr. Wilkins slid back the heavy metal door of B Ward, building no. 6, the horrible smell of the place staggered me. It was so wretched that my first thought was that the air was poisonous and would kill me. I looked down to steady myself and I saw a freak: a grotesque caricature of a person, lying under a sink on an incredibly filthy tile floor in an incredibly filthy bathroom. It was wearing trousers, but they were pulled down around the ankles. It was skinny. It was twisted. It was lying in its own feces. And it wasn't alone. Sitting next to this thing was another freak. In a parody of human emotion, they were holding hands. They were making a noise. It was a wailing sound that I still hear and that I will never forget. I said out loud, but to nobody in particular, "My God, they're children."

Wilkins looked at me and said, "Welcome to Willowbrook."[79]

On entering an institution, one's first impression was of desolation. There was no furniture, no special little spaces for the "residents'" possessions. In some institutions, the shoes were jumbled unpaired into a single box. In the late 1950s when Wolf Wolfensberger, at the time a psychologist in the institutional system, tried to put up a picture to liven up the surroundings in one of the places he worked, the staff immediately snatched it down.[80] Wolfensberger remembered in the institutions where he worked—such as Muscatatuck State School in Butlerville, Indiana— the sea of beds "one next to the other, with virtually no space in between and scarcely any other furniture." After fifty members of the Alabama legislature visited the Partlow State School for the Retarded in Tuscaloosa in 1959, they wept. The children at Partlow slept "on small cots because there is not room for larger beds, and the cots are jammed together, row on row."[81]

Everyone was shocked at the kind of odor that assailed Rivera. Wolfensberger said, "There was the unforgettable impact of the powerful stench produced by a mixture of stale or not-so-stale feces, perspiration, decayed urine, and bodies and clothes that hadn't been washed for a long time. Feces could sometimes be seen hanging from the ceiling where thrown. . . . Such odors had eaten into the very walls of these buildings so that even in areas from which residents were absent the stench was often intolerable. In breathing this odor one became malodorous oneself. Stench comes out of one's nostrils and one's mouth and clothing. So when you came back from visiting an institution, you would strip naked, pop all of your clothes in the washer and wash your hair and so on. I remember once when all of that didn't work, the stench was still there. It turned out to be in the eraser of a pencil."[82]

So overpowering was the stench that first-time visitors often vomited. A lawyer representing the state on a first-time visit to Pennhurst in Pennsylvania "was reportedly so visibly shaken by what he was experiencing on the ward that he excused himself to the men's room."[83] When Ohio governor Michael DiSalle went to visit one of the MR institutions in that state, he ended the visit by going "outside and vomit[ing] at the curb because of the stench and the horrible situation he saw inside, and he said that this has got to be changed and began to make arrangements for transfer of some of these patients out into better quarters."[84] To be sure, other kinds of institutions such as mental hospitals—where schizophrenia was (wrongly) said to have a supposedly distinctive odor—stank as well. But in these MR institutions the level of neglect was so extreme, with conditions so unsanitary (residence in an MR institution later became an automatic indication for a hepatitis B vaccination), that one's nostrils alone indicated one was in a place of horror.

The visitors' second impression concerned the loneliness of the children. These little boys and girls had been abandoned there, usually in infancy, and for comfort they had only each other and the severe warders who stood observing them behind glass plates. As Pearl Buck said of Vineland, "I have to endure heartbreaking moments every time I go to visit my child, for inevitably some other little child comes and takes my hand and leans against me and asks, 'Where is my mamma?'"

A warder explains to Buck that the little girl's parents never visit. "Her grandmother came to see her two years ago and that's the last."

Buck said, "The little thing's heart is slowly breaking. . . . There are other children who come to tell me, eyes glowing, 'My daddy and mummy came last week to see me!' Even the ones who cannot speak will come to show me a new doll that the parents brought."[85]

Vineland was a relatively well-run private institution where the children did receive attention, but in the public institutions the loneliness of the children engraved itself forever in the memories of the visitors. When Rabbi Bernard Raskas of St. Paul went up to the MR institution in Cambridge, Minnesota, he was taken to a ward where the children were all wearing boxer helmets to keep them from hurting their heads if they had seizures. "So I went up to one boy who was about ten. . . . We started to talk, and he didn't know I was a Rabbi, and he said, 'I got a picture of you.'"

The two had never laid eyes on each other before, and the Rabbi asked the little boy what he was talking about. The boy opened up "an old battered Sunday School text and showed me a picture of Jesus." (It wasn't the Rabbi because Jesus had more hair.)

The Rabbi asked, "Why do you say this is a picture of me?" The boy replied, "Because you came to see me when nobody else would." Touched, the Rabbi turned aside with tears in his eyes.[86]

"Almost everywhere you went in the children's unit," Wolfensberger said of another institution, "the children would crowd upon the visitor wanting affection and bodily contact. They were climbing up all over your body and when you left it was almost impossible because their hands wouldn't come loose. You pry one hand loose and it would come right back. Unless you got help from the attendants at the doors, there was no way to get out. It was common for visitors to depart those units all choked." The adult residents themselves, said Wolfensberger, had often been in the institution since early childhood and had gotten in the habit of calling the attendants "mommy and daddy."[87]

"Forgotten children" became a familiar administrative category. In 1961, the Fernald School in Massachusetts adopted a "substitute parents" program "to visit the 'forgotten children,' and take them out on visiting days." This program "brought about a great change in the morale of these children."[88]

Compounding the tragedy for these "forgotten children" is the realization that most of these admissions had been unnecessary in the first place. Although the role of institutional care today is still debated—some severely retarded children do seem to benefit from it—for the great majority there was never a need for confinement in institutions, away from their families and communities where someone would have loved them.

Children with severe retardation often have many physical handicaps, such as the inability to walk without assistance or to feed themselves at the same pace as others. Given the routine brutality and indifference built into institutional life, existence on a ward for the severely retarded often resembled an antechamber of hell. The following describes the early 1960s "idiots'" ward (for those with under-20 IQs) at the Pacific State Hospital in Pomona, California:

> A blond teen-ager flits about rapidly flapping his arms in a bird-like manner, emitting bird-like peeping sounds all the while. A large Buddha-like man sits motionless in a corner, staring straight ahead. A middle-aged man limps slowly in a circle grunting, mumbling, and occasionally shaking his head violently. . . . A blind youngster sits quietly digging his index fingers into his eyes, twitching massively and finally resolving himself into motionless rigidity. A red-haired patient kneels and peers intently down a water drain. . . . Others smile emptily, many lie quietly, still others from time to time erupt into brief frenzies of motion or sound.[89]

Some neurological conditions affect patients so severely that development is stymied regardless of how much personal contact they receive. Yet for the enormous midrange of conditions causing MR, development does follow stimulation. And these children were receiving virtually no stimulation. Life at Pacific State Hospital was bleak even though, under psychiatrist George Tarjan, it was one of the best-run of the American MR institutions. After the "idiots" had finished breakfast they would be herded into an empty and shadeless asphalt play yard surrounded by an eight-and-a-half-foot wire fence. There they were watched but otherwise left almost entirely to their own devices. Aside from an unused tetherball and a couple of volleyballs, there were no toys or other play equipment. "At least 20 patients do nothing but sit, rock, or lie quietly. The activity of the remaining 30 or so consists of running, pacing, or shouting, and this typically in a manner oblivious of their surroundings. Aside from an occasional general outburst when, for instance, two patients bump into each other or when one pushes or strikes another, there is little interaction between them."[90] Sports and organized physical activity were missing entirely from the lives of the boys and men on this ward.

For the severely retarded, a particularly disagreeable aspect of institutional life was the surgical operations performed on them for the sake of the warders' convenience. Kerlin himself in 1892 had evidently been among the earliest of advocates of lobotomy, the surgical destruction of a portion of the brain.[91] Although such procedures at that time would have been extraordinary, the advance of surgery and the discovery of antibiotics made surgery for the indication of convenience commonplace by the mid-twentieth century. The superintendent of one MR institution routinely ordered hysterectomies for all female patients so that staff would not have to deal with menstruation.[92] According to Burton Blatt, who emerged in the 1970s as a major voice of change, at one institution the medical director instructed that seven healthy teeth be extracted from a patient "to prevent her from eating the threads of the day-room rug." At some institutions, it was the task of the staff dentist to "extract the teeth of those who bit themselves or other people or ate 'inedible' matter." Blatt himself had "seen and spoken with innumerable girls and boys— ten, fifteen, twenty years old—with hardly any teeth in their mouths, because teeth have been removed in years past for committing such 'offenses.'"[93] At the Sunland Training Schools in Florida, it had been the practice right until the 1970s to perform gastrotomies, or stomach incisions, upon severely retarded children in order to speed up feeding times. "A tube is put in, feeding time is shortened, and the budget is reduced in that institution."[94] Such interventions, which defy every canon of medical ethics and common decency, had become routine on wards for the severely retarded, demonstrating the concrete side of the concept of dehumanization. The retarded were bereft of their humanity in these institutions.

For the less severely retarded, life in an institution resembled that in a reform school or prison. Indeed, in these institutions many of the attendants and orderlies, the so-called "bug-house bums"—unemployed construction workers drifting in the tides of the Great Depression or downwardly-mobile bank clerks in the eddies of the 1940s—tended to circulate from one kind of institution to the next. "This type of attendant is a floater who drifts from one hospital to another, all over the country," said one observer in 1939. "He remains on each new job until dismissed for drunkenness, for the cruel treatment of a patient, or for some moral offense. Between hospital jobs he works as a bootlegger, panderer [or] contact man in the numbers racket. . . ."[95]

"Half Moon Haven"—the fictional institution in Martin Russ's 1959 novel *Half Moon Haven*—was filled with such types. Russ had served for some time on a ward for "high-level morons" at an institution in upper New York State, possibly Letchworth Village in Thiells. The institutional violence common to MR asylums, prisons, and reform schools emerged most starkly in his novel. Systematic violence kept the adolescent male wards toeing to a military-style discipline. On the first day on the job Russ saw another attendant "whack a patient named Kidde on the side of the head. Kidde was a small boy and this sent him reeling into the bushes. His eyes watered from the sting and he blushed, but other than that he gave no indication that anything unusual had happened. . . ." As time passed, Russ realized this discipline was essential to achieve the institution's concept of order: "The ideal patient never spoke a bloody word from dawn to dusk and responded instantly to orders."[96]

For dinner call at Half Moon Haven, the residents arrayed themselves "into a neat and rigid formation. There were two parallel ranks, one on either edge of the walk."

"Eyes straight ahead," Turnipseed (a warder) blared. "Toes touching the heels of the boy in front of you."

But boys being boys, they would commit infractions. "Paul Bork's back began to ache from standing so long at Attention and when he slouched forward to ease it, Di Angelo [a warder] quietly knocked the wind out of him. George Helfand reached into his pocket for a handkerchief and was pummeled in the ribs by Flagg. Ferrara tried to pass his neighbor a hickory nut and was felled like a sapling by Di Angelo. Moravic coughed and was propelled comically into the prickly bushes by Flagg. That's the way it was at supper call, exhilarating but very exhausting."[97]

In every other respect save intelligence, these were normal little boys. Many of them had been in the institution since early childhood and would remain there until they died, never having known another world.

Among the most brutal warders in many institutions were the less retarded patients who were sent to "terrorize and beat up the more severely retarded ones in order to keep them in line." Wolfensberger remembered "retarded workers raising their fists and moving menacingly towards someone who made a move to get up, and that person would then cower right back onto their seat or [the] floor."[98]

Such violence sometimes led to retaliation by victims against their tormentors. Wolfensberger described his experiences at the Greene Valley Hospital and School in Greeneville, Tennessee, in the early 1960s, a progressive and nonviolent institution. As the hospital took in transfers from other institutions, the patients would be led off the trucks in chains, marching backwards because their former warders feared they would try to bite. "We sat them down to a meal with knives and forks. The former warders said, 'Above all don't give them knives and forks. . . .'" But the newcomers did well at Greene Valley. The violence they exhibited before coming to Greene Valley was institution-bred, and it vanished in the more humane clime.[99]

The circumstances at most other institutions would have been outrageous for anyone to bear. But it was especially galling that many people in wards for the mildly retarded were not retarded at all. They were unwanted. Their families or the authorities had placed them in MR institutions because of behavioral problems. In 1912, for example, George Wallace, director of the Wrentham State School, deplored that "in Massachusetts it has become too easy a matter to get a child into an institution for the feeble-minded and I do not believe we who are at the head of institutions can idly sit by and allow children to be railroaded into our institutions regardless of their mental condition simply because they have been a little wayward."[100]

Typical was Kathleen R. of Toronto, who in 1926 was eighteen years old. Subject to "fierce fits of temper," her parents unable to control her, she had spent her adolescent years in various "industrial schools" and reformatories. As she turned eighteen, she had become truly unmanageable, running away from one industrial school on eight occasions. A physician who examined her in August of that year said, "This patient has been a social menace since the age of 15, when she was first arrested for sex promiscuity. According to her own statement she has followed an indiscriminate sex career continually since that time. She did two years in the Alexandra [Industrial] School and was out only two weeks when she was arrested on Yonge Street in Toronto at two a.m. when making an appointment with several men." Although her IQ had never been tested and there were no references to retardation in her chart, the physician casually added, "She belongs to the moron class." On September 1, 1926, Kathleen R. was admitted to the mental hospital in Toronto, evidently with a view toward later transferring her to an institution for mental retardation.[101] It is highly unlikely that Kathleen R. had any form of retardation at all, merely that she had violated the sexual norms of puritanical Toronto in the 1920s.

Social dumping would be a steady theme throughout the horror period. This indeed was the whole problem with such terms as "high-grade moron," meaning a person who was indistinguishable from the rest of the population until an IQ test spied him or her out. The apparently scientific language of the clinic and the laboratory became a screen behind which undesirables could be whisked away. As George Stevenson said in 1947, "Many a social agency today is relieved to get a diagnosis of mental deficiency on a troublesome case so that it can unload it on an institution."[102] The Toronto case cited above suggests the ease with which such a diagnosis could be procured.

As late as 1974, readers of the *Miami Herald* were shocked to learn that, among sixty-two hundred patients at the six Sunland training centers in Florida, there were hundreds who were not mentally retarded at all. "They're the physically handicapped, the poor, the 'troublemakers.' But mostly, they're the unwanted," said the *Miami Herald*. "Yet they've been confined to institutions for 10 years, 20 years and longer." In the past an individual could be placed at Sunland with great ease, at the say-so of a physician, a psychologist, or even a "responsible citizen." Under Florida law the person had no right to a lawyer or a court hearing. (In other states hearings were pro forma, the supposedly retarded person in absentia.)

At Miami Sunland, Sheila, age twenty-seven, had a disorder that confined her to a wheelchair. "She is vibrant, charming and an excellent conversationalist," found the journalist.

"I don't know why she hasn't been placed in a foster home from here," added Bruce Hobler, the Sunland director.

Said an aide, "I work with her every day and there's nothing wrong with that girl. She really wants to get out. Sometimes she sits down and cries."[103]

These are appalling stories. They establish how recklessly basic freedoms, such as the freedom from unjust confinement, were denied these poor, downtrodden, and forgotten people who were too inarticulate or timorous to speak for themselves. And once they were in an institution, they had little way of getting out again except for the unlikely event that their families wanted them discharged. Canadian MR reformer John Fotheringham recalls of the MR institution at Orillia, Ontario, "All residents were certified as incompetent, and if they escaped, they were brought back. Once, when I was in the Orillia Hospital, they brought back a woman who had escaped three years previously. She was discovered working in a restaurant as a waitress and supporting herself."[104] Just imagine. For three years she had led a normal existence on the outside and then was dragged back to the stinking hell of the Ontario Hospital at Orillia.

Yet the MR institution did not merely confine. It molded. Once inside, both the retarded and the nonretarded ended up learning the same kind of enfeebled behavior, or "learned helplessness." There is experimental evidence that the crowding and confinement of an institution produce bizarre behavior even among normal people. In one study, college students exposed to "inescapable noise" ended up showing the same symptoms of helplessness and depression that one encountered in MR institutions.[105] The noise bouncing off the undecorated tile walls (so easy to clean!), the linoleum floors in rooms without furniture, and the congestion of hundreds of patients pressed together in a dayroom without organized activities sufficed in and of themselves to explain the pacing, the stereotypical hand motions, and other compulsive behavior that many residents had learned in the institutions. As Gunnar Dybwad testified at a deinstitutionalization case in 1972, "Individuals who come to institutions and can walk stop walking, who come to institutions and can talk will stop talking, who come to institutions and can feed themselves will stop feeding themselves; in other words, . . . [there is] a steady process of deterioration."[106]

The MR asylum thus stunted the psychological lives of both the retarded and the nonretarded within its walls. But even more appalling was its lethality. Mortality in institutions was much higher than in the general population. This was partly because some forms of mental retardation carry with them potentially fatal physical defects. Down Syndrome, for example, tends to cause congenital heart problems and circulatory ailments. A study carried out in British Columbia between 1952 and 1981 showed that one-third of the people with Down Syndrome had died by age thirty. Their risk of dying from circulatory disease was sixty times greater than that of an age-matched control group; they had a risk of infectious death seventeen times greater and died of congenital anomalies thirteen times more often.[107] Many retarded people are also born with neurological defects that may cause epilepsy. Therefore, epilepsy was the most common cause of death in MR asylums before the World War II, followed by tuberculosis (TB).[108]

Many of these deaths were not inevitable, however. They were affected by the quality of care. In potentially fatal epileptic seizures (or status epilepticus), phenobarbital—available since 1911—could have been injected intravenously. As for the numerous TB deaths, there was no isolation of infectious patients within the institutions. Such causes of mortality were by no means inherent in the conditions causing mental retardation.

The advent of antibiotics after World War II, and of later medical advances such as operations for hydrocephalus and heart defects, reduced the mortality rate among MR patients. The new wave of younger physicians in the 1940s who replaced the indifferentist old guard probably behaved in a more dedicated, caring way. Among these young idealists was Robert Cooke himself, who became a resident physician at Southbury Training School in 1944. Cooke later recalled, "We tried to bring state of the art medicine to every patient."[109] Yet ironically, the improved survival of the inmates added to the horror. Whereas retarded children previously had often not made it beyond adolescence, after World War II their survival into adult life grew commonplace. In New York State, the average age at death of mildly retarded children ("morons") in MR asylums rose from 24.7 years in 1928 to 34.8 in 1958, an increase of 41 percent. For the moderately retarded (the "imbeciles"), the average survival rate increased by 35 percent.[110] However, the improved survival rate of this latter group in particular, who often required special nursing care, overwhelmed the institutions' ability to cope, and the quality of life in the large MR warehouses deteriorated even beyond what it had been in the 1920s and 1930s.

Interestingly, the survival rate of the most severely retarded, the so-called "idiots," rose only 6 percent. This was doubtless owing to a covert but nonetheless real policy of neglect verging on infanticide that seems to have prevailed at many institutions: if these children did not live beyond the age of twenty-one, it was because the system decided they would not. In some institutions, for example, the staff would wet the severely retarded down with a hose and then leave them in the cold, in the mistaken belief that exposure to cold causes pneumonia (it does not).[111] Filthy living conditions, indifference by staff to medical care, and denial of nutrition were so systematic in these stinking institutions that one scholar has likened them to the Nazi death camps.[112] Looking back over this era, Robert Burt, a professor at Yale Law School, called U.S. policy toward the mentally retarded just one step short of infanticide: "We did not kill retarded children. We buried them alive in hidden public residential institutions."[113]

"The Schools Won't Take Our Children"

For MR children who stayed at home, the most burning issue was not institutional neglect but education, or rather their lack of access to it. "The schools won't take our children," said one mother to Pearl Buck. "What shall we do?"[114]

Schooling represents one of the few points of light in the early history of mental retardation. Yet it illuminates how desperately needed help was around 1960, because the early points of light became mostly extinguished in the years after the Great Depression.

Around the turn of the century, progressive individuals did see hope for the retarded: in the form of public education. The first special-ed classes were established in 1896 in Providence, Rhode Island, followed by isolated efforts in several other cities.[115] But the true birthplace of special education in the United States was the Vineland Training School in Vineland, New Jersey, with its psychologically-minded administrators. "Vineland" meant actually two institutions: the private New Jersey Home for the Education and Care of Feeble-Minded Children (later the New Jersey Training School for Feeble-Minded Children), founded in 1887 by S. Olin Garrison, a Methodist clergyman; and the public State Institution for Feeble-Minded Women at Vineland, which New Jersey created a year later.[116] Vineland is important because the staff at the private school propagated the notion that the mentally retarded could be helped through special education. Four individuals played a particular role: superintendent Edward Johnstone, Goddard himself, and two younger psychologists, Wallace Wallin and Edgar Doll. Their early triumphs stand in contrast to the later marasmus into which special education would fall.

These special-ed pioneers show what a handful of dedicated individuals could accomplish. Johnstone had come to Vineland in 1898 to run the education program, becoming director three years later after Garrison died. He is among the first Americans to assert that people with MR could learn. In 1902, Johnstone began offering special classes in the summer to train teachers of mentally retarded children.[117] This was the first such program in the country.

Goddard, who remained at Vineland until 1918, was internationally known for his study of the Kallikaks. Less well known is that in 1906 he established a psychology laboratory at Vineland. There, three years later, he introduced Alfred Binet's and Théodore Simon's IQ test to the United States.[118] The debate about the validity of the test for anyone continues today. Its misapplications in the field of MR were certainly legion, with tests often being mischievously applied to keep MR children out of school. Yet the IQ test was useful in helping worried parents establish what was wrong with their child.

Edgar Doll, a pupil of Goddard's, pioneered the study of differences between children who were just slow ("pseudo-feebleminded" was his term) and those who were genuinely retarded. He was also among the first to challenge Goddard's hereditarian theories, emphasizing instead organic lesions—such as from birth injury—in the causation of mental retardation.[119]

The last of these pioneer psychologists associated with Vineland was J. E. Wallace Wallin, who played a strategic role in the development of special education. With a Yale Ph.D. in experimental psychology, Wallin came briefly to Vineland in 1910 as a substitute for Goddard, who was traveling in Europe.[120] Like Doll, Wallin was skeptical of Goddard's theories, in particular disliking the notion of "IQ 50" as some kind of fiendish cutoff beneath which the child was deemed uneducable and not a candidate for admission to special-ed classes in public schools. Parents dreaded this cabalistic number, despairing if their child failed to attain it. Yet Wallin had quite successfully taught children who were deeply impaired, discovering only later that they had IQs of 35 and lower. In 1921, he founded a program at Miami University in Oxford, Ohio, for training teachers of the mentally retarded, one of the few sources that reached parents in local communities.

Thus, in one way or another, the impetus for special education radiated from Vineland Training School in New Jersey. In 1911, New Jersey became the first state to mandate special-ed classes for mentally retarded children. Wallin and Goddard drafted the legislation.[121]

When in 1911 Goddard standardized an American edition of the IQ scale, he gave the special-ed movement a powerful though, ethically, somewhat problematical boost. Vast numbers of people were discovered to be "retarded" on the basis of their inability to make the types of subtle verbal distinctions for which the test called. Wallin, for example, tested a group of successful Iowa farmers and found them all to be "morons." With tongue in cheek he asked, "Who is feeble-minded?"[122] Looking back to the 1910s and 1920s, Fred Kuhlmann, head of the national organization of MR asylum superintendents, later said that with Goddard's IQ test, "We found the moron. . . . The mental test revealed the moron in undreamed of numbers. The percentage of the general population estimated to be feeble-minded jumped at once from a fraction of one percent to several percent." It now seemed folly to keep building institutions. The retarded were so numerous they could never all be segregated.[123]

The only solution was to try to educate them. Here the special-ed narrative diverges somewhat from the asylum narrative, which from 1890 on plunged into unrelieved gloom. The years 1900 to 1930 saw progress in educating mentally retarded children. It was only after 1930 that things started to fall apart.

Following the leadership of New Jersey, by 1930 as many as fourteen states were legally mandating special-ed classes within public schools. In the United States as a whole, the number of children in such classes quadrupled from 24,000 in 1922 to 100,000 in 1936, the number of cities offering such classes rising from 133 to 643.[124] The White House Conference on Child Health of 1930, at which numerous Vineland alumni played a role, featured special education prominently among its main recommendations and represented the capstone of the whole special-ed movement.[125]

Then came the Depression, and these gains were eroded as cash-strapped states and communities withdrew their funding for special education. New Jersey had more children enrolled in special-ed classes in 1918 than it did in 1946.[126] For the mildly retarded there were some losses; for the moderately to severely retarded, who previously had enjoyed public school classes mandated by state law, it was as overwhelming defeat.[127]

By the early 1950s, availability of special-ed classes become paltry indeed. On paper, many states provided for MR programs in the local schools. Yet the programs were "permissive," in that the local community had the option of implementing them or not.[128] In 1957, Lawrence Derthick, Commissioner of Education, told a U.S. Senate committee hearing that when he was a local school superintendent in Tennessee, it had required "tremendous effort to get classes for these children." And even after the classes were funded, he couldn't find the specially trained teachers for them. "We had to do the best we could to select teachers and train them on the job." Countless children, said Derthick, were excluded from adequate public education because they were mentally retarded. "Those children are just as important to our Nation as any other children," he said.[129]

As for university programs to train teachers for the mentally retarded, little was available in the 1950s. Around 1957 there were "only 28 instructors giving full time to the preparation of teachers of the mentally retarded" in the whole country. According to the Office of Education, many of the universities offering training programs on paper were "inadequately staffed and otherwise ill equipped even for the training of undergraduate students in the area."[130] In 1953, there were 794,000 retarded children in the United States, of whom only 14 percent were in "special schools and classes."[131] That means that six out of seven retarded kids were at home all day, every day, watching from the window as their brothers and sisters went off to school, trapped along with their parents in a nightmare of isolation, deprivation, and exclusion.

Rosemary

On September 13, 1918, Rosemary Kennedy was born at the Kennedy family home in Brookline, Massachusetts, a suburb of Boston. Unfortunately, Dr. Frederick Good, the young professor of obstetrics at Tufts University who was the family's obstetrician, was late in arriving. Rosemary's head was trapped in the birth canal; her brain became deprived of oxygen, and she was born retarded.[132] This was not an uncommon cause of MR in the days before hospital deliveries became the norm, making possible the rescue of an oxygen-starved child with an emergency caesarean section. As Eunice Kennedy Shriver later reassured the grandchildren of Joseph and Rose Kennedy, "If the doctor had arrived on time, Rosemary would be like the rest of us."[133]

There was much about the life of "Rose Marie" Kennedy, as Rosemary's parents originally intended to call her[134] (the family called her simply "Rose"), that was typical of mental retardation in the years before 1960. Other characteristics were unique, a consequence of being born to a well-to-do, highly athletic, and very competitive family.

As with most MR children—Down Syndrome being the big exception—Rosemary seemed to be a normal baby. "It was only slowly," her mother later said, "as she grew to be a toddler and beyond, that I began to realize she might be handicapped.

"She was slow in everything, and some things she seemed unable to learn how to do, or do well or with consistency." For example, she was unable to steer her sled, and as she started to learn to read and write, "the letters and words were extremely difficult for her." Rose was informed that Rosemary's IQ was low, but Rose received no further details.[135]

When Ted Kennedy was seven and Rosemary twenty-one, he would joke with her about being an "empty head."

"Am I?" she asked.[136] She had little awareness of herself as being different.

It must be emphasized that Rosemary was only mildly retarded. The list of things she could do well was much longer than the list of things she couldn't do well or do at all. She was, for example, responsible enough to take six young children to the beach while visiting at a friend's house. "Rose[mary] would take each one of the children in the water, swim with them, and then bring them back to the beach and say, 'Wait here.' . . . Then she read them all a story." She was said to have "the daintiest table manners," and, as adolescence set in, she aspired to keep up with her sisters when it became time to go on dates. Her mother took her to an Arthur Murray Studio regularly "until Rose[mary] could dance well enough to go to parties."

It's of particular interest that Rosemary loved sports. Her mother played tennis with her for hours, something Rose Kennedy never did with her other daughters.[137] "At Hyannisport," Eunice recalled, "I would take her as crew in our boat races, and I remember she usually did what she was told. She was especially helpful with the jib. . . ." Rosemary was also an excellent swimmer and took classes along with her four sisters twice weekly. "She loved it, enjoyed winning, and got quite angry if any of her sisters beat her in the races."[138]

In 1935, Eunice and Rosemary traveled to Europe together on a holiday. "We went on boat trips in Holland, climbed mountains in Switzerland, went rowing on Lake Lucerne. . . .

"Rose[mary] could do all these things—rowing, climbing—as well or better than I. She could walk faster and longer distances than I could. And she was fun to be with." By the end of that summer, Rosemary was showing great signs of improvement. She had not become agitated or irritable "over the strain of keeping up with a busy itinerary. Our hopes climbed."[139]

In 1938, the sisters again returned to Europe as their father became American ambassador to Britain. The following year Joseph Kennedy was invited to attend the "coronation" (as his daughter Eunice remembered it) of Pope Pius XII, and decided to bring the family along. "Five girls and Mother, all went to the department stores. We bought ourselves five black dresses with long black sleeves, black stockings, black gloves and black veils. We flew to Rome, drove to St. Peter's and all were thrilled by our chance to 'meet the Pope.'" Rosemary included. She participated fully in all these events.[140] Of course she was not on par with the others, but she came across to outsiders only as a bit "shy" and certainly had no striking peculiarities of appearance or behavior.[141]

After the family returned to America in 1940, Rosemary, now twenty-two, began to experience a worsening of her condition. She evidently resented her inability to keep up with her inexhaustible siblings. In the words of two Kennedy biographers, "She began to have tantrums, and then rages which developed into near-clonic states during which she smashed objects and struck out at the people around her." Once, in the summer of 1941, she attacked her grandfather John Fitzgerald ("Honey Fitz"), hitting and kicking the frail old man "until she was pulled away."[142] Family intimates recalled "long absences at night when she'd be out wandering the streets and violent verbal exchanges."[143] Apparently in the course of these wanderings she was having sexual contact with men.[144]

Her alarmed parents experienced the same frustration that every other family with a mentally retarded child underwent of going from doctor to doctor in a melancholic attempt to obtain a diagnosis and learn about treatment. "My mother took Rosemary to psychologists and to dozens of doctors," said Eunice Shriver. "All of them said that Rosemary's condition would not get better and that she would be happier in an institution where competition was far less. . . ."[145]

These violent outbreaks made acute an issue that had been simmering within the family since at least 1933: whether to put Rosemary in an institution.[146] Her father, Joe Kennedy, apparently opposed it. When various psychologists recommended that Rosemary be put away, Joe said, "What can they do in an institution that we can't do better for her at home—here with her family." He felt that, in Eunice's words, "Rosemary should have every opportunity that the rest of us had, even though she could not make the most of such opportunities."[147]

By the fall of 1941, however, his daughter's behavior had overwhelmed even Joe Kennedy's determination to keep her at home. He settled on one last desperate measure before sending her away: lobotomy. Surgical destruction of the prefrontal lobes of the brain in order to cure mental illness had become a stylish operation within psychiatric circles late in the 1930s. Under circumstances that remain obscure, in the fall of 1941 Joe Kennedy had his daughter admitted to St. Elizabeth's Hospital, a psychiatric hospital in Washington, D.C., where an unnamed neurosurgeon—possibly James Watts—lobotomized her.[148] This was certainly an unusual strategy, not typical of the recommended treatment of MR in those days. This action on the part of Joe Kennedy, Sr., perhaps more than any other, has earned the financier the scorn of historians. Some writers argue that it was an evil way of dealing with the sexual coming-of-age of a mildly retarded young girl.[149] Other observers feel the lobotomy, which counted at the time as state-of-the-art treatment, represented more a loving father's efforts to gain the best possible care for his daughter.[150] It is impossible to sort these claims out with the evidence available at present. We know merely that Rosemary was not told what was going to happen, and that her mother did not learn of the operation until 1961.[151]

The operation considerably worsened Rosemary's condition. At some point in the early 1940s, the family did in fact institutionalize her, apparently in Craig House, a private psychiatric hospital in Beacon, New York. In 1949, she was sent to the St. Coletta School in Jefferson, Wisconsin.[152] Thus in their encounter with mental retardation, the Kennedy family had at last rejoined mainstream America.

In their fears and anxieties as well, the Kennedys were typical of the rest of America in confronting mental retardation. "Mother worried about Rose[mary]'s future," recalled Eunice in 1962. "What would happen to her if anything happened to Mother and Dad?"[153] In 1975, Rose Kennedy expressed a particular interest in the problems of elderly people with mental retardation. Eunice said of her mother's concerns, "Many other parents are concerned also as to what happens to their retarded children when they [the parents] die."[154] (Indeed this was a general concern. One remembers Pearl Buck's anxieties about what would happen if her daughter happened to outlive her: "What if she lived to be older than I? Who would care for her then?"[155])

Finally, the Kennedys had in common with most other parents their sense of shame at the presence of mental retardation in the family. Until the 1960s, they were deeply embarrassed about Rosemary, trying through the most absurd stratagems to explain her disappearance from the public stage as owing to some socially acceptable reason. In 1957, the family told the *Saturday Evening Post* that Rosemary was "teaching" at St. Coletta's.[156] Likewise, Kennedy biographer James MacGregor Burns put out the story in 1959—wittingly or unwittingly—that Rosemary, "a sweet, rather withdrawn girl," was helping to "care for mentally retarded children" at St. Coletta's.[157] After John F. Kennedy's election to the presidency in 1960, the official line became that Rosemary was suffering from "cerebral palsy."[158] (At the time the cerebral palsy lobby was trying hard to keep CP from being stigmatized by any association with mental retardation.) Although news of Rosemary's condition had already leaked to insiders within MR circles (Joe Kennedy had been making public references to it in radio speeches as early as 1951[159]), it was through Eunice Shriver's article in 1962 in the *Saturday Evening Post* that the Kennedy family announced to the public the true story of Rosemary's condition. So powerful was the social stigma against the mentally retarded that this influential and very enlightened family, already extensively involved in the MR movement, did not feel able to associate itself with the condition until two years into JFK's presidency.

Thus we come to the Kennedy family's own efforts in the area of mental retardation. The official version is that the family, saddened by Rosemary's fate and sensitive to the plight of the mentally retarded, did its best to help out.[160] That is not exactly the way it happened.

2

Joe Senior

The story of the Kennedy family's efforts on behalf of the mentally retarded commences with a real estate transaction in Chicago. On July 21, 1945, Joseph P. Kennedy, Sr., financier and father of nine, bought the Merchandise Mart in Chicago for $13 million.[1] Built in 1930 by Marshall Field & Company for wholesalers in household furnishings and for offices, the Mart, with its eighteen floors of space and a twenty-three-story central tower, was the largest commercial building in the world. During the Great Depression, it had earned the title of "Chicago's No. 1 real estate white elephant."[2] By the end of World War II, Marshall Field & Company wanted to dump it in order to realize a large tax write-off.

With the Merchandise Mart, Joe Kennedy acquired a property well positioned for the postwar commercial boom that he correctly foresaw. Knowing that the low-paying government tenants—who in the 1940s occupied about 40 percent of the building—would soon be moving out, Kennedy's strategy in the years to come would be to sign up high-paying corporations such as NBC that were looking for suitable Chicago head offices. Six months after Joe Kennedy scored this coup, business writers were estimating the return on his investment at 23 percent a year. The financier had now acquired a money-spinner to build his postwar real estate empire.[3]

But what to do with the profits of the Mart? On May 14, 1945, two months before finalizing the deal on the Mart, Joe Kennedy incorporated in Washington, D.C., a private foundation, the Mercié Foundation, dedicated—as he put it in his application for tax-exempt status—to "the relief, shelter, support, education, protection and maintenance of the indigent, sick and infirm." The foundation was also to encourage "habits of thrift and self dependence among the poor."[4] Five months later, on October 29, 1945, the Mercié Foundation was renamed the Joseph P. Kennedy, Jr. Foundation.[5]

The Kennedy Foundation, as it is generally referred to, was to play an important role in recycling the revenues of the Merchandise Mart. By permitting the foundation to buy one-quarter of the Mart, Joe ensured that a quarter of the Mart's profits went into tax-free funds that could be used partly for charity, and partly to subsidize the political activities of his son Jack. Joe himself was to get an eighth of the Mart's revenues, his wife Rose another eighth; one-quarter would go to Joe's trust fund for his children, another quarter to the "Joseph P. Kennedy Trust Funds." The quarter to the Kennedy Foundation would be tax exempt. The other three-quarters were taxable at the "partnership" rate, a lower rate than the corporate rate, from which Joe Kennedy petitioned to be exempted.[6] Thus, fully one-quarter of Mart revenues could be used for charitable, covert political, and even personal financial purposes: for example, the Kennedy's Palm Beach house was for many years owned by the foundation.[7]

In March 1946, Joe Senior further turned his foundation into an arm of his business empire by giving it the power to do commercial transactions, especially to borrow or loan money on behalf of other companies and to engage in all kinds of real estate deals.[8]

Running the foundation as part of his business, both headquartered at 230 Park Avenue in New York, Joe Kennedy possessed absolute control over it. He conducted its activities through phone calls from poolside at his Palm Beach home or by dictating letters at the family estate in Hyannisport. But in formal terms he was not associated with the foundation at all, for every foundation must by law have officers, such as president and treasurer, and trustees. He himself never served in any of these positions.

At the beginning, the foundation was not primarily a family affair. In 1945, he appointed as president and vice president two obscure cronies—Edward O'Leary and Thomas Delehanty—who ran his liquor importing business, Somerset Importers, in Manhattan.[9] In 1946 or early 1947, Jack Kennedy became president of the foundation.[10] Among the other trustees were the usual gaggle of retainers such as Paul Murphy, then a young lawyer, and James Fayne (Joe Senior's adviser on stocks and investments).

Other members of the Kennedy family were not uninvolved in the foundation, merely not prominent at the beginning. In 1947, Joe made his daughter Eunice a trustee. Eunice, a recent graduate of Stanford University and at age twenty-six the eldest of the three mentally-competent daughters living in the United States, was an interesting choice. (Of the financier's other daughters, Pat was then twenty-three and Jean nineteen. Rosemary was twenty-nine; a fourth daughter, Kathleen, twenty-seven years old, resided in England.) Had Joe at this point already identified special qualities in Eunice? And did she somehow disappoint him in her twelve-month tenure? Her name vanished from the list of trustees after 1947 and would not reappear for many years to come.[11]

In any event, all the flimflam about officers and trustees was merely window dressing, for Joe Kennedy himself made the decisions and signed the important letters. The trustees did not meet, or advise, or play any practical role.[12] Until 1960, four of the five trustee slots were occupied by nonfamily members, so clearly the financier did not set out to create a strong family identification with the foundation.

How important is the paper trail here as a marker of what actually went on? People with long memories insist that even in the early days, Eunice's role was larger than the documents show: that in informal conversation she shaped her father's thinking and helped steer him toward causes she had researched, and that her energy and drive—as the most vibrant member of the younger half of the family—made her in reality an important force, regardless of what the roll of trustees may indicate. Family confidant and adviser, the pediatrician Robert Cooke, told me much later, "I know she remained active in pursuing information for her father."[13]

History has not been kind to Joseph Patrick Kennedy, Sr., chairman of the Securities and Exchange Commission in 1934–35, Ambassador to Great Britain in 1937–40, and patriarchal founder of America's First Family. In the work of some writers he has emerged as a demon, a ruthless speculator, a womanizer, and a wartime poltroon.[14] Yet the man's life must be considered in some kind of balanced perspective for, like other Kennedy family members who similarly have been demonized, he was a rich and many-sided character. And his values and attitudes were not chiseled into granite: he possessed the ability to change. As the years passed, he underwent a kind of conversion from a hard-as-nails tycoon to a man genuinely devoted to improving the lot of the mentally retarded. And with this softening, a human side always apparent to his family became visible to the outside world as well.

In 1945, Joe Kennedy was fifty-seven. He had a "shock of graying red hair crowning a strong face, the wide friendly grin emphasized by crinkles of mirth around his eyes," as his adviser Lee Moni later recalled.[15] Jackie Kennedy, JFK's widow, remembered Joe Senior from her visits to Florida or the Cape as "always in Sulka lounging clothes or shorts and matching shirts. . . . I loved him," she wrote, "when he was off to Hialeah [a racetrack] in his pale blue gabardine suit . . . he would saunter out with one hand in his pocket and salute you, 'Hello Gorgeous!'" Above all she recalled Joe Kennedy's manners: "He had the most beautiful manners—the manners and ease of Kings."[16] One could hear even in his voice the presence of one who was accustomed to commanding, to making things happen. Said his first secretary of the days when Joe was a young bank president, "When he arrived at the bank everyone would be on the qui vive. His voice would boom out for whomever he needed at the moment. There was a silencer put on the mouthpiece of his telephone so that people could not overhear what was being said."[17] Thus did friends and family assemble the portrait of a man who was overarchingly self-confident and habituated to power, to owning the horses that raced at Hialeah as well as betting on them.

Why would such a man have even bothered with a charitable foundation? For one thing, many of his friends were doing it. Joe Kennedy belonged to a generation of self-made entrepreneurs who came of age in the 1920s and who by the 1940s—their immediate lust for acquisition slaked—were looking for ways to burnish their community reputation and family name. Some, like Sam Noble who established his foundation in 1945, or J. E. Mabee who in 1948 chartered his foundation—based on an Oklahoma oil fortune—had come from poor families. Others such as Conrad Hilton and Charles Stewart Mott were more middle-class in origin, from families that had been able to give their children a good education.[18] Although Joe Kennedy fell between these economic and social rankings, he was nonetheless part of the same wave of American wealthy carried upward by the prosperity of the 1920s who survived the Great Depression. Organizing a family foundation was the thing to do among his social circle.

The years 1940–50 saw the great wave of setting up foundations in the United States. Where did the Joseph P. Kennedy, Jr. Foundation fit in? In 1953 it had assets of $2.5 million. Of the 7,300 foundations that existed in those years, the assets of 640 others were roughly in that category, with another 78 really large ones having assets of over $10 million. Indeed, it was the 1940s in particular that saw the establishment of hundreds of other such midsize family foundations, so Mr. Kennedy was a bit of a sociological phenomenon.[19]

But Joe Senior also seems to have been animated by a genuine sense of philanthropy, a desire to give community service as a token of thanks for what he had profited from the community, or for what God had given him. It was in 1919, as young Jack seemed close to death from scarlet fever, that Joe made his first charitable offering, vowing that if his son recovered, he would give the Catholic schools of Boston the fifty-seat school bus they had been requesting. This was, according to one source, "his first major philanthropic gift."[20]

On his motives, Joe Kennedy was close to inscrutable. He never explained to the Catholic church why he was making contributions nor did he stipulate what they were to be used for.[21] But he does seem to have had a genuine sense of charity, as opposed to opportunistic giving. Learning in March 1956 of the death of his friend Dr. Ephraim Shorr, an endocrinologist at Cornell Medical College in New York, Kennedy wrote to a friend, "I had seen him the Friday before he died and I feel his death very greatly. He was a stimulating man and a true disciple of the theory that a man could fulfill his destiny by helping his fellow men."[22] As philosophies of philanthropy go, it was not a complicated one, but Joe Kennedy seems to have believed in it.

Finally, Kennedy gave because he wanted to boost his children up the ladder, especially the males. He hoped that polishing the family name on a brass foundation plate would lend greater luster to their own reputations. Whenever grants were announced in press conferences, it was almost invariably Jack who stood on the podium; or Bobby, who was president of the foundation after 1954; or Ted, president after 1961—never Joe Senior himself.

It follows that Joe Kennedy's charitable donations in the late 1940s and 1950s were a mixture of genuine philanthropy, whimsy, and political calculation. There is no doubt that he was a serious philanthropist. From the very beginning, the family foundation gave millions of dollars to religious charities, both Catholic and Protestant alike, all over the country and particularly the eastern seaboard. The following is a sampling from the letters sent out on Christmas Eve, 1946: for Mother Hamilton, treasurer of the Convent of the Sacred Heart in Albany, there would be $5,000; for Francis Cardinal Spellman of New York, an unrestricted donation of $10,000; for the Reverend John Cavanaugh of Notre Dame in "Notre Dame, Indiana," a donation of $5,000, and so on.[23] Over the years Joe Kennedy gave great sums of money to Archbishop Richard Cushing of Boston (Cardinal after 1958.) Joe Kennedy was also openhanded with Protestant and secular charities, and by 1958 had given over $800,000 to causes as diverse as the Associated Jewish Philanthropies ($450,000 in 1947) and the Boy's Club of Boston ($25,000 in 1954).[24]

Kennedy also gave money for basically whimsical reasons: because he was close to this director or that cleric socially or because he had heard good things about a private school or because he wanted peace in his relations with his Massachusetts neighbors. He gave, for example, $150,000 to build a skating rink in Hyannis that opened in 1957.[25] Even more imaginative were the grants that did not appear on any list for official distribution, such as paying the tuition at Notre Dame for many of the thirty-one cadets expelled in 1951 from West Point in a cheating scandal.[26] This kind of scattershot charity lacked focus but was not otherwise unennobling.

Quite a different matter, however, was funding the foundation made available for Jack Kennedy's political activities, not direct subsidies of his campaigns but money to fill the coffers of various organizations that could be of political use to the young congressman, and after 1953 senator, from Massachusetts. In fact, Jack seems to have made some of these grants more or less on his own hook as president of the foundation. For example, in March 1951 Jack asked one of his father's assistants to "draw up a check in the amount of $5000.00 against the Joseph P. Kennedy, Jr. Foundation, payable to the Italian-American Charitable Society, Inc.

"I made a commitment in this amount to Judge Frank Tomasello, of Boston, who is the President of the Society. . . ."[27] What purpose could this money possibly have served save the currying of good political will?

Courting the black vote would be of greater importance to Jack Kennedy in the presidential campaign of 1960. In 1958, he asked his father (via his brother-in-law Sargent Shriver) to make a grant to Xavier University of Louisiana, a small black college in New Orleans. Congressman Hale Boggs from Louisiana was said to be especially keen on this. A grant such as this might have played a crucial role with the black vote in Louisiana, a state that Jack Kennedy carried in 1960 by a very slight margin over the combined vote of the Republicans and the States' Rights Party.[28] (Boggs became the majority whip in the House in 1961 just as JFK took office.)

During the presidential campaign of 1960, efforts to use the foundation as a tax-free slush fund came to a sudden and embarrassing end. Sometime in 1959, Kenyan nationalist leader Tom Mboya first met Jack Kennedy at a conference near San Francisco on African affairs. Mboya told the senator that he was trying to raise funds to bring a group of Kenyan students to the United States for study. Jack was sympathetic. In August of 1960, when Mboya again returned to the United States for fundraising, he decided to visit Jack at Hyannisport. (In the interim Mboya had requested funds from the State Department and had been turned down.) On August 10, Kennedy promised $100,000 in foundation money for the airlift. Three days later, evidently at Richard Nixon's instigation (Nixon was then Vice President under Eisenhower), the State Department reversed itself and accorded the Kenyan students their money. The whole story became public, and it looked as though Jack Kennedy were bidding against the federal government in an effort to influence the black vote. As Republican Senator Hugh Scott thundered against the Kennedy Foundation on the front page of the *New York Times,* "If a foundation which belongs to a family has a faucet which can be turned on by Mr. Kennedy . . . to gain some advantage with any group of our people, they can do the same with the farmers.

"They can organize a farm study group and pay a lot of farmers with make work money and get the farm vote. . . ."[29] The story was a major embarrassment.

The Kennedy Foundation never again attempted to use tax-exempt funds to win favor among political groups, though not necessarily just because Jack Kennedy, as President of the United States, had to stand at arm's length from his family's money. There were other brothers and brothers-in-law whose campaigns could have used the funds. By 1961, however, Eunice Shriver had taken charge of the foundation. And to Eunice, such dissipation of monies that could have gone to the cause of mental retardation was an act of sacrilege. Never again was the foundation's name mixed up in politics.

Joe Kennedy Discovers a Cause

From the outset, Joe Kennedy had been interested in giving to causes associated with mental retardation, though he did not make them a principal focus until the late 1950s. This interest came about because of Cardinal Richard Cushing of Boston, the crusty cleric who has become a piece of American folklore.[30] Cushing, fifty-one in 1946, was seven years Joe Kennedy's junior. He had grown up in Boston, was ordained as a priest there in 1921 and a bishop in 1939, and was consecrated archbishop of the Boston archdiocese in 1944. Cushing was among the first influential Americans to speak out about the plight of the mentally retarded (for whom he preferred the phrase "exceptional children"), and he emerged as a major advocate in the 1950s. In 1955, noting that the House had approved an appropriation on behalf of research into MR, he immediately wrote Massachusetts Congressman John McCormack asking if this money could actually be used to help children.[31] Cushing also established close ties to Congressman John Fogarty of Rhode Island, head of the House appropriations subcommittee on health and the principal advocate of the mentally retarded in Congress. They routinely congratulated each other for various public appearances on behalf of MR; it was "Dear John" and "Your Excellency" between them.[32] Thus Cushing established himself in the 1950s as a principal public figure in the cause of mental retardation—this at a time when the Kennedy family was virtually invisible on the public scene.

But Cushing knew in private, of course, of the family's interest and sought the financier Joe Kennedy out for money. Here lay the origin of Joe Kennedy's charitable involvement with MR.[33] Cushing needed Kennedy as a benefactor, and Kennedy in turn depended upon Cushing for advice, for example, on how to deal with Rosemary. In retrospect, it's perhaps not so curious that the two should have found each other. Both were hyper-energetic and all-controlling men, patriarchal by nature and political by choice. Cushing was heavily involved in Jack Kennedy's various political campaigns in the Massachusetts. Cushing also took a bossy hands-on attitude to projects in his archdiocese. Indeed, Joe Kennedy finally became so put off by Cushing's meddling that he decided to involve the foundation in fields where Cushing's reach did not extend, such as university research.

At Cushing's behest, however, Joe Kennedy launched his earliest ventures in MR. The Sisters of St. Francis of Assisi ran the various St. Coletta schools for the mentally retarded in the United States. In 1947, Cushing persuaded Kennedy to help finance a new St. Coletta school in Hanover, Massachusetts. The school opened that same year as the St. Coletta School by the Sea, later renamed the Cardinal Cushing School and Training Center. Ten years later Cushing extracted from the financier a three hundred-bed dormitory for the school; Jack Kennedy showed up along with a throng of more than five thousand people for the opening ceremony. Over the years the St. Coletta School in Hanover became the darling in the Cardinal's collection of charitable institutions; he expressed the wish to buried on its grounds.[34]

St. Coletta remained the bridge between the two men: it was at Cushing's behest that Rosemary was placed at the St. Coletta School in Jefferson, Wisconsin.[35]

Cushing also led Joe Kennedy into his first big venture regarding humane care and training for the mentally retarded, persuading the financier late in the 1940s to contribute several hundred thousand dollars to establish a hospital for handicapped children in Brighton outside of Boston. The Joseph P. Kennedy, Jr. Memorial Hospital—or the "Kennedy Home" as it came to be known—was to be run by the Franciscan Missionaries of Mary and staffed by the faculty of Tufts medical school. The hospital did not specifically focus on mental retardation, and in fact ended up with cerebral palsy as its main concern; nonetheless, many of the young patients were mentally retarded. This institution marked the real beginning of the Kennedy family's financial commitment to the cause of mental retardation.[36]

In the Brighton project, the charitable and the political converged. Brighton was an important community for Jack Kennedy politically. The most influential organization there was the Brighton Women's Club, whose annual banquet Jack attended regularly. As Boston politician and Kennedy man Thomas Broderick recalled, "A home for retarded children practically was initiated at the head table sometime around '48 or '49 when the Cardinal was there. He used to attend every year too. At that time he was an Archbishop. That's when they really got together, he and Jack. And of course . . . Jack gave one hundred and some odd thousand dollars as the initial amount of money to start that home for retarded children, which is now the Joseph P. Kennedy Home out there in Brighton. . . . I've never mentioned it because that's one thing that Jack would never, you know, you'd never discuss with him." [37]

Cushing's own version of the origins of the Brighton home, as told to Ted Kennedy, was that "shortly after the Second World War" he met the family for the first time. "As a result of the death of this very promising young man [Joe Jr.], I gradually became a friend of your family. Ere long they conferred with me concerning a memorial for 'Joe, Jr.'" [38] Thus arose the concept of the children's hospital in Brighton.

Cushing then became so wrapped up in the Brighton hospital that he came to regard it as his own private domain. In 1957, he gently chided Eunice, "By the way, Eunice, it is not the 'Kennedy Home' but the 'Joseph P. Kennedy, Jr. Memorial Hospital' and, furthermore, it is one of the greatest specialized hospitals in the country. We are now building a Research Centre there. . . . The next time you come to Boston notify me in advance so that I can bring you around to some of these new projects." [39] The next time Eunice Kennedy happened to stop by, the archbishop showed *her* the Kennedy family charities! So exalted was Cushing about "his" pediatric hospital that he later rejected Sargent Shriver's suggestion that the Brighton hospital might want to work together with the Harvard Medical School on a program in mental retardation. [40] Joe Kennedy complained in 1954, "The Home in Boston is so completely under the domination of Archbishop Cushing that I would hesitate to do anything about it [regarding a Catholic psychiatrist who was seeking an appointment]. This Home has not brought me nearly the satisfaction I thought it would." [41]

Launched into the world of MR philanthropy by Cushing, Joe Kennedy went on to establish further Kennedy MR "homes" far afield from Boston, setting up a second in New York. The family's third large MR project in the early years was the St. Coletta School in Palos Park, a suburb of Chicago. In 1949, the nuns at St. Coletta's had started "educating and training God's exceptional boys." Their efforts had come to the attention of Joe Kennedy, who in 1952 gave them a grant of $1.5 million dollars. Of course the nuns renamed the school in honor of Joseph P.

Kennedy, Jr.[42] Throughout the 1950s, Eunice would take visitors to the school or campaign on its behalf in various charities, thus serving her own apprenticeship in working with MR.

As a result of grants like that given to the nuns at St. Coletta, Joe Kennedy began to acquire a certain public profile in the MR cause. As John Royal, an NBC vice president, wrote from New York after the Palos Park grant was announced, "Congratulations on your wonderful gift to the Retarded Boys of Chicago. If you get a few spare dollars, could you build something for retarded old men, or retarded pretty girls of any age?"[43] The parents' organization—the National Association for Retarded Children—also tried to gain Joe Senior's support, but to no avail.[44]

Despite his public profile and these few residential schools he helped establish, Joe Kennedy was only minimally involved with MR right through the mid-1950s. In 1957, for example, the foundation gave only 17 percent of its grants to causes associated with mental retardation.[45] The foundation's official line, sent out to disappointed applicants, was that only projects "for the benefit of underprivileged children" were supported, with nothing being said of mental retardation.[46]

Nor did Joe Kennedy seek an identification with MR before the mid-1950s. In fact, he often found administering the foundation such a nuisance that he sought no profile of any kind for it, for fear of encouraging a swarm of applications. As Joe's lieutenant James Fayne told Sargent Shriver in 1952, "The Boss says no on any publicity about the Foundation's work. He does this because in the past any mention of the Foundation's program was followed by a flood of appeals to be included in its yearly spending."[47] It was actually under the rule of Joe Kennedy's ambitious son-in-law, Sargent Shriver, that public identification of the Kennedy family with MR causes first began. Joe Kennedy was much more in line with the old-style philanthropists, who preferred to do things out of the public eye and often in the belief that the most blessed form of philanthropy was to give anonymously. He gave a number of gifts anonymously.[48]

It is difficult to understand why, in those early days, he bothered at all. Joe Kennedy had chartered his foundation with a combination of political instinct and dutifulness about philanthropy, and until the mid-1950s the foundation seems to have brought him relatively little gratification. He did not, for example, attend the various benefits his children put on to raise money for the MR cause.[49] Nor, at the outset, did he seem to have any more emotional commitment to the MR cause than to any of the other causes he backed; he seemed far more interested in his sons' political careers.

Getting into MR

In the late 1950s, Joe Kennedy acquired a powerful sentimental commitment to the lot of the mentally retarded and thus seems to have undergone something of a conversion experience. Two developments occurred: (1) he began giving almost his entire foundation budget to causes associated with mental retardation, and (2) he determined that the best way to spend that money was not on the care of the mentally retarded in institutions, but on research dealing with the causes of mental retardation.

From the mid-1950s onward, the foundation's spending on mental retardation increased sharply, rising from 17 percent of the budget in 1957 to 66 percent in 1960.[50]

Furthermore, Joe Kennedy seems to have included family members in grant making more than before, beginning when the Kennedy Foundation gave a new MR school to the sisters of Notre Dame de Namur of Washington, D.C. In 1954, Monsignor John Spence, director of education for the Washington archdiocese, realized that special education for Catholic children with MR there was nonexistent. A survey of the Catholic schools turned up 843 children with some variety of learning problem. Two of the Notre Dame de Namur nuns volunteered to organize a pilot project; one of them was sent to St. Coletta's in Wisconsin for training.

In September 1955, the archdiocese opened a fifteen-seat classroom, called the "Holy Spirit School," for retarded children. The school featured oversized desks and other special physical apparatuses for the students. "Some were brain-damaged, some emotionally disturbed, and others multiply handicapped." Among the pupils was Michael Folliard, son of *Washington Post* reporter and White House correspondent Edward Folliard.

In October 1956, Edward Folliard met Bobby Kennedy on the campaign trail in Elkins, West Virginia, where Bobby was scouting to learn about the mechanics of a presidential campaign. Folliard told Bobby about his mentally retarded son and said that he admired Joe Kennedy for giving to the MR cause. Folliard also told Bobby that the D.C. nuns needed help.

Bobby Kennedy said nothing. Folliard thought to himself, "My God, I put my foot in it."

Later, at Senate hearings where Bobby was working as the committee counsel, Folliard bumped into Joe Kennedy. It turned out that Bobby had in fact briefed his father on the needs of special-ed institutions in the District of Columbia. The financier asked Folliard for details. That afternoon Folliard asked one of the nuns to write a letter listing the school's requirements, and the next day Folliard handed the letter to Bobby. Shortly thereafter, Joe Kennedy sent Folliard a telegram saying that he should stand by for further developments.

"A day or so later," recalled Folliard, "I got a phone call from Ethel Kennedy. She wanted to stop by. She had some of her children—there were three small ones then. Could they stay somewhere? My wife and I went to get them. Ethel had a station wagon. We drove to Holy Spirit and looked over the school. Ethel could see that it was inadequate, but she was delighted with the Sisters and the children."

A few days later, Ethel phoned Folliard: "Grandpa is willing to go for a half-million." That was the beginning of the Lieutenant Joseph P. Kennedy Institute in Washington.[51] (It also marks an initial stage of Bobby Kennedy's own involvement with MR.)

Why the hard-bitten tycoon underwent this change of heart is unknown. His interest in MR occurred much too late to be associated with Rosemary's condition. One possibility is that he was moved by the wrenching appeals that he started to receive once it became known that his foundation was handing out money to institutions set up to improve the quality of life for the mentally retarded.

Consider one Chicago mother who in December 1951 wrote Joe Kennedy about her mentally retarded son Charlie, apparently in his late teens, with an IQ of 27. A few months prior, he had been expelled from the St. Coletta School in Chicago on the grounds that he was "unruly, did not want to obey, ran away, refused to work or study, that he was almost perfect physically and strong, and a man should be able to handle him, it was not a woman's job."

Charlie's story went back a long way. At age ten, he had gone into the state institution at Dixon. "He was only there two or three months at the longest," said his mother. "Call it mother instinct or whatever it is one feels. I knew in my heart something was wrong. I nearly always notified them I was coming on a visit but that time decided to make an unexpected call which I did. As I walked into the cottage . . . a man about 21 years old was striking [Charlie] across the face with a yardstick. The man had shoulders twice the size of an average young man. I was furious but managed to hide my feelings for my child's sake. He had a mark across his face."

Charlie's mother requested that the administration allow her to take her son home, but her request was denied: "No! He is a ward of the State. You cannot take him out for a year." She explained that her son had been placed there voluntarily, but still they refused to allow her to take him home.

As she said goodbye to Charlie that day, she said that he "fell on his knees and begged me to please take him home. They were mean to him. If he couldn't go home, ask God to let him die."

Two weeks later she returned to the institution. "Now I decided to take matters into my own hands. It was the month of November. Charlie did not even have a jacket on. I got to the edge of town and for the first time in my life I actually thumbed a ride into town [Chicago]. I had kidnapped my own child."

Back at home, this mother received threatening letters from the institution, which she ignored. "The police came with a search warrant but they did not try too hard. I refused to let them in. A welfare worker came to the house and demanded that I return the boy. I said, 'Over my dead body you'll take Charlie back to that torture chamber.'"

For five years, she kept Charlie at home. Then she managed to get him into St. Coletta's, where he spent "two wonderful years" before being expelled.

The point of this mother's letter was not to complain to Joe Kennedy about Charlie's expulsion from St. Coletta's but to plead for Joe's help in regard to what occurred after the expulsion.

"About two weeks ago I was busy getting supper about 5:30 p.m. Someone knocked at the back door. Thinking it a child I told Patricia our youngest daughter to answer. I turned around to see who it was. When I saw two very serious looking policemen I told them to come in."

The mother asked the police officers, "Did Charlie throw stones?"

No.

"Did he take something that did not belong to him?"

No.

"I told them I did not know how he could be into much mischief as he never leaves the yard and just from habit I go to the back window a hundred times daily to see if all is well."

It turned out that he had administered a spanking to a seven-year-old who had made a rude remark to him, and the child's parents had called the police. The child had not been injured.

"The children," explained Charlie's mother to the police, "do not mean to be cruel but they are without realizing it. Going and coming from school the boys taunt him, call him names and dare him to come out and fight. He says, 'Go on leave me alone, I'm minding my own business.' He told his father some day he would spank one of them so they would remember. We thought it just talk."

The police took Charlie down to the Stockyard station for questioning. Charlie's mother said that as her son left, she "just stood there like someone in a daze, and tears running down my cheeks. . . . I stood there like I was rooted to that floor for I don't know how long, staring at the door and not believing what just happened. There had never been any kind of trouble with our family, never at any time."

Charlie spent the night at the police station and the next day was taken to court. The father of the seven-year-old, who now had been apprised of the situation, refused to press charges. Nonetheless, Charlie spent a second night at the station. Finally his mother raised $200 bail, which she borrowed from a loan company, and brought Charlie home. It was just before Christmas. The judge decreed that after the New Year, Charlie would have to return to Dixon. Could Mr. Kennedy not help and get the court order changed?[52]

Many such letters arrived. Only a heart of stone could remain unmoved.

Such pleas for help may explain why, in the late 1950s, Joe Kennedy reoriented his own approach to the family charity. Not only would he focus mainly on MR, but he would redirect money from the provision of services for the mentally retarded—such as schools and residential institutions—to research on the causes and prevention of MR.

Joe Kennedy's decision to get involved in MR-related science seems to have been made sometime in 1954, and perhaps in relation to his growing unhappiness about losing control of such homes as those in Palos Park and Hanover after having financed them. "So when I sum it up," he complained to Maurice Sheehy in January 1954, "I find that after I have furnished the money to build these homes, then somebody else takes over. Perhaps that's all for the best. Therefore, I don't know what I could do that would have any bearing on what we have done. . . ."[53] But the following year, in 1955, he had figured out what he might do differently. He proposed to Archbishop Cushing the organization of a research unit—to be named in honor of Cushing—at the Kennedy hospital in Brighton.

This research unit arose in a way that would typify the Kennedy family's approach to charity thereafter: acting only after consulting academic experts. In November 1955, Joe talked with Howard Rusk, the New York rehabilitation specialist, about how one should go about funding scientific research. Joe wanted to set up an advisory council for the Brighton hospital and asked Rusk for recommendations. Rusk put forward the names of three well-known neurologists and internists: Derek Denny-Brown and Paul Yakolev of Harvard, and Dean Hayman of Tufts.[54] Yakolev had been clinical director of the Fernald State School for the Retarded in Waltham, Massachusetts, from 1938 to 1947, and was the only one of the three with a background in MR.

This episode represented the first time that Joe Kennedy turned to academic specialists for advice about "scientific philanthropy"—how one gives money in order to get at the roots of a problem rather than merely relieving it. It established the pattern that the Kennedy family would follow for decades to come: when one feels uncertain about uncharted waters, convoke a group of academic specialists and let them give advice. Joe Kennedy told Rusk that with such a group of experts, "We would have a research committee that would instill great confidence and would be of great prestige in the conduct of the work."[55]

Cushing was flattered at having the unit named after him, for it accorded perfectly with his own ideas about how to move ahead on MR.[56] "My dear Friend, Joe," he wrote in December 1955. "The possibility of the Archbishop Cushing Research project, financed by the Kennedy Foundation, really thrills me." Cushing agreed that only the "very, very best" would do for the advisory committee.[57] Three months later, in February 1956, Cushing announced that the Kennedy Foundation had given the archdiocese a $1,178,000 grant, much of which would go to the Archbishop Cushing Research Department of the Brighton hospital for "a research program related to mental retardation and physical defects due to brain injuries."[58] This was the first substantial grant in the nation's history for research into the causes of MR.

Emboldened by the apparent success of the Brighton experience, in 1958 Joe Kennedy decided to press ahead full-steam on the scientific side. In the spring, he drew again upon Howard Rusk for advice on another expert committee that could propose further research projects for the foundation to support. Rusk suggested three names, this time all psychiatrists: Bernard Wortis, who was head of the department of psychiatry at New York University; Kenneth Appel, a professor of psychiatry at the University of Pennsylvania in Philadelphia; and Francis Braceland, head of an exclusive private nervous clinic in Hartford, Connecticut. This committee—together with Sarge, Eunice, and Pat—met in Joe's Park Avenue offices several times over the spring and summer in order to come up with a plan for the financier to pursue.[59]

Joe Kennedy was simultaneously getting advice from Cushing. In May of 1958, he asked Cushing to "give me the benefit of your thinking on the establishment of the Kennedy Foundation as a research organization from now on." Many people had been importuning Joe Kennedy for money for buildings. "So, the sooner we get into research, the better it will be."[60]

There is no doubt that in this period Joe Kennedy was himself becoming thoroughly familiar with problems in the MR field, rather than delegating information-gathering to his son-in-law or daughter. As Cushing wrote to Bishop William Molloy, who was considering applying to the foundation for money, "Everything else you mentioned about the [building] project is well known to Mr. Kennedy because he is more familiar with the needs of retarded children than most of those who appeal to him for aid. His appreciation of the problem is that we should get at the root source of retardation in so far as children are born with this handicap."[61]

By the fall of 1958, it was clear that the Kennedy Foundation had embarked upon an entirely new course: funding science rather than service. In September, Joe Kennedy told Mother Stella Maris of the Mount Saint Agnes College in Baltimore, "I am sure that you have a rough idea of the work we have been doing—confining our interest almost exclusively to mentally retarded children. We are now changing our policy and are going into the scientific research on the question of mental retardation to see if something can't be done for these children."[62]

How had this crucial switch occurred? There were two influences on the financier. One was his wife Rose, whose own contribution to the MR story risks being forgotten because she didn't leave a paper trail or have any executive authority. But in the 1950s, Rose had tried to function as a quiet public advocate for the mentally retarded. Kennedy scholar James Hilty—whose mentally retarded sister died at age two and whose mentally retarded brother is now sixty-one years old—said, "My mother spoke briefly with Rose Kennedy in 1960 at a mental retardation symposium at which Rose described herself as the parent of a 'retarded' child whose condition was similar to my brother's." Rose recalled the encounter, and later at another meeting greeted Mrs. Hilty "by again mentioning their mutual concerns as mothers of 'retarded' children."[63]

When I interviewed Ted Kennedy, I told him of my plan—which I believed to be justified—to place his sister Eunice at the center of the story. He was silent for a minute, then made a face and said simply, "I hope that the contributions of my mother won't be forgotten in your story."

But of course the second influence on the financier Joe Senior was his daughter Eunice, whose advice seems to have been crucial in the timing of the switch to science. The redeployment of funds in the late 1950s to MR research occurred almost certainly as a result of her and Sarge's growing influence in the operations of the Kennedy Foundation.

What was it that led the Kennedys toward the MR cause? Against the conventional wisdom, it was not so much Rosemary, although memories of her fate were doubtless still vibrant in the family. It was the accumulated grief of the parents, expressed in countless pleading letters —plus the influence of Cardinal Cushing—that dragged Joe into the area of mental retardation. Perhaps the prodding of his wife plus the restless energy of his daughter Eunice and son-in-law Sarge Shriver then prompted the old man to make MR the foundation's main commitment.

Why would Eunice have been so interested in this neglected cause?

3

Eunice and Sarge

At some point in the spring of 1958, Joe Kennedy asked his daughter Eunice and son-in-law Sargent Shriver to take responsibility for the Joseph P. Kennedy, Jr. Foundation's new program on prevention of mental retardation through scientific research. And thus the torch passed from the first generation, that of the founder, to the second generation, that of the seven surviving children. A spirit very different from the father's came to light. If Joe Senior had casually attended to MR as a kind of afterthought, in the hands of his eldest surviving daughter Eunice the cause became an incandescent torch.

So this is the story of a woman. Eunice Kennedy transformed from a wife and mother, scarcely visible behind the overpowering figures of her father and her husband, to an independent actor, moving and shaking events in center stage in a spotlight of her own. Her story was not unlike the passage of so many American women of the 1960s and 1970s—from invisibility to command. Yet unlike the many other women who embarked in those years on the journey toward liberation, Eunice Kennedy did so not in the service of a career but of a cause.

At the beginning of the story, in the late 1950s, Eunice was Mrs. Sargent Shriver. Occupying the limelight was not this most dynamic of Kennedy women, but her even more dynamic husband. As Eunice and Sarge got going, therefore, Eunice got going in the shadows.

Eunice

Born July 10, 1921, in the family home in Brookline, Massachusetts, Eunice was the fifth of the nine Kennedy children.[1] Joe Junior, Jack, Rosemary, and Kathleen had preceded her. As they grew up, Eunice never was really part of the initial "golden trio" of Joe, Jack, and Kathleen. She gravitated instead to a role as natural leader of her younger siblings: Pat, who was three years her junior; Bobby, four years; Jean, seven years; and Ted, eleven years.[2] Recalled one family friend of Eunice's headship of this band, "If anyone in the family wanted to do something but was afraid to ask, Eunice was the one who would jump up and say, 'I'll speak to Dad about that, don't worry.'" One scholar makes her "the female counterpart of Joe Junior."[3] By 1960, Jack would be sidelined from clan life as President-elect, Joe and Kathleen were dead, and Rosemary was in a home for the mentally retarded in Wisconsin. It was therefore partly the happenstance of fate and birth order that positioned Eunice to take charge. But it was also a matter of character and personality.

Eunice had received a proper Catholic drilling, attending the parochial grade schools of Brookline, followed by a series of exclusive Catholic boarding schools, such as Brantwood Hall in Bronxville, New York, and the Convent of the Sacred Heart in Noroton, Connecticut. In 1939, she graduated from the Roehampton Convent of the Sacred Heart in London, where her father was serving as ambassador to the Court of St. James's. Returning to America that September, she enrolled in a convent school, the Manhattanville College of the Sacred Heart, in Manhattanville, New York (later in Purchase), where her mother had attended and where Joan Kennedy would later enroll. Eunice's upbringing to this point had been intensely and exclusively Catholic.

At Manhattanville, the chronic health problems that would dog Eunice all her life—Addison's disease (an adrenal disease that also plagued her brother Jack), stomach ulcers, colitis, and a tendency to succumb to nervous exhaustion—now caught up with her in a serious way. She lost a semester at Manhattanville because of illness. In the belief that the California sun would do her good as it had Jack several years earlier, Rose sent Eunice out to Stanford University in Stanford, California.[4] There Eunice joined the Lagunita sorority and studied social science, graduating in 1944.[5] She was twenty-three, a young beauty with a serious bent toward secular, not Catholic, activism.

At some point during those years—perhaps while going into Harlem one day a week to work with black kids when she was at Manhattanville, perhaps in the liberal climate of Stanford—Eunice decided to occupy herself with the social services. Later, she often referred to herself as a "social worker," even though she had never been formally trained as one. Why she elected the secular side of social work rather than the religious is unclear. Given her competitiveness with her brothers, who all were setting out to make their mark in politics, it was probably because she didn't want to distance herself too much from the race with them.

Thus, Eunice landed in wartime Washington, D.C. Her first job was at the "special war problems division" of the State Department. It consisted of helping officials deal with the anxious relatives of soldiers held prisoner of war in Germany.[6]

In 1946, Eunice aided in Jack's congressional campaign in Massachusetts, then the brother and sister moved into a house together on 31st Street in the Georgetown district of Washington. Simultaneously in 1946, Attorney General Tom Clark was establishing a commission to study juvenile delinquency. Eunice's father prevailed upon someone in the Department of Justice, perhaps Clark himself, to take her on as a staffer, and in January 1947 she began as a "dollar-a-year-girl" (meaning she worked without a salary) to help organize the department's sports program for the Young America project. As she said in an interview, her initial job was to help Clark "get the Nation's youngsters into the game," presumably in order to stamp out juvenile delinquency.[7] She also was to handle relations between the Department of Justice's National Conference for the Prevention and Control of Juvenile Delinquency and similar local-level conferences.[8]

It grew into a big job, actually a project for the whole Kennedy family, as Joe Kennedy conceived things. He geared up John Dowd's public relations firm in Boston to organize publicity on behalf of his daughter. (Dowd complained that the naive Eunice sent him "the wrong kind of picture in which she appeared full length in a family grouping, rather than all by herself in a head-and-shoulder pose."[9]) To make sure that Eunice's performance redounded to the reputation of the family, Joe Senior sent his new employee, Sargent Shriver, to Washington to help her out or supervise her. "Dear Sargent," wrote Joe Kennedy in March 1947. "It looks as if we got you into a plenty tough job, even though it is very interesting." The financier himself would also be coming to Washington, "and maybe help out Eunice on some questions of organization." Why all this effort to help Eunice with a sports program for wayward boys? "We want to make a success of that job."[10] The first venture of Joe's daughter into the big world, in other words, was a family enterprise.

In 1947, Eunice was twenty-six. What did she look like? How did she seem as a person? At five feet ten inches and 130 pounds, Eunice gave an impression of tawny elegance, or rather, if she did not always appear elegant, at least she gave the impression that she was capable of doing so. *Vogue* later described her as "a marvelously boned, high-cheeked, slender woman with the appearance and movements of someone whose habitat is the open air. . . . She has a lean and free-moving body with the smoothness and unity usually seen only in professional athletes."[11] The accompanying photograph captured a perfectly coiffed society woman.

Subsequent family life, however, would disarray the coiffure a bit. In the 1950s and 1960s, Eunice became anything but *bien soignée*. The Cardin creations that hung in her closet were often replaced by the reality of Eunice and the five kids wedged into a shuttle flight from Boston to Washington, tourist class. Of one such flight it was said that "Mrs. Shriver was typically disheveled, her hair in her eyes and a pencil protruding from behind one ear. One of her shoes even had a missing toe ornament."[12] She was known to be "particularly indifferent to display," and, as one journalist put it, "seems happiest banging about the old house at the Cape wearing a venerable skirt and sweater, and a pair of men's shoes she inherited from an old friend of her father's."[13]

What distinguished Eunice was not her wardrobe but the sense of personality and energy that she projected. "Eunice Kennedy Shriver's personality is so strong that it greets you before she does," began one admiring piece. "Not an ounce or ray of this strength is wasted; she channels it so that all the activities of her life are fueled and flamed with maximum efficiency."[14] Another writer said, "She speaks with a quick down-East accent and high breathlessness, uncannily like John F. Kennedy's voice. Of all the Kennedys she looks the most like the last President, and her manner is like his, vibrant and compelling, with the impression of rushing against time."[15]

Capping this image of vibrancy was the famous Kennedy smile, a genetic trademark perfected by five years of monthly orthodonture in New York. Eunice attributed the smile to the efforts of her mother: "A lot of Mother's things have paid off, both in general and in special ways. For instance, that so-called 'flashing Kennedy smile' that got to be part of the trademark after we grew up and some of us entered public life. You don't flash unless your teeth are good. Mother monitored our intake of sweets.

"Then the tooth brushing. After every meal. . . . I remember it as part of the morning drill. She'd always come down in her robe, for breakfast with us, to make sure we had the right food and ate it and then brushed our teeth."[16] Thus equipped, Eunice marched into adult life with a golden smile that was, in fact, used highly selectively, for she was also known for being brusque, imperious, and impatient in a quite unsmiling way.

Most of all, though, despite a history of chronic illness, Eunice Shriver was famous for her enthusiasm for competition and for excelling. She was said to be "the most competitive" of the Kennedys.[17] In this, ventured a *New York Times* writer, "She reminds people most of President Kennedy and their hard-driving father." As a family friend told the journalist, "She could have been a tycoon. She could have been another Joe Kennedy."[18] Reflecting the values of the 1950s, which held it impossible for women to be President of the United States, her sister-in-law Ethel opined, "It's a shame she wasn't a man, because she'd make a great President."[19] And her brother Teddy, speaking in regard to the Democratic convention, quipped, "I'm not supporting anybody before the convention, but if Eunice should decide to run, I might have to reconsider."[20] A headline in the *Ladies' Home Journal* that year blazed, "The Kennedy Who Could Be President (if she weren't a woman)."[21] Thus, Eunice was a woman whose drive was presidential caliber.

Rather than channeling this relentless energy into political competition, as her brothers did, Eunice sublimated it into sports. Winning at sports was a theme woven into Eunice's life from early childhood. In the Kennedy household, the pressure to excel was intense. Joe Senior exhorted his children to win—to play fairly, of course, but in the end to beat the competition. As Eunice recalled of those days of swimming and sailing about Hyannisport, the kids were taught that "coming second was just no good."[22]

At Manhattanville's Sacred Heart and at Stanford, Eunice played on the school tennis team. And in 1947, as she embarked upon the attorney general's conference on juvenile delinquency, she told the *Washington Post* that her "favorite sports now are tennis, sailing and horseback riding."[23] Throughout her adult life Eunice played fiercely at sports, dragging her balky children nearly every night onto the grass of their Maryland estate, Timberlawn, to toss a football.[24] (*Time* reported in 1972 of Eunice at the family touch-football games, "She is particularly noted for a deft maneuver of hauling in a pass and then ducking behind a tree to elude her pursuers."[25]) Sargent Shriver later mused, "I'd never been with a woman who really tried to beat the hell out of a man on a tennis court. I used to say, 'What's the matter with her?'"[26]

These personal details help us understand the nature of her commitment to the cause of mental retardation. There is no mystery about why Eunice became involved with MR in the first place: her father steered her towards it. But if we ask why she went after it with such single-minded determination, the answer is a little more complex, and involves both her attitudes towards religion and her relationship with her parents.

The depth of Eunice's personal piety was not really publicly known, mainly because she was loathe to discuss it in nonreligious settings for fear of alienating potential allies or of appearing archaic in a secular society.

But there is no doubt that one of the bedrocks upon which Eunice's commitment to MR rested was her faith. She got this from her mother. Rose was said to attend mass virtually every morning. As John Throne, former executive director of the foundation, recalled, "I went with Rose to Sweden in 1966 and she drove the secret service and the Swedish police crazy because she'd be up at four a.m. for early mass. I think she went every day to mass."[27] Eunice had absorbed much of Rose's legendary piety, although she did not attend mass daily. It is said that Eunice had once contemplated becoming a nun—until Sargent Shriver proposed to her in 1953.[28]

Her deep preoccupation with religious questions spilled over into her daily life. Though she almost never mentioned religion as a reason for helping the mentally retarded—preferring instead to dwell upon their humanity—she tried to bring concerns of a fundamentally Christian nature to the hard world of Washington politics. For example, in the 1960s Eunice unsuccessfully tried to persuade James Shannon, head of the National Institutes of Health (NIH), to install a program on morals and ethics at NIH.[29]

Her faith was also evident in her personal life, in the form of spontaneous and unacknowledged acts of charity. Sargent Shriver's driver, Richard Ragsdale ("Rags"), remembered one such act. Rags normally would drive Sarge from Timberlawn into D.C., and Eunice would drive herself. One day Rags knew that Eunice was coming in right after him and told the parking lot attendant not to barricade her car after she arrived.

"The parking-lot attendant," said Rags, "was a refugee from El Salvador or some place and didn't speak any English, and so when Mrs. Shriver finally came to get her car, she couldn't get it out."

She told Rags, "Go get the manager."

Rags went and got the manager and Eunice discovered that the reason for the problem was the man's lack of knowledge of English. "So she voluntarily paid for a course of English lessons at the Berlitz school for this guy which cost about $2500."[30]

Eunice also maintained the traditional Catholic probity toward human sexuality. She opposed abortion. She was a strong believer in premarital chastity as well. Michael Novak, the conservative Catholic social philosopher, recalled that on the occasion of his first visit to Timberlawn in 1970, Eunice asked him to explain to her son, the sixteen-year-old Bobby Shriver, "why premarital intercourse is wrong."[31] (Whether Bobby Shriver, who remained for many years a bachelor, followed these precepts is uncertain.[32]) No hint of scandal ever clung to Eunice or her husband Sarge. In matters of faith and morals, she remained her mother's daughter.

Thus Eunice's involvement with mental retardation was driven by ethical and religious wellsprings within her own psyche. Though she was reluctant to say it in so many words, she believed that helping the mentally retarded was an aspect of her Christian mission. Part of the enthusiasm with which she fulfilled that mission was derived from the zealotry of the Jesuits.

Another part of Eunice's commitment to the mentally retarded, however, came from her desire to show her dominating, overcontrolling parents what she was really capable of on her own. This analysis is more speculative, for in public Eunice never made more than the most deferential remarks about her mother and father, the very mirror of filial devotion. But the picture that emerges from both public and private family documents is that of an overbearing father and a meddlesome, intrusive mother—quite the opposite of the portrait of Rose as detached and withdrawn that has been given us by other writers.[33]

While Rose's household was religious, it did not actually swim in piety. For example, Eunice had the opportunity to make marginal comments on the screenplay of a TV special, to be called "The Matriarch," starring Katherine Hepburn. (It was never produced.) Her marginalia give some insight into the true level of religiosity in the Kennedy household in the 1940s and 1950s. At one point the text has Rose saying, "Joe, this is a day to 'make a joyful noise unto the Lord.'"

Eunice wrote in the margin, "Not Ma."

At another passage where JFK is being inaugurated, Joe says, "I hate being late."

Thereupon Rose is supposed to murmur, "We were on time for the only thing that matters today . . . the moment Johnny put his hand, here . . ." The ellipses are provided in the text. Rose is mandated to speak softly and touch the Bible.

Eunice commented, "No, too soft, 'religious.'" (She also noted that her mother always called the President "Jack," never "Johnny.")

Elsewhere the screenplay had Rose reading from the Psalms as London was being bombed. Eunice wrote simply, "No, no, no."[34]

More accurately, Rose's religious beliefs resulted in a highly intrusive style of parenting. Rose believed that parenting must be taken seriously, because parents influenced their children both in the here-and-now and for the kingdom to come. In 1967, in an interview, she mentioned to CBS's Harry Reasoner the "tremendous" responsibility of the parent. "What you say has influence not for a day or for a year, but for time and for eternity."[35]

Given this awful impact, no misstep was too small to remain uncorrected. Rose instructed Eunice at one point in 1959 not to let her daughter Maria go "up and down in the elevator in her nightgown. I do not think that it looks very well. If I were to come into an apartment house and find a child thus, I would think the apartment a very strange one and the parents of the child rather careless."[36] This note was written as a business letter, typed by Rose's secretary in Palm Beach.

On another occasion, Rose rebuked Eunice about an outfit she had worn: "Will you please be sure that your yellow pants are not too tight in the seat.

"I thought they looked a little 'snuggy' the other evening, if you know what I mean."[37] Again, a secretary typed this communication in the form of a business letter.

Eunice, a grown woman of thirty-six with two children, was accepting instruction from her mother in how she was supposed to dress.[38] One might surmise that Eunice felt herself very much under the thumb of this intrusive mother, and that an occasion to break out of this role of perfect-Catholic-daughter-and-mother would not be unwelcome.

With her father, Eunice's problem was different. Joe Senior was certainly authoritarian but somewhat indifferent. Or at least he was indifferent to seeing his daughter bound ahead in the domain that mattered to her but that he considered to be the province of his sons: secular success.

Eunice began her 1965 tribute to her father with the overwhelming sentence, "My father is the most involved, dynamic, powerful, energetic, competitive, organized, and delightful man of vision I have ever known."[39] Every public utterance she ever made about him was somehow awestricken such as, for example, a declaration supposedly made to their mother: "You were in charge of us and raised and trained us while we were children. And then, when we began turning into young people, Dad took charge the rest of the way."[40] In private, Joe was unstinting with advice about how a suitable Kennedy woman should behave and appear. In regard to a forthcoming fashion show in 1958, Joe Senior let his views be communicated to Eunice, via Rose: "Dad says that Cassini is to do the show, so why not have him do a dress for you. You like his clothes and he would be terribly interested. . . ."[41]

Yet Joe Kennedy was, in the last analysis, really not that interested in his daughters' activities, loving though he may have been to them. He once said of Eunice, "If that girl had been born with balls she would have been a hell of a politician."[42] But Eunice, for better or worse, was born female. And her father, like many others of his day, did not see her as much more than a housewife.[43] In his correspondence with Cushing, Joe would gush over the progress of his "sons," never of his "children." In accordance with his views about the sexual division of labor, Mr. Kennedy named his three sons—and none of his daughters—executors of his will,[44] and made his three healthy daughters—and none of his sons—Rosemary's legal guardians.[45] Nor did he ever mention his daughters to the Cardinal, save in the most ancillary of ways. Lacking any awareness of these issues, Ted Kennedy claimed of his father, "His standards were the highest *for each of his sons.*"[46]

Eunice once wrote her father rather plaintively, "Dear Daddy, I know you are very busy. I also know you are advising everyone else in that house on their careers, so why not me?"[47]

Why not me? Eunice used to joke to her father about being President herself. Rita Dallas, who nursed the financier after his stroke in 1961, reported how much JFK and Eunice "loved visiting their father together, and he got a great kick out of hearing them challenge each other. The President always went through his speeches with Eunice, seeking her opinion. They would huddle together in the library [at Hyannisport] and then stop back at Mr. Kennedy's room, so Eunice could say of Jack, 'He's pretty good, Daddy . . . but I could do it better.'"[48]

Was the source of Eunice's drive her desire to demonstrate herself the equal of her brothers? One tries to eschew the psychologizing that has marred so many books about the Kennedys. Yet there is evidence that Eunice might have brooded in her heart about her father's inattentiveness to issues that really mattered to her. Eunice, presidential material in her own right who possessed all the qualities save the requisite gender, was determined to show her father what she could really do. She accepted the MR cause as a way of carrying out that demonstration.

Sarge

In 1950, Eunice moved with her sister Jean to Chicago. Jean was to work at Merchandise Mart, Eunice to busy herself with various religious matters at the Chicago archdiocese, including a spell of social work at the House of the Good Shepherd and helping with the St. Coletta School at Palos Park.[49] Eunice also became caught up in promoting the Mart—suggesting, for example, in 1950 that the male models at a men's fashion show be auctioned off to a "Here's how to get your Man" theme.[50] In Chicago, she saw more and more of the young assistant manager of the Mart named Sargent Shriver. On May 23, 1953, they were married.

Sargent Shriver, thirty-seven at the time of his marriage, was in many ways the exact opposite of his wife: amiable where she was abrasive, emollient and well-spoken where she was curt and laconic, a Maryland aristocrat by descent where she had come from the rough-and-tumble Boston Irish. Their joint success in the cause of mental retardation signifies that these apparent differences were really quite superficial;

deep down Sarge and Eunice were unified by powerful ties of moral conviction and force of character.

The Shrivers arrived in Maryland in 1693. The family built a grain mill in Union Mills in 1797, and subsequent generations would form a large and genteel Maryland clan. There were Shrivers protesting against the Stamp Act in 1765 and riding with Jeb Stuart's Confederate cavalry in the Civil War. With a long and distinguished lineage behind her, Sarge's mother Hilda Shriver (whose maiden name was also Shriver; she and her husband were second cousins) felt she could hold her head up when her son married one of the famous Kennedys: "We go back three hundred years in Maryland, when they were still in Ireland," she told Harris Wofford, who at the time was an assistant of Sarge's.[51]

But the Shrivers had never been wealthy. Sarge's father, Robert Sargent Shriver, Sr., started out as an officer of a local bank in Westminster, Maryland. Sarge's mother came from a somewhat loftier branch that had entertained at table the likes of Teddy Roosevelt, William Howard Taft, and other distinguished names of the day. In 1921, the Shrivers moved to Baltimore when Robert became vice president of the Baltimore Trust Company. In 1929 it was onward to New York. Then, just as the father was in the process of organizing a Wall Street commercial bank, the family was wiped out in the Crash of 1929.[52] Thus, despite the family's lack of great wealth, Sarge Shriver came from a family of genteel background. In a Kennedy-Shriver union, there was no question of wealth marrying wealth, though breeding in the Shriver background was aplenty.

The Shrivers also did not have a deep family background of Catholicism. Sarge's father converted to Catholicism at the time of his marriage, but what distinguished Robert Shriver religiously was a lively interest in questions of religion and morality. He was said to be "an active doer of good works." As Sarge grew up, these matters were often discussed at the family dinner table.[53] Sarge, therefore, emerged from his upbringing with a consciousness of the importance of public service. He later told *Time* magazine, "For 250 years my family has been in public office. We've always been bankers, businessmen, public officials. It's a natural thing."[54]

Sarge attended Cathedral High School in Baltimore until the family moved to New York in 1929. There was just enough money from 1930 to 1934 to send him to Canterbury, a selective Catholic prep school in New Milford, Connecticut. Doing well at Canterbury, Sarge won a scholarship to Yale and graduated cum laude in 1938. During his school years, he had to work at all kinds of jobs to keep his head above water. In the summers of 1932 and 1933, he operated a corn-cutting machine at a relative's canning factory in Owings Mills (Sarge's daughter Maria Shriver—now a television personality—has Owings as her middle name). At Yale he was editor-in-chief of the campus newspaper, the *Daily News*. "I've always sent money home," he told reporters in 1963. "I've had to earn my own way."[55]

It was by force of personality rather than family name that Sarge Shriver became a "big man on campus" at Yale. He was a member of the correct fraternity, Delta Kappa Epsilon; was "tapped" by the private society Scroll and Key; and generally cut a figure as an outgoing, activist type, not a "brain" but a young man interested in ideas, philosophy (he was the secretary of the St. Thomas More Society), and sports. As the historian of his Yale class later wrote, "Sarge Shriver took over the *News* and put his cards right on the table, by outlining his position as Christian, Aristotelian, Optimistic and American. Whew. Well, we knew where we stood, at any rate."[56]

Shriver went on to earn a law degree from Yale in 1941, working briefly on Wall Street thereafter. But meanwhile, there were other things on his mind. In the shadow of war, he enrolled in the V-7 program of the U.S. Navy Reserves, serving as an apprentice seaman in the summer of 1940 on the battleship the USS *Arkansas*. He then finished law school and in June of 1941 went on active duty with the U.S. Navy. Six months later Pearl Harbor was bombed.

In the Pacific theater, Shriver saw plenty of action. He started out on a destroyer, became anti-aircraft officer on the battleship USS *South Dakota*, and was wounded in the fighting around Guadalcanal (yet according to one biographer "refused to put in for a Purple Heart"[57]). In October 1943, he shifted to the submarine service, helped sink several enemy ships and, in fact, in early 1945 found himself looking through the periscope at Tokyo Bay. Through an administrative accident he was assigned back to San Diego, and by the time the snafu had been cleared up, it was too late to get back into combat.[58]

Decommissioned at the war's end, Shriver found himself with a taste for excitement that rejoining his classmates in a Wall Street law firm would not satisfy. Having come through a number of narrow escapes, Sarge as a thoroughly religious man also found himself asking if God had spared him for some purpose. "I had a lot of guys killed right near me," he later told a reporter. "That's very sobering, to be as close as you and I are, talking in this restaurant, and suddenly you're blown away and I'm still sitting here and there's no reason for it in the world. None. I mean absolutely zero.

"I wanted to be assigned to a fleet submarine in the war zone [in early 1945]. Instead they put me on a boat in San Diego. I thought I was screwed. But every one of those subs I wanted to get on was sunk. With everybody on board. Every single one. Every single sub. . . . So, you go through life and those things keep happening. You can either become very fatalistic or you say to yourself, no matter what I think of myself, I'm being kept alive to do something."[59]

With this curious combination of zeal for action and a sense of mission, Sarge sought out a job in journalism. He had worked as a stringer for *Time* magazine while at Yale, and being on friendly terms with the family of Malcolm Muir—who was the editor-in-chief of *Newsweek*—Sarge was able to get a job as assistant to Edward J. Barrett, *Newsweek*'s publisher. The ambitious young journalist then met Eunice Kennedy at a cocktail party in Manhattan sometime in 1946. She mentioned Sarge to her father.

Joe Kennedy was on the lookout for energetic young men to help run his empire, particularly to turn the Merchandise Mart around. In January 1946, the financier wrote to Paul Murphy: "What we want in our Merchandise Mart is our own organization—topside people who can handle our own business effectively."[60] Surrounding oneself with the best people available had hallmarked Joe Kennedy's career, and in Sarge Shriver he identified one of those rare "topside people." On the pretext of asking Shriver to evaluate for possible publication a diary that Joe Junior had kept while in Spain during the Spanish Civil War, Joe invited Sarge to breakfast at the Waldorf-Astoria in New York.

Joe asked if the memoirs could be published.

Sarge drew in his breath and said no. "That took two and a half minutes. I was worried about getting down to *Newsweek* on time. Then [Mr. Kennedy] said, 'I've just bought the Merchandise Mart. I'm looking for guys to work for me.'"[61]

Sarge at first turned Mr. Kennedy down. He still had hopes of a career at *Newsweek,* on the face of it a socially more acceptable choice than playing major-domo to a man who had a public reputation as one of America's great robber barons. Then something went sour for Sarge at *Newsweek*. In November 1946 he wrote to Joe Kennedy, "Frankly I want to get another job." Sarge said he had begun exploratory negotiations with his old law firm. "It is true, however, that I'd much rather go to work for you. . . . I'd be more than glad, in fact I'd prefer, to call you at your convenience in Hyannisport."[62]

Joe Kennedy took Sarge on as a kind of all-purpose general assistant, sending him first as a personal representative to Chicago, then in 1947 to work with Eunice in Washington, then again in 1948 to Chicago as the assistant manager of the Merchandise Mart. Shriver would remain in Chicago for the next twelve years. His job there was to drum up new business for the Mart and to function as a midwest listening agent for Joe Kennedy, and also to act as regional manager for Jack Kennedy's political campaigns.

The business association was to evolve into a remarkable friendship, although Sarge always called the financier "Mr. Kennedy." Through Joe's tutelage, Sarge came down from his philosophical ivory tower and learned how the world worked, learned "to respect a dollar," as he later put it.[63] In return, Sarge was able to serve Joe Kennedy as an employee with razor-sharp wit and captivating charm, and with absolute fidelity—if Sarge ever said anything negative about his father-in-law, it is not a matter of written record.

Not only did Sarge respect Joe Kennedy for his business acumen and his ability to size people up, he loved the financier in a profoundly Christian sense, often praying for him.[64] On Christmas Day, 1950, Sarge wrote to Joe and Rose Kennedy, "My job has permitted me to work on the St. Coletta's project . . . to support my mother and make her happy; to help Eunice a little with some of her activities; to enjoy the friendship and gaiety of Jean; to hear wonderful music and see the best theatre . . . in fine, to occupy a position of dignity and opportunity where I have no one but myself to blame for any failures or faults.

"I hope some day to look back on a life in which I may have done for some just a few of the things you have done for many. If and when I do you can be sure I'll remember that you gave me the chance and showed me how, and that without your interest and support my life would have been unhappily different and poor indeed."[65] Such praise would be considered toadying were it not for the tone of complete gratitude and sincerity in these letters.

In a way, Joe Kennedy reciprocated this love for Sarge, although he did not write him heartfelt letters. Joe arranged for Sarge to marry his daughter Eunice.

When Eunice arrived at that cocktail party in Manhattan in 1946, her sister Kathleen came up to her and said, "There's the most divine man here. He's just right for you!" Eunice's said of her first impression of Sarge, "He was bubbling, bursting with energy, and very attractive."[66] Sarge was about six-feet tall with an athlete's chest and muscular arms. His biographer describes him in those days as "a very handsome man, with a twinkle in his eye and a magnetic smile, always impeccably garbed."[67] (In 1964, Sarge was named one of the ten best-dressed men in America in the annual list issued by the Custom Clothiers Association of New York.[68]) It must be stressed, however, that Sargent Shriver did *not* have the Kennedy style. In the judgment of Anthony Lewis of the *New York Times,* Sarge was "not a Kennedy in looks or manner. His neutral voice, slightly touched with Maryland, and his open, informal style are far from the boyish but patrician, reserved figure of John Kennedy."[69]

Perhaps that is why Eunice did not take to him at once.[70] For her, it does not seem to have been love at first sight. She was being courted by other men.[71] As for Sarge, it is impossible to know what he might have thought about his wife: the soul of gentlemanliness, he never said. Sarge saw Eunice socially somewhat in 1947 on the Georgetown dinner party scene, and of course became friendlier with her as he helped her at the Justice Department. Staying on in Washington for sixteen months, "it wasn't only the job that kept me there," he said.[72]

Friendship blossomed into romance after the two began working together in 1950 in Chicago, Eunice living in an apartment that Sarge, at her father's behest, had fixed up for her and Jean, Sarge himself staying in a suite the Kennedys retained at the Ambassador East Hotel on the Near North Side. Sarge would "move out temporarily whenever some member of the Kennedy family came to town."[73]

Joe Kennedy's assistant James Landis believed it was Joe himself who had picked Sarge as a marriage partner for Eunice.[74] Eunice and Sarge were married in May 1953 at St. Patrick's Cathedral in New York City, with Cardinal Spellman officiating and seventeen hundred guests present. Eunice toasted the groom at the wedding dinner with, "I searched all my life for someone like my father and Sarge came closest."[75]

In reality, however, Sarge was quite unlike Joe Kennedy. For one thing, despite the flurry of movement with which he surrounded himself, Sarge was very much an intellectual. Harris Wofford recalled from late 1960 when Shriver was in charge of the talent search for the new administration, "He would regularly read in his bed long after midnight, turning from the endless memos of the talent search to something philosophical, religious or literary. Stirred by a passage in Saul Bellow or a verse in a poem, he would read it aloud, and a conversation would spring up until sleep put it out. Often it would continue first thing in the morning when Shriver would take me along to mass, his common routine (which he thought good for my Episcopalian soul)."[76]

In religious matters, Sarge not only possessed intense faith but also was highly reflective about his beliefs. He adhered to the tradition of liberal, socially active Catholicism of the French theologian Yves Simon, who had struggled to achieve faith amid "the atrocious moral history of our epoch."[77] Regarding the Vatican II papal council, which convened between 1962 and 1965, Sarge Shriver wrote, "No longer can we seek the spiritual kingdom of God by turning our back on the social realm of man. We must instead go into that realm—as social beings involved with other social beings."[78] Just as Eunice had considered at one point joining a Christian order, Sarge had contemplated it as well. "I've always thought Sarge might have been a misplaced Franciscan," said Donald Stedman, who worked for the family foundation briefly in the early 1960s.[79]

Rather than retreating inside a monastery with his faith, Sargent Shriver carried it into the streets. He believed racism wicked, and in Chicago he was constantly initiating interracial councils and other civil rights programs in order to bring blacks into the American mainstream. He battled against the relentless secularism of the media, once firing off a letter to his sister-in-law Pat in 1973 in which he opposed an English TV series called "The Ascent of Man" as being overly adulatory of progress: "It seems to me that Professor [Jacob] Bronowski is perpetuating the post-Renaissance, post-Reformation Age of Enlightenment, deification of science and scientists, adulation of progress, and other bromides, which may be at the heart of our philosophic and spiritual problems. Even the title 'The Ascent of Man' perpetuates the idea that we human beings today are somehow superior to Aristotle and Plato, that we have ascended somehow or other from their condition."[80] On another occasion, defending the Peace Corps, he said, "The belief in a civilization based on the God-given dignity of the individual being, the readiness to sacrifice to enable such a civilization to live. . . . This has been waiting to be tapped, this is what the Peace Corps is tapping."[81] Of course any politician could say this, but it is clear from an examination of his personal correspondence that Sargent Shriver actually believed it.[82]

In short, it is impossible to understand Sargent Shriver without grasping that his basic motivation to do well and to do good came as an expression of his religious faith. He was concerned with advancing the interests of the Kennedy family, but only insofar as he saw the family lending itself to just causes. As he said in 1958, "The only genuine elite in this world, or in the next, is the elite of those men and women who have given their lives to justice and charity."[83] Sarge was conscious of belonging to an elite, but it was not the elite of Hyannisport and Palm Beach.

Finally, Sarge Shriver differed from his father-in-law in that Sarge proved himself to be a charismatic leader of men and women. He inspired an entire generation of idealistic young people at the Peace Corps and the War on Poverty in the early 1960s to follow him in the vision of a cause. One of them, Harris Wofford, later said, "Shriver was not a tidy administrator, but he was a great executive. He did not delegate powers through an orderly chain of command, but he empowered people. He released their energies, backed their efforts, and drew on their insights. Wives of staff men tended to be jealous because Shriver harnessed their husbands' energies and loyalties—and weekends."[84] Another of Sarge's lieutenants, Michael Novak, retained this same sense of charismatic style.

"To work with Shriver has always meant an enhancement of life—sheer fun and growth. It has also meant a touch of something else. . . . A touch of class, a willingness to reach, no fear of flying."[85]

In the early 1950s, as Sarge Shriver was about to marry the boss's daughter, many of these qualities were only mildly apparent. But Eunice must have seen in Sarge a man whose energy and commitment would match her own. At this point neither had yet singled out mental retardation as the focus of their moral force. Both were groping across an array of causes—young kids in trouble with the courts (the Shrivers would take three foster daughters from the slums of Chicago into their home), or campaigning on behalf of civil rights (the Shrivers made a point of including blacks in their social gatherings on Chicago's lily-white Gold Coast). In picking Sargent Shriver, Eunice could not have better prepared herself for the struggle to come on behalf of the mentally retarded.

Getting Going

Sometime in the late spring of 1958, Joe Kennedy asked Eunice and Sarge—but most particularly Sarge—to take responsibility for organizing a research program for the family foundation on the causes of mental retardation.[86] The program would be situated in universities, and the previous policy of supporting residential institutions would be discontinued. This represented a momentous change in the lives of the Shrivers.

The immediate problem was the Shrivers' almost total ignorance of the scientific side of MR, and of how one went about organizing programs in universities. On the face of it, Sarge was the assistant manager of an office building, Eunice a housewife who worked occasionally for religious charities in Chicago. It would, under other circumstances, have seemed incongruous for such people to sit down with university presidents and talk about scientific programs. Beneath the surface, of course, realities were entirely different: these were Kennedys, and they had the self-esteem to negotiate with anybody they liked. As one of their advisers later pointed out, it was not at all incongruous for the Shrivers to conduct such negotiations "because university presidents smell money, and when they smell money it doesn't matter who you are. It was the Kennedy name. They had total access to anyone they wished based on the name. It was a powerful thing."[87]

There was nothing of the blunderbuss about the Shrivers. Aware of their ignorance, they immediately set out to remedy it. Eunice in particular badly felt the need for information. As early as the big meeting in New York in the spring of 1958, which her father had organized with his own MR advisers, she was uncomfortable about overrelying upon psychiatrists. She wrote later in an unpublished account:

> I remember in 1958 [Dad] decided he wanted to go into research in mental retardation with the Foundation. He felt that was the only way to really do something effective to help these children. Until that time he had run the Foundation as he wished, and pretty much alone. He mentioned at lunch one day that he was going to try to see Dr. Rusk to talk about the problem. I asked if I could go and he said yes. We attended a meeting for about two hours and when the meeting was over a decision was made about a director to be hired to work out a program for the Foundation.
>
> I objected. I felt that as a result of this discussion the program was going to be a mental health program, that the director was going to be mental health oriented and although I was active in mental retardation I knew that mental health people were not really interested in mental retardation.[88]

On the way back from the meeting to the hotel, Eunice then made her objections clear to her father. "I thought we should staff our office and our research center for mental retardation with people previously interested [in the subject]. However, I didn't know how to do this."[89]

In the summer of 1958, Eunice and Sarge began a crash course in mental retardation. They first turned to local resources in Chicago, attending meetings of the Group for the Advancement of Psychiatry (an activist group within the American Psychiatric Association). They also sought the advice of James Campbell of the University of Illinois Medical School and Jerome ("Jerry") Schulman, a physician who belonged to what was then a rare breed: a pediatric neurologist.[90]

They began to depend on Schulman in particular. A New Yorker by background who had trained in pediatrics at the Jewish Hospital in Brooklyn, then in psychiatry at Johns Hopkins, in 1957 Schulman had just taken a post as assistant professor of pediatric neurology at Northwestern University's medical school in the Chicago suburb of Evanston. He was also the director of the child guidance clinic at the Children's Memorial Hospital in Chicago. Schulman was therefore right at the heart of what the Shrivers wanted to learn about. They started out by taking him on trips to various MR institutions and universities. (After about ten such trips Schulman started pulling back a bit, fearing the loss of his independence to the Shrivers' beck and call.)[91] These trips, under Schulman's guidance, were a hands-on learning experience for the Shrivers as they saw who was doing what.

The Shrivers then invited two other MR specialists to serve, alongside Schulman, as a kind of informal board of advisers. One was Richard Masland, a neurologist. In 1955 the organization of parents of retarded children, NARC, had asked Masland to conduct a survey of the nation's universities to see what new developments science might have to offer their children. Masland had brought Seymour Sarason, a Yale psychologist, and Thomas Gladwin, an anthropologist at the National Institute for Mental Health (NIMH) in Bethesda, into the survey. In December 1958, Basic Books in New York City, the noted publisher of psychological books, brought out the three men's work under the title *Mental Subnormality: Biological, Psychological and Cultural Factors*. Masland, thirty-eight in 1958, was very much a rising star. In ten years he had climbed the academic ladder to a full professorship at Bowman Gray Medical School in Winston-Salem, North Carolina, and in 1957 was summoned to Washington, D.C., to become the assistant director of the National Institute of Neurological Disease and Blindness, one of the NIH institutes. Masland was a perfect "Kennedy man," as the Kennedys liked to think of the academics who advised them—energetic, a "topside figure," and yet not a sycophant or toady but having cool objective judgment. "I had great respect for the Shrivers," Masland said in a later interview. "I was very happy to help them in any way that I could. There was never any friction. I helped when I was asked to."[92]

Sometime in the summer or fall of 1958, Eunice got in touch with Masland and asked him, like Schulman, to accompany them on a number of site visits. Masland finally sent the Shrivers a long letter on how they might include the universities in MR research. He said that a big stumbling block had been the isolation of MR from any kind of university environment. It would make sense, he said, to set up within several outstanding universities MR research centers. The centers would be multidisciplinary, because MR itself affected all the social and biological aspects of an individual's life. The universities should be major ones in order to lend respectability to such research.[93]

The Shrivers brought one more specialist on board, psychiatrist George Tarjan, probably because they wanted somebody who had garnered actual experience with mentally retarded children. Tarjan was superintendent of the Pacific State Hospital in Pomona, California. Forty-six in 1958, he counted as a progressive young institution director with an avid interest in research. Tarjan was also intent on incorporating some of the new insights of the parents' movement. Hungarian by birth, he was by all accounts a remarkable man. One colleague described him as "incredibly perceptive." "His knowledge, his insight, his ability to persuade . . . of all the people I know he probably was one of the best advisers along with [Robert] Cooke that the Shrivers and the Kennedy Foundation ever had."[94] Tarjan would go on to become director of MR research at UCLA's Neuropsychiatric Institute and, much later, serve as president of the American Psychiatric Association. (It was said that he "eventually became the president of every group he joined."[95]) But in 1958 he was merely a rather obscure institution director whom the Shrivers had tapped because they heard he was good.

On November 9, 1958, the Shrivers and Joe Senior met with these three key advisers—Schulman, Masland, and Tarjan—in New York City. Each of the experts had prepared a paper indicating how the foundation might best approach the universities. The participants opted for Tarjan's plan, apparently because it was quite limited. Tarjan recommended that universities set up professorships in the area of MR to be named after the Kennedy family. Schulman was opposed to calling them chairs for "mental retardation." "This does not sound right for the name of a professorship," he said.[96] After the meeting, Schulman reworked Tarjan's paper and added a few of his own ideas. It was to serve as a basis for approaching Harvard, continuing an initiative on "mental health" that Joe Kennedy had begun with Harvard in February of 1958.[97]

The negotiations with Harvard went nowhere. Joe Senior was already quite irritated with Harvard for having refused to give Joe Junior a varsity football award before the war, and for later turning down Ted Kennedy's application to law school.[98] Also, Schulman had warned Sarge about universities' practices of accepting grants and then "raiding" them for general operating funds, so that the donor's purpose remained unaccomplished while the original project sank in a morass of academic bafflegab.[99] So Sarge was suspicious as he approached Harvard.

In December 1958, Sarge and Tarjan saw McGeorge Bundy, dean of Harvard's Faculty of Arts and Sciences. Predictably, Bundy was enthusiastic, but the worst fears of the Kennedy people were soon realized. It was apparent that Harvard was willing to yield the Shrivers no control at all over who would be appointed to the new professorships or what they would do research on. Also, Harvard had shied away from MR as such and wanted the program to study "human development." Masland recommended that Sarge turn Harvard down.[100] Although negotiations dragged on a while longer, that was really the end of it. There never was a Kennedy program for MR at Harvard.[101]

In the meantime, another venerable Boston institution had reared its head: the Massachusetts General Hospital. Raymond Adams, the professor of neuropathology at Harvard and head of the neurology service of the Mass General, had been following these negotiations with interest. In fact David Crockett, the hospital fundraiser, had previously sounded out the Kennedys for money. Thus, just as the Shrivers were negotiating with Bundy and medical school dean George Berry, Adams played his hand. "[Berry] got wind of this and was mad as hops," said Adams later.[102]

Although Adams had little previous interest in MR, he was concerned with organic brain disease in children as a general phenomenon. He and Crockett summoned the Shriver negotiating team to the Mass General for an all-day session. In this parlay the basic division of labor that would prevail between Sarge and Eunice was already clearly outlined. In Adams's recollection, Eunice was "always in the foreground" of public view. "But it was clear that she depended very much on Sargent Shriver's good judgment. So she would often go into a huddle with him." That was as much of the process as Adams saw. We know from the documents that Sarge, who carried the ultimate signing authority, would check back with his father-in-law before sealing the deal.[103] The hospital received over a million dollars.

The money was to be used to set up a laboratory for research in mental retardation within the Mass General, to be headed by Adams. It was the first such laboratory in the world and had the advantage of combining basic research into metabolic disorders causing MR with clinical contact, the patients being either at the Mass General or nearby at the Fernald State School in Waltham, an MR institution. It was to be called the "Joseph P. Kennedy, Jr. Laboratories for Mental Retardation." Although the Kennedy family had donated the start-up funds, this lab, like the several other centers the family had sparked, would in the future be supported by federal and state funds. The first grant was usually all that was given.

What moved the ball along so quickly at the Mass General was the confidence that Joe Kennedy and the Shrivers placed in Raymond Adams, a towering scientific figure as well as a physician who commanded great personal respect. Adams was forty-eight in 1959, having come to the Mass General eight years earlier as chief of neurology (and becoming professor of neuropathology at Harvard in 1954). Joe Senior had apparently told Eunice, "If Dr. Adams will commit himself personally to supervise the research, I'll authorize the Foundation to make the grant."[104] Schulman put it more snidely, but in language that Joe Kennedy might have appreciated. Writing on the subject of Sarge's simultaneous negotiations with the University of Wisconsin, Schulman said, "It appears to me that what we are 'buying' in this instance is quite different than in Massachusetts General. At Massachusetts General we bought a man; that is Ray Adams. In Wisconsin we are 'buying' the medical school."[105]

Weighing the relative importance of dynastic and philanthropic factors is complex. The aging Mr. Kennedy seemed genuinely delighted at the chance to help. After the grant was announced he phoned Adams to say he was very pleased to hear that the award had been made "and that," as Adams recalled, "if I needed help for anything just to call him."

"I am not a piker," the financier added.

Organizing the Kennedy Labs at the Mass General gave MR a sudden prominence in scientific circles. Such figures as Hugo Moser, who later became superintendent of the Fernald School, or Edwin Kolodny, later director of the Shriver Center for research on mental retardation (which is on the grounds of what is now the Fernald Center in Waltham), had served as residents under Adams. As Adams said in 1993, "All of our residents for several generations now have had to work there for a time."[106] One bears in mind that the Harvard Medical School was among the most famous in the world. Its pediatrics and neurology departments served as beacons for their disciplines. And it was absolutely unprecedented to have these prominent departments focus on a disorder like MR that, until then, had not really come out of the closet.

The contact with Raymond Adams during these arduous negotiations in 1959 also turned out to be the beginning of a beautiful personal friendship. Eunice chose Adams as her family doctor, even though he lived in Boston. Both she and Sarge continued to hold him in great respect, always calling him "Dr. Adams" while he called them "Eunice" and "Sarge." Over the years the foundation would often turn to him for advice about how best to make grants, although Adams discouraged too close an association as endangering the doctor-patient relationship. "You have to have a certain delicate line," he said.

The research center at the Mass General was the first fruit of a year of frenetic activity for the Shrivers. Receiving advice from Adams and Masland, from the fall of 1958 onward they crisscrossed the country, visiting universities in order to establish candidates for further centers based on the Mass General model. Although Sarge would generally stand back and let Eunice occupy the spotlight wherever they happened to be, it was Sarge who ultimately ran the show. As Joe Kennedy wrote Howard Rusk in April 1959, "I have sent your letter to Sarge Shriver who is now doing most of the work of setting up the program for the Foundation."[107] Jerry Schulman, along on many of these trips, later said, "Eunice would make it clear that she was sort of boss. I remember the time, we were in a big meeting around the table and she said, 'Sarge, go get me a glass of water.' And he trotted off and got it. It was totally inappropriate. That one incident stood out in my mind because I felt very embarrassed." Yet on the whole, said Schulman, it was "more Sarge" who moved things along. "I have tremendous respect for him. He's intelligent, extremely hard-working, and energetic. He can meet all day."

And Eunice?

"She was very actively involved but I don't think she has the same sort of incisiveness that he did. He more ran things but was deferential to her."[108]

And so in the summer of 1959, the Shrivers raced from university to university. One week, for example, took them from Brandeis University in Waltham, Massachusetts, to Yale in New Haven, Connecticut, to the University of Wisconsin in Madison.[109] They started to become well known in Chicago for this ceaseless voyaging. "Eunice Kennedy Shriver," prattled the *Chicago American*, "refuses to slow down her activities, although she is expecting her third baby in August. She and her husband . . . have visited twenty U.S. cities, awarding grants from the Joseph P. Kennedy, Jr. Memorial Foundation. The latest was $800,000."[110] Most of this travel was done from Friday evening to Sunday evening, so that Sarge would be back at his desk on Monday morning. (He was by this time head of the Chicago school board.)

This period of travel resulted in the Kennedys funding a number of different research institutes and laboratories for mental retardation, especially in Wisconsin, Stanford, Chicago, Georgetown, and Johns Hopkins. It's worth tarrying for a moment at Johns Hopkins in Baltimore, because that is where they met Bob Cooke.

Dr. Robert E. Cooke, forty years old and professor of pediatrics at Johns Hopkins when he first met the Shrivers in 1959, would stay with them for the rest of their days as their scientific *éminence grise*. Of all the academics who clustered about the Shrivers, Cooke has perhaps been most their match in terms of force of personality and style. A man of movie-star looks and dean's-corridor grooming, he projected the Kennedy image of fast-lane dynamism. As someone with first-class intelligence and strong moral convictions, he could hold his own in any after-dinner debate at Timberlawn, the Maryland estate to which the Shrivers moved in 1961. One of Cooke's former residents later said, "Eunice didn't have many long debates with Bob Cooke because she knew she wouldn't get anywhere."[111]

Cooke, born in 1920 in Attleboro, Massachusetts, had gone to high school in Boston, getting an M.D. from Yale in 1944. In his pediatric residency at Yale, he was a student of Grover Powers, the founder of modern pediatrics in the United States. (Powers was NARC's scientific adviser, and it had been at the request of Powers that in 1955 Richard Masland agreed to do the MR survey of the nation's universities for the parents' organization.) In terms of Cooke's scientific development, equally important was the work he did at Yale under Daniel Darrow, the physiologist who pioneered the study of salt and water balance in children. It was in this field that Cooke made his own scientific mark.

Cooke later said, "As a consequence of those experiments there was a major change in the feeding practices for infants throughout the world with a substantial decrease in morbidity and mortality everywhere."[112]

In 1956 Cooke left Yale for Johns Hopkins to become the professor of pediatrics, occupying one of the most distinguished pediatric chairs in the country. It was at this point that Cooke included in his medical profession a focus on mental retardation.

Around 1950, Cooke and his wife had two severely retarded children of their own. They were born with cri du chat syndrome (cry of the cat), a condition characterized by a small head, a catlike cry in infancy, and a customarily short life expectancy (though one of Cooke's children is still alive at this writing). As is so often the case among people who are personally involved with mental retardation, Cooke found himself turning professionally to this orphan field. In 1956, he became a scientific adviser to NARC and in 1957–59 received from NARC a $10,000-a-year grant as the "Grover F. Powers Research Professor."[113] Cooke was therefore already highly visible within MR research when Richard Masland, acting on behalf of the Shrivers, asked him in 1959 if he would like to propose a program at Johns Hopkins for the Kennedys to support.[114]

On November 9, 1959, the Shrivers together with their advisers Schulman, Campbell, and Masland traveled to Baltimore to see Cooke and the members of his proposed team. Cooke made a big impact on them. "Dr. Cooke is . . . without any doubt, one of the leading pediatricians in America," Sarge wrote to Joe Senior. "All of us were greatly impressed by him." Sarge also pointed out that at Johns Hopkins, a "top-flight" place, "We have a better chance of attracting good people into research work on mental retardation."[115]

So the Johns Hopkins program went ahead. But more important, the Shrivers decided to make Cooke their right-hand man. Later in November of 1959, Sarge asked Cooke if he would join a scientific advisory council the family was setting up.[116] By the following summer, in the midst of the presidential campaign of 1960, it had become "Dear Sarge" and "Dear Bob." But it was "Dear Mrs. Shriver" for quite a while to come. Then, in early fall, Eunice requested from Cooke a crash course on how a private foundation might help in the MR cause.[117] That was the real beginning of the psychological tie that would bond Cooke to the Shrivers for the next thirty years.[118]

In November 1960, Jack Kennedy won the election. Apparently at Eunice's recommendation, Cooke became part of the transition team on health care as JFK took office. Thus, the basic alliance among Eunice, Sarge, and Bob Cooke was cemented.

Very Human Ambitions

In the early days of the family's work, Eunice tended—or was obliged—to let her husband and father carry the ball. Even Eunice herself would later forget that at the beginning she had not been a major player. She permitted, for example, a volume to be published in 1969 that claimed, "In 1950 Mrs. Shriver became the executive vice president of the Joseph P. Kennedy, Jr. Foundation." She said that the foundation "has had a first objective from the outset [presumably 1950]: to seek the prevention of mental retardation by identifying its causes. . . ."[119] Why such insistence on a big fib? Was Eunice reluctant to revisit the early years, before the dramatic transformation that was later to occur in her own role? Was her early involvement just idealism?

Eunice once said of her early trips to MR institutions, "I have seen sights that will haunt me all my life. If I had not seen them myself, I would never have believed that such conditions could exist in modern America . . . adults and children . . . in barrack-like wards, their unwashed clothes and blankets in rags."[120]

Trying to account for Eunice's commitment to MR, Sarge said much later, "My wife would give me hell, but I think she got interested in these people because no one else was willing to give them the time of day. They appealed to her because they were so 'hopeless.' She saw she could do something, with special education or athletics. . . .

"So when she saw these children, wearing these football-like helmets, some of them so retarded they couldn't even speak, she said, 'Jesus, what the hell are we wasting our time [getting started] on this for.'"[121]

These idealistic moments give us a quite incomplete picture, however, of the nature of the Kennedy family's attachment to the MR cause. It was probably not coincidence that the Kennedy Foundation began to acquire a national image of identification with MR at exactly the time that Jack Kennedy was running for President. Family members were clearly aware of how the foundation's charitable activities could benefit his campaign. In 1959, Frank Sleeper, at the time a reporter with the *Press Herald* in Portland, Maine, was serving on the publicity committee of an international conference on MR. Could Senator Jack Kennedy attend? "Sen. Kennedy," Sleeper pointed out, "if he'd make himself available, might want to appear on national TV shows such as Garroway's Today to help publicize it and to help get himself some more favorable publicity. We might dream up some family appearance in connection with the Kennedy Foundation and the whole problem of the retarded." Perhaps even Rosemary could be brought in.[122]

Sarge's reply to this was cool but not discouraging. "I think Mr. Sleeper is 100% correct in his comments concerning Senator Kennedy. The Senator takes a great interest in the work of the Foundation and helps it in many ways, but for the reasons indicated by Mr. Sleeper [fear that the publicity might backfire], we have been careful not to give anyone an opportunity to claim that the Foundation's activities were influenced by the Senator's situation."[123]

In reality, the foundation's activities were manifestly influenced by Jack Kennedy's situation. Later that summer of 1959, Sarge was discussing with Joe Kennedy how to handle the announcement of the grant to the Mass General. Sarge was plumping for a press conference at Hyannisport on Labor Day, even though that might be inconvenient for the hospital people. Why? "I personally," said Sarge to Joe Senior, "believe that the newspapers will print much better nationwide if they can get a photo in which you, Bobby and Jack all appear. That kind of picture would be easiest to get, I suspect, over the Labor Day weekend." Jack Dowd's PR firm in Boston would tee things up with the Boston papers, "alerting them to the fact that a good story will be released for Sunday, September 13. I think we would get good coverage in New York as well as in Boston and other cities. Certainly the wire services would carry something on it."[124] At the time that he wrote those lines, disinterested philanthropy was the furthest thing from Sarge Shriver's mind.

Quite apart from the political fortunes of Jack Kennedy, there was the reputation of the family generally to think about. The family wanted the same profile in the MR cause that, for example, the Macy family had with medical research. As Sarge explained to one correspondent, "The Josiah Macy Foundation might be used as an example of a foundation which, through conferences, develops new ideas in various fields of medical research in somewhat the same way in which the Kennedy Foundation would like to develop new ideas on mental subnormality."[125] They sought a dynastic identification so that when the public thought "MR," they would think "Kennedy." It was therefore essential that the various research centers the family was establishing had "Kennedy" in the title. As Jerry Schulman recalled of those hectic days in the late 1950s, "They were interested in putting their name on everything. The motivation in terms of finding cures or research was also there, but they had this strong feeling of name. In the long run, although not the most honorable motivation, it turned out to be the most important thing."[126]

But there was more. The Kennedy family was not just to be identified with mental retardation as a cause, but to possess it. In a highly competitive family, there was competition to keep others out, almost like winning a sailboat race. As Sarge Shriver explained to his father-in-law in discussing the need to move ahead with a research center at Johns Hopkins, "[Another] point which to me is extremely significant is this: The National Association for Retarded Children and the National Foundation (formerly the infantile paralysis crowd) are beginning to take an interest in the field of mental retardation, an interest similar to ours. We think they will soon begin to try some of the ideas we are working on. Consequently, if we are to establish ourselves firmly as leaders of research in mental retardation, I think we'd better do it at the best places. Hopkins is certainly one such place. If we don't start a program there, one of these other national organizations certainly will do so."[127] Win that sailboat race! In the struggle against MR there could be only one winner, and that winner would be the Kennedy family.

To have one's family name shine, to come across as a kind of saintly figure interested only in the welfare of the downtrodden—these are very human ambitions. Who among us could turn his back monkishly on such temptations? Mental retardation was such a tremendous national problem that anyone who actually got results in this area might be pardoned lapses of family vanity. Eunice got results. And she got them because of a dramatic transformation in her life that occurred in 1961. All of a sudden she emerged from the shadows cast by her dynamic husband, from the meddlesome control of her father and mother, to stand in the center of the spotlight herself.

4

Camelot

Three things happened in 1961 to change Eunice Shriver's life. In January, her brother was inaugurated as President of the United States. In March, her husband became preoccupied with his new job running the Peace Corps. And in December her father suffered a stroke that rendered him unable to communicate. All of a sudden, Eunice Shriver found herself standing clear of the males in her family and in the center of power.

During the three brief years of John F. Kennedy's presidency, later referred to by Jacqueline Kennedy as "Camelot" in evocation of Alan Jay Lerner's and Frederick Loewe's 1960 Broadway musical of that title,[1] the history of mental retardation entered a new phase. As Sargent Shriver put it after Camelot had ended, "For the first time in history mental retardation—the least understood, most feared and most neglected scourge of mankind—came under the guns of the chief executive of the most powerful government in the world."[2] For the first time, the awesome force of the American federal government was enlisted on behalf of the retarded. People with MR began to experience a new visibility and a growing acceptance. If the years before 1960 had been characterized by exclusion and isolation, after the Kennedy presidency people with mental retardation would acquire the possibility of showing what they could achieve as accepted members of the community. This was an historic accomplishment: the ability to demonstrate one's human worth despite the presence of a great handicap.

It was in the spring of 1960 that Sarge Shriver started working full-time in Jack Kennedy's campaign. In April he had managed the Kennedy forces in the Wisconsin primary, going next to Washington to become "issues manager" in the central campaign office. In October Sarge resigned as head of the Chicago school board. Though the Shrivers would retain a residence in Chicago, henceforth their base would be a rented fourteen-room estate called Timberlawn in Rockville, Maryland.[3]

After Kennedy won the presidential election, Sarge became his chief talent scout, recruiting such heavy-hitters as Robert McNamara for secretary of defense and McGeorge Bundy as special assistant for national security affairs at the White House. Although Sarge still had time to help on MR issues, his energy had essentially been diverted toward politics.[4] In March 1961 he was appointed head of the Peace Corps, and at this point he ceased being the family's chief MR executive.

Thus, several preconditions for Eunice's emerging as her own woman had been realized. Her father was away in Palm Beach; her hyper-energetic husband was in D.C. eighteen hours a day; and she herself was now no more than a phone call away from the presidency, spending weekends with her brother at the Cape. She had passed from being Mrs. Robert Sargent Shriver, Jr., the Chicago socialite, to Eunice Shriver, vice president of the Kennedy Foundation.[5]

"What About Your Own Son?"

Under Camelot a number of different measures in support of the MR cause went forward simultaneously, although they are best discussed here one at a time. The first concerns the setting up of an institute for child health on the "campus," as it is called, of the National Institutes of Health in Bethesda. The institute would focus on developmental problems of childhood, giving MR a big play. Most immediately, however, it accorded Eunice Shriver a chance to test her new power.

In July 1960, just after Jack Kennedy won the Democratic nomination, Eunice initiated her campaign to secure high priority for MR in what she hoped would be a Democratic administration. She asked Bob Cooke to send Jack "some ideas on the health and welfare of children, presumably to use these ideas in the campaign."[6]

After beating Richard Nixon in November, the President-elect decided to set up a transition task force on health care. It was called the President's Task Force on Health and Social Security, and Jack appointed Wilbur Cohen, professor of public welfare administration at the University of Michigan, to head it. In 1935, as a young man, Cohen had been one of the architects of Franklin Roosevelt's social security legislation, and in 1960, at age forty-seven, he counted as left-of-center in the spectrum of American politics. (The American Medical Association later opposed his nomination as assistant secretary at the Department of Health, Education and Welfare, or HEW, on the grounds that he favored "socialized medicine.") Eunice, concerned that Cohen's interest in the elderly would cause a loss of focus on children, prevailed upon her brother to appoint Bob Cooke to the task force.[7] Others serving on the task force in addition to Cohen and Cooke included James Dixon, the president of liberal Antioch College in Ohio, and Joshua Lederberg, an eminent—and socially conscious—molecular biologist whom Sarge had gotten to know in his negotiations with Stanford. The general tenor of the task force was activist and interventionist.[8] To the enthusiastic approval of the others, Cooke proposed "a center for child health."[9]

As head of pediatrics at Johns Hopkins, Cooke had been closely following government policies on child health. It troubled him that NIH, under its hard-driving chief James Shannon, had been hitherto inattentive to children's issues. Shannon was disease-oriented, believing that NIH's role was to target specific illnesses such as heart disease and cancer. (The institutes for those diseases had previously received the lion's share of the NIH budget.) Even before November 1960, Cooke had been badgering Shannon to do something about child health, but Shannon opposed carving out new institutes on the basis of age and scornfully told Cooke, "There aren't any major problems in children."

"That really raised my hackles," said Cooke. "When a month later I got Cohen's call I was loaded for bear, ready to do something about NIH."[10]

In December the task force on health presented its recommendations in Washington to Abraham Ribicoff, the newly designated secretary of HEW. "Ribicoff," said Cooke, "was not interested in a national institute of child health, but Ted Sorensen [one of JFK's key advisers] sat in on the meeting. He liked the idea. Here was this youthful administration putting all its emphasis on old people."[11]

Shortly after taking office, JFK created the new institute of child health with an executive order. But what was it to be called? Shannon, who objected to the proliferation of institutes, wanted the new creation subordinated to an administrative division at NIH for "general medical sciences." He thought "National Institute for Mental Retardation" much too narrow, "Institute for Child Health" somewhat narrow, and favored "National Institute of Human Development."[12] Eunice and Bob Cooke, mingling in negotiations behind the scenes, feared that MR would be lost in the fog of "human development."

Here another of Kennedy's lieutenants, Myer ("Mike") Feldman, entered the picture. Feldman had started out in 1946 as Kennedy's informal adviser on Jewish affairs, becoming in 1958 a member of his Senate staff.

In 1961 Feldman, forty-four, was appointed to the special counsel's office of the White House over which Ted Sorensen presided. Feldman had a reputation for arrogance and abruptness, but in everything concerning the President's relations with the federal bureaucracy he was the great facilitator.[13] As one observer later described him, "Mr. Feldman, of course, was the hatchet man for the President and did all the political maneuvering. He had a fantastic memory for people and occurrences, promises, who was good and who was bad in maneuvering political devices. He had two phones on his desk, and they were ringing constantly, and he could almost carry on two conversations at once."[14] Within the White House, Feldman would be the chief force for action on mental retardation.

In the debate over the child health institute, Feldman worked out a deal: the general medical science department would become an institute in its own right, a coveted status, if in turn the child health group could also be granted status as an institute.[15] The NIH would thus grow not by one institute but two, a solution that mollified Shannon while delighting the Kennedy people.

Now Congress had to approve. In his health message to Congress on February 27, 1962, President Kennedy said that he would press forward with the new "Institute for Child Health and Human Development" that had been introduced the previous year.[16] Following that announcement, Eunice and Bob Cooke constituted themselves as a lobbying team and, joined by Sarge and Bobby Kennedy (who had just been appointed Attorney General), began visiting Congressmen.[17] In particular, Eunice and Cooke went to see the two men who controlled all health legislation in Congress: Senator Lister Hill from Alabama and Representative John Fogarty from Rhode Island.

Hill was chairman of two strategic Senate committees, the Committee on Labor and Public Welfare and the subcommittee on appropriations for health and education (which was a part of the Appropriations Committee). The former committee passed health legislation; the latter subcommittee, which Hill had headed since 1955, funded it. Hill's support for medical research had made him known in the Senate as "Mr. Health." Having once contemplated studying medicine himself, and having grown up in the home of a physician father, Hill was fascinated by medicine. He was said to go home at night and read medical textbooks.[18] So the Kennedy people found a sympathetic listener in Hill.

In the House of Representatives, John Fogarty from Rhode Island was the big man to deal with. In 1949 Fogarty had become head of the House subcommittee on health and welfare appropriations. Just like Hill, Fogarty had pressed for more money for health research over the years. Yet unlike Hill, Fogarty had a particular interest in mental retardation.

Arthur Trudeau, an old high-school friend of Fogarty's in Providence, had a mentally retarded son. As early as 1954, Trudeau had started bringing Fogarty to meetings of the Rhode Island parents' group. At congressional hearings on health appropriations in 1955, Fogarty had thrown HEW Secretary Oveta Culp Hobby off balance by suddenly asking her what the department was doing for mental retardation. Over the next several years, the former bricklayer from Providence slammed one of the few pre-1960 pieces of MR legislation—a bill on training teachers for the mentally retarded—through Congress.[19]

Fogarty had originally been opposed to the new child health institute out of loyalty to other federal agencies that found themselves threatened by it, such as the national institutes for neurology and mental health and the Children's Bureau.[20] However, thanks to judicious lobbying by Cooke, Fogarty was won over and the success of the new institute in the House was assured.[21]

In August 1962 the bill to establish a National Institute for Child Health and Human Development, or NICHD (the second "H" is usually omitted from its acronym), passed the House. To ensure that the institute's intended focus on child development and MR would not be lost, Oren Harris, the Arkansas congressman who was the bill's floor manager, attached an amendment stipulating that the institute not do research on the elderly.[22] The bill, supported by Senator Robert Kerr of Oklahoma, passed the Senate on September 28. Three weeks later President Kennedy signed it into law.[23]

The entire exercise was a neat initial illustration of Eunice Shriver's ability to maneuver effectively in the corridors of power. In one year's time she had gone from being a Chicago housewife to executing an end-run around someone like Jim Shannon, the most powerful health bureaucrat in the federal government. She could now line up such great czars as Hill and Fogarty. Persuasive though he was, Cooke alone would not have been able to steer a major bill through Congress. But given the backing of the Kennedy family (and with the help of Wilbur Cohen, who by now was the assistant secretary responsible for legislation at HEW), opposition simply fell away.

Opposition was aplenty within the bureaucracy. No established agency likes a tough new kid on the block. The National Institute for Mental Health, for example, resented the loss of MR research to the newcomer, although NIMH had, in Cooke's words, "given very, very weak support" to MR in the past.[24] The Children's Bureau, which was the HEW agency that had been responsible for child health, hated the whole idea of the new institute and put pressure on Cooke to make sure that NICHD didn't destroy the bureau. (The head of the Children's Bureau was later appointed to the NICHD advisory council.)[25]

It would be Eunice, needling her brother for the new institute, who sliced through such normally fearsome bureaucratic opposition. She quickly acquired the authority to give orders to Mike Feldman, who in turn gave orders to Wilbur Cohen. In August 1963, the President himself suffered the loss of his newborn son Patrick Bouvier Kennedy to hyaline membrane disease, a disorder that keeps the lungs from inflating properly.[26] Together at the Cape with Eunice that autumn, Jack Kennedy had a report on NICHD with him. Eunice recalled, "I remember out on the boat one day, he said to me why did he have to support another national institute; why were they proposing it to him and why should he back [it] . . . because it was going to cost a lot more money and he was having trouble with the budget; and what were some of the reasons. . . .

"I told him about virtually nobody studying anything about infant mortality or with very little knowledge about prenatal disease and that sort of thing. And I said, 'What about your own son? You probably wouldn't have lost one of your own children if we knew more about prematurity.'"

The President said, "Are they going to study that kind of thing at the NICHD, prematurity and that sort of thing?"

Eunice replied, "Yes, Jack. And that's what's going to stop it."

The President said, "Well, that seems to really be worthwhile."[27]

The Panel

Virtually the last thing Joe Kennedy did on behalf of mental retardation before he had his stroke in December 1961 was to suggest a national commission. Now that his son had become President, he figured that a commission might profile MR as a cause in the same way as had Herbert Hoover's two commissions on executive organization in 1947 and in 1953, on which Joe Senior had served. Joe and Herbert Hoover had been close personal friends, and Eunice had met the former President as a student at Stanford during the war. So it seemed a sensible strategy to try such a commission on MR. As Eunice told Cooke, "My father said we ought to create something like the Hoover commission, and call it a President's Panel."[28]

Cooke conceded that his own recollections of the origins of this commission, which would become the President's Panel on Mental Retardation (PPMR), "may be denied by some people." And indeed in Eunice's own recreation of events, it was she and not her father who came up with the idea for the panel: "In 1960 I was in St. Elizabeth's Hospital in Boston recovering from surgery when I read in the newspaper the report of the Mental Health Association to the Congress. There was no mention of the mentally retarded. . . ."[29]

Eunice felt something should be done about that, and, by her account, she phoned Cooke and asked him if the foundation could support a similar kind of national conference. Eunice says that she then phoned her father, who "found the idea excellent." While down in Palm Beach for Christmas 1960, she said that she explained her plans further to her father.

"He listened and then said 'Go to Jack. This movement needs the federal government behind it.'"[30]

It was quite unnecessary for Eunice to throw the veil of Kennedy Foundation mythology over the origin of the President's Panel (although it is interesting that she did so). Whoever thought up the idea, the actual creation of the panel was clearly the result of Eunice nagging her brother. As Bobby Kennedy once joked, "President Kennedy used to tell me, 'Let's give Eunice whatever she wants so I can get her off the phone and get on with the business of the government.'" John Throne, who became executive director of the Kennedy Foundation in 1963, recalled these conversations with Bobby. Throne added, "She was always ragging him [the President] to do this and that."[31]

Donald Stedman, Throne's predecessor as foundation director, confirmed these impressions when I asked how the Kennedy Administration had come to set up the President's Panel. Was it because of Eunice? "I think so," Stedman replied. "It's fair to say it didn't take long for the President with a good bit of prodding from Eunice to set up something that had already been very close to their heart and attention."[32]

It is likely that Jack Kennedy did not have a great deal of personal interest in the issue of mental retardation. As Elizabeth Boggs recalled, "I went down to testify [at a meeting of the Senate's Health and Welfare Committee in 1957] on the teacher training bill, and Senator John Kennedy was on the committee that had this legislation under review. The person who was the moving force behind it was Senator Lister Hill, who was chairman of the full committee. . . . Senator John Kennedy came out of the executive session and did not attend the hearing. He didn't have to tell the world that he had a retarded sister in order to support that legislation, and yet he didn't [support] it."[33] Only in February of 1960, heading into an election, did anyone in Jack Kennedy's office make contact with the National Association for Retarded Children, the chief standard-bearer on behalf of the retarded, which had existed since 1950 and had been very active in lobbying the Congress since 1955.[34]

As President, JFK would enthusiastically ask various members of the panel about their work on MR. But then, that was his style with everyone, and on everything. As a patrician who never wanted involuntarily to make anyone feel ill at ease, he expressed interest in subjects he knew to be close to their hearts.[35] In retrospect, the President probably sought out the kind of historic identification that Franklin Roosevelt had with polio, or that Eisenhower had with heart disease and cancer,[36] without necessarily himself becoming passionately involved. The one who was passionately involved was Eunice.

Eunice wanted a national panel on mental retardation. Sometime in late 1960 or early 1961 Eunice and Bob Cooke went to New York to see former President Herbert Hoover and discuss with him how such a panel might be set up. As Cooke recalls, "President Hoover was very sympathetic and rather helpful actually."[37] Around this time Eunice apparently broached the idea to JFK, and her brother said, "Call Mike Feldman and let's get a meeting set for next week at the White House."[38] Feldman would retain the oversight of the panel, JFK being far too busy to concern himself with the details of organizing it and keeping it out of political trouble. The close alliance that developed between Feldman and Eunice drove forward every aspect of the panel's work. Later in life they would become the best of friends and go out to the movies together on Saturday nights.

Throughout the summer of 1961, Feldman, Eunice, and Sarge worked to set up this MR panel. A front-burner question in any Kennedy enterprise was the publicity. Who should handle it? They obtained advice from several of JFK's friends who were knowledgeable about publicity, eventually hiring Victor Weingarten's agency in New York to "build news value" into the panel's activities.[39] Edwin Bayley, a staffer in the White House press office, told Weingarten how tough it would be to get coverage. "Reporters generally [are] quite cynical about commissions in general and exercise hard news judgment about such stories. In other words, our news would have to compete on an equal basis with all other events out of Washington."[40]

There was also the question of who should direct the panel. Sarge and Eunice contacted Richard Masland, who by now was head of the neurology institute in Bethesda, and Masland recommended a man who, on the face of it, was not the most obvious candidate: Leonard Mayo, director of the Association for the Aid of Crippled Children in New York, a foundation for children with disabilities.[41] Mayo, sixty-two at the time, had himself been born at an MR asylum, the Berkshire Industrial Farm in Canaan, New York, where his father was director. Mayo had spent time as an MR institution staffer, working from 1923 to 1924 at the Maryland Training School for Boys in Loch Raven, then moving into social work administration in New York City. Mayo taught at Columbia University in the 1930s, at Case Western University in Cleveland in the 1940s, and in 1949 became head of the Association for the Aid of Crippled Children in New York. Yet when Bob Cooke asked Mayo in the spring of 1961 to head the panel, it was not because Mayo was an MR expert, but because he had his finger on everything happening in the area of disabilities. Mayo possessed, moreover, a tremendous capacity for getting people together and encouraging them to compromise. Boggs said, "To the end of his life he was in demand to be moderator and summarizer at conferences."[42] For a group as divergent as the panel required—and for an agenda as diffuse—Mayo was perfect. George Tarjan agreed to be vice chairman.

Complicating Mayo's task was Eunice's insistence that the panel complete its work within one year, an almost unheard-of lead time for an undertaking of this magnitude. But Eunice had the sense, correctly as it turned out, of racing against time. "We wanted to try to get something done," she said later. "The need was enormously urgent, and if you get a year, you can really do a lot if everybody really hustles. Why would you need more than a year?"[43]

The panel was to have twenty-seven members, plus Eunice as "consultant." The members were chosen rather haphazardly over the summer of 1961, depending on whom Cooke, the Shrivers, Mayo, and Tarjan knew "to be good." So political criteria were downplayed. There was no black person on the panel, even though that might have been appropriate. JFK resisted later demands to add this or that constituency to the panel.[44]

Among the twenty-seven members of the panel were two quite different constituencies that normally would not talk to each other. There were the basic scientists—people such as Seymour Kety, chief of the Laboratory of Clinical Science at NIMH, and Joshua Lederberg, professor of genetics at Stanford, both of whom were doing research on underlying brain biology. (They could never figure out why they had been invited in the first place.[45]) Then there were the behavioral scientists and educators, who tended to assume that MR was caused more by social deprivation than by brain disease. Rounding out the panel were activists from various constituencies, such as Elizabeth Boggs from the parents' group and Monsignor Elmer Behrmann, director of the Catholic Guidance Center, a Catholic MR clinic and school in St. Louis.

On October 11, 1961, JFK held a press conference to announce "a national plan in mental retardation." "Although we have attacked on a broad front the problems of mental illness," he said, "although we have made great strides in the battle against disease, we as a nation have for too long postponed an intensive search for solutions to the problems of the mentally retarded. That failure should be corrected."[46] The announcement was timed to coincide with the annual meeting of the parents' group in San Francisco. That night a group of NARC executives huddled in the executive director's hotel suite to catch a rebroadcast of the President's news conference on the eleven o'clock news. They sat electrified as the President of the United States announced that mental retardation, for so long shoved into the closet of shame and forgetfulness, was to be a national priority.[47]

The *New York Times* carried the story the following day on page one: "White House Panel to Prepare Attack on Mental Retardation."[48] The coverage was not inappropriate. This presidential message of October 11, 1961, represented a true turning of the page in the history of mental retardation. Rosemary Dybwad, secretary of NARC's international relations committee, wrote excitedly from Switzerland that the presidential message was appearing "in more and more publications of overseas organizations. First in Israel, Geneva, Ireland. . . ." Eunice forwarded to the President a copy of Dybwad's letter with the notation, "Jack, I thought this letter would interest you. Over 300,000 copies of your message on M.R. have been distributed."[49]

In October and November 1961, the panel received prominent play as the President announced first its composition, then the agenda for its first meeting—a meeting that featured Eunice entertaining panel members for tea at the White House.[50] By early November the panel had divided into two task forces, one on research, the other on service.[51]

And then progress stopped. Throwing twenty-seven vastly disparate strangers together around a table to derive recommendations for a problem as huge as MR carried a large downside risk: that they would come up with nothing. "I do remember a couple of meetings," recalled Cooke, "where I just thought this was the living end, that it was going just terrible. We were going absolutely nowhere. There was just one platitude after another being put on the table. We had one meeting in Baltimore, I think, and it was just horrendous. I know Mrs. Shriver's blood pressure must have gone up and down about a thousand times during that session. I remember talking with her in the middle of it, and she said something like, 'We've just got to change this, you know, we're going absolutely nowhere, just talk, and nothing constructive."[52]

Around the beginning of 1962, the panel was split into six task forces, each with its own chairman. Divided into such areas as "law," "prevention," "behavior," and so forth, they would grapple with precise questions and come up with exact recommendations.[53]

Disagreements among the various task forces nearly tore this tidy scenario apart. The science-oriented "researchers" squared off against the education-oriented caregivers. The education-behavior camp, already suspicious of the new NICHD that was being erected independently of the panel, accused the researchers of wanting to build mini-NIH's and of ignoring the human misery of the real world. The scientists accused the educators of ignoring the very real biological and genetic component in severe MR. As Bob Cooke, himself biologically-oriented, summarized his adversaries' position, "The educator said something like this, 'I'm the one who handles ninety percent of the mental retardation problem; it's really an educational problem. I don't recognize genetics. I don't recognize this and the other defects that you physicians talk about."[54] One recalls here that Cooke had two children with tiny brains who required special care.

By September 1962, Mayo was to integrate these opposing views into a single report, due in the President's office on October 16, a year to the day from the time of JFK's MR message. Judge David Bazelon, head of the law committee, tried to bring the two camps together. "You want to be humane to those who are here and take care of them, but you must be careful to leave plenty of resources for prevention. You have to stop the flow. And you can only do that by prevention; you can only get prevention by research."[55]

The tension in particular between Seymour Kety, head of the biology task force, and Anne Ritter, a psychologist at the Kennedy Child Studies Center in New York on the behavioral task force, was so acute that agreement seemed impossible. Mayo had gone off to Turkey for a conference. Eunice Shriver called him there at a banquet of an organization of which he was president. He left the banquet and found a phone in a bar. She had been trying to get through to him for two days. "Mrs. Shriver . . . said that disagreement had again broken out between the research panel on biological sciences and that on the behavioral or social sciences . . . that if possible I should come home and see if I could work it out."

Eunice added, "I don't want you to feel pressed to return. But I think if you can't come now, we'll postpone our appointment with the President to give him the report."

Mayo recalled, "This gave me cold chills even though I didn't know what was coming, but I knew that to postpone an appointment with the President was not desirable."

"I think I'll come home," Mayo said to Eunice.

"When?"

"Tomorrow." Mayo said later that it was "one of those flashes of intuition that a person gets when one knows instantly what one ought to do."[56]

Mayo returned to Washington, reconciled the warring sides, and completed an immense report that included ninety-five specific recommendations about improving the lot of the mentally retarded and about prevention.[57] The morning of October 16 arrived. Yet the John F. Kennedy whom the panel members found as they trooped into the Cabinet Room of the White House was not the same jaunty and outgoing man they had met a yet earlier. "All of us were struck by his rather sober demeanor," said panel member Edward Davens. "He was in an entirely different mood than at the meeting a year previously when he gave us our marching orders. He did not smile or crack jokes in his usual fashion; he was very polite and reserved. He obviously had read the report, and had been briefed on it. He discussed the recommendations intelligently. . . . But there was something about his mood which was just so different that most of us could not help wondering what was the underlying reason." At lunch the puzzled panel members discussed just what seemed so different. "We finally settled on the word 'grave'; he had an air of great gravity about him."[58]

Davens thought no more about it until a week later when he picked up the morning edition of the *Baltimore Sun* and discovered what the President had had on his mind. "At 7 o'clock that morning he had received the news from his staff of incontrovertible evidence that Russian intercontinental ballistic missiles had been sighted on Cuba and the Cuban crisis was on."[59] Just as the Cuban missile crisis was beginning, John Kennedy had been able to spare two hours to discuss the question of mental retardation. This is a remarkable comment, either on the President's commitment to the mentally retarded, or on his loyalty to his sister Eunice.

It was Eunice who had lashed the panel forward from the very beginning. "The point was," she said, "to get a report and get it to Congress. . . . We concentrated on just that one objective, to get the report and try to get hundreds of millions of dollars which were needed. What difference does anything else make really?"[60] Far from being a peripheral "consultant," Eunice was really the head of the panel. Her name was at the top of the panel's letterhead, along with Mayo's and Tarjan's.[61] Panel member Nick Hobbs, a psychologist from Peabody College in Nashville, referred to her admiringly as "the prime mover."[62] Leonard Mayo, speaking on the phone to Sarge Shriver one morning, said, "Well, Mr. Shriver, I want you to know one thing. . . . [What] makes this Panel unique is that Mrs. Shriver is not only interested in it, but is certainly one of the instigators of it. . . . So she may be a consultant on paper, but as far as I'm concerned, she's the chairman of the board."

"Well," said Sarge. "I see I don't have to draw any pictures for you."[63]

It was, in short, Eunice Shriver's sense of mission that drove these crucial events in 1961 and 1962 ahead. She realized that the country was in a time of flux, that the "New Frontier" as John Kennedy called it—Camelot as it was retrospectively dubbed—represented a narrow window in which genuine change was possible. "Ten years ago," she told a group of mental health workers in 1962 at Washington's Statler

Hilton Hotel, "there was a general belief that mental retardation had to be accepted in a spirit of weary fatalism. But this attitude is no longer justified. The years of indifference and neglect, the years of callous cynicism and entrenched prejudice, are drawing to a close. The years of research and experiment . . . are upon us now with all their promise and challenge." She concluded by echoing the words of her brother's inaugural address, "Let us go forward together. . . ."[64] As Eunice Shriver stood before this group of psychiatrists, telling them of the panel's exciting work, she had for the first time come into her own. Now it was she in center stage, her husband and overpowering father far from the limelight.

Coming into one's own—especially in the fish bowl of Washington politics—is fraught with pitfalls. Eunice had experienced both politics and the national media mainly from being interviewed and from hearing family conversations. There were lessons to be learned. After the panel convened in the White House for the first meeting of all its members on October 18, 1961, Edwin Bayley was given the job of press relations. "This was very difficult," he said later, "because Eunice is not the easiest person in the world to deal with. She's insistent and, I felt, unreasonable. . . . She thinks it's the most important thing in the world, and she doesn't understand why it isn't a headline in the *New York Times* every day."

Bayley said that for the meeting on October 18, "I pulled every string I could. I practically pleaded with friends in the press to write something about this meeting." Two or three White House reporters did cover it, "a couple of fellows who were on the Saturday afternoon shift who are about the third string men in the bureaus. And some of them wandered in and out, and maybe sent a paragraph. But she envisioned interviews with every one of these famous people and pictures all over the paper."

The next day Bayley got a call around 9 a.m. from Eunice. "She'd gotten the *New York Times,* and she was just livid, screaming at me, 'There isn't anything in the paper.' And I hadn't seen the paper yet; she got me out of bed."

Bayley explained to Eunice all he had done, that he had talked to the *Times* reporter but, he added, "They must have just decided that it wasn't news." Bayley hung up, got the paper, searched through it, "and on page fourteen I found a story about six inches long. So I thought she must have missed it, so I called her back, and I say, 'The story is in the *Times.* It's on page fourteen."

"Well," said Eunice. "I know that little story, but I meant the big story. Why wasn't it on page one?"[65]

Eunice Shriver was just at the beginning of her own journey into the limelight.

The Puniness of Federal Efforts before Camelot

The panel members saw themselves as pioneers and quite naturally wanted to minimize the contributions of the federal government under Eisenhower and previous administrations to the MR cause. Eunice claimed that before the Kennedy Administration nothing really existed. "It took me three days to find out where the Department of Special Education was, dealing with the retarded," she said. "I couldn't find what floor it was on, or the office it was in, or where it was, or anything about it. It was just a laughing, roaring joke. I thought that was shocking and so did, I think, everybody else on the panel."[66]

Eunice was substantially correct that very little had preceded her brother's administration. Yet before 1960 a number of government agencies had at least skeletal programs in place for helping the mentally retarded, and these would become the platforms on which the massive new aid programs after 1960 would be built. The federal social service bureaucracy was enormous even in 1960, and HEW programs dealing with the mentally retarded were flung across five different areas: the vocational rehabilitation program, the social security administration, the office of education, the hospital construction program of the Public Health Service (PHS), and the National Institutes of Health (also situated administratively within the PHS).

The federal vocational rehabilitation program began with an act of Congress in 1920 directed toward such goals as job training and providing artificial limbs to the physically handicapped. In the 1920s "voc rehab" belonged to the fashionable liberal causes; in 1925, U.S. Secretary of Labor James J. Davis called vocational rehabilitation a "moral obligation of organized Government."[67] Getting injured people back to work was the keynote of voc rehab before World War II, and the mentally retarded were disqualified from such back-to-work programs on grounds of being permanently disabled: it was thought they would never be able to work, so there was no point in spending voc rehab funds on them. (Also, only adults were eligible.) The states, not the federal government, would be responsible for the mentally retarded.

The first crack in this wall of indifference to voc rehab for the mentally retarded came in 1943, when the Barden-La Follette Act authorized rehabilitation grants to a few individuals with MR. Funded in 1945, the act permitted a slow but steady increase in the number of mentally retarded people who received some kind of rehabilitation training so that they could take jobs in the community.[68] In 1960, for example, almost three thousand people with mental retardation were able to join the workforce as a result of this program.[69]

The modest success achieved by voc rehab in this area was largely due to Mary Switzer, a member of that cohort of brilliant, usually single female administrators who came to Washington during the Great Depression and made their marks in the postwar era. In 1950, Switzer became director of the Office of Vocational Rehabilitation. She was an example of what John Gardner, a later Secretary of HEW, called an "entrepreneur in government." (Sarge Shriver was another.) Switzer would acquire close ties to mental health and to the National Institutes of Health. Gardner said of Switzer, "She was a leader, an innovator, a builder, a risk-taker. She had a generous, loving heart, the shrewdness of a high-stakes poker player, and the gall of an eighteenth-century pirate."[70] Mary Switzer's interest in MR may have been prompted by her sister Ann, who was the executive director of The Arc (sometimes also known as the Association for Retarded Citizens and ARC) in Connecticut.[71] In 1954, Mary Switzer convinced Congress to accept a voc rehab program that established almost two hundred local rehabilitation centers, increasing funds available to retarded adults as well as to those with physical handicaps.[72]

Mary Switzer was a major player within HEW as the panel's work approached completion. Switzer was fearful that Eunice Shriver's thrust on mental retardation under the Kennedy Administration might squeeze out voc rehab. She made it clear that she wanted all the mentally retarded within the purview of her programs, and that meant MR children as well.[73] Mary Switzer, therefore, good though her heart may have been, was an example of a potential bureaucratic roadblock around whom the Shrivers would have to maneuver. (Indeed the panel's report appeased her with generous kudos to voc rehab, recommending that the federal government match state expenses for vocational rehabilitation of the mentally retarded, including children.[74])

Then there was the Children's Bureau, established in 1912 within the Department of Labor to investigate all matters relating to children, including the mentally retarded. In the early days, the bureau's involvement with MR was limited to conducting a few surveys. But in 1935 the new Social Security Act offered the possibility of directly helping the mentally retarded with its programs for crippled children (a number of whom were also retarded), and for improving maternal-child health, though few funds actually flowed in those directions. In 1946, the Children's Bureau was shifted from labor to social service agencies, from which in 1953 HEW would ultimately arise. Simultaneously, the Children's Bureau saw its budget pumped up. In 1954 the bureau also began to fund a small network of diagnostic clinics for MR.[75]

The Children's Bureau did become involved in one alluring initiative. In 1948, the social service bureaucracy spawned the Interdepartmen-

tal Committee on Children and Youth. This committee became allied
with the Macy Foundation in funding a series of conferences. In 1955,
Fogarty's sharp questioning of Secretary Oveta Culp Hobby caused this
committee to spin off a subcommittee on mental retardation, with Joseph
Douglass, an assistant in Hobby's office, as chairman and Martha Eliot,
chief of the Children's Bureau, as acting chairman. (A year later Eliot
was in command of the subcommittee.) In February 1956 the subcommittee staged a small MR conference at the Nassau Inn in Princeton,
paid for by the Macy Foundation and organized by Frank Fremont-
Smith, the Macy Foundation's medical director.[76] The conference led to
nothing in particular and is worth remarking on here only because it was
cosponsored by the Menninger Foundation (of the Menninger family of
psychiatrists in Topeka, Kansas). Between 1954 and 1959 Eunice Shriver
was a member of the board of governors of the Menninger Foundation.
Neither Eunice nor any member of the Kennedy family attended the
conference, but Eunice almost certainly knew of its existence, and of the
Macy Foundation's involvement. Possibly, therefore, it was Eunice who
alerted her father and Sarge that a rival foundation was about to take MR
away from the Kennedys!

On the whole, however, these early efforts by the Children's Bureau
were quite limited. As Michael Begab, who was hired in 1957 (at Fogarty's
behest) to run the Children's Bureau's MR programs, later commented,
until the late 1950s the bureau did not include mental retardation "as
an integral part of their program activities, either in their child welfare,
maternal and child health, or on crippled children's programs. Some of
the states did so, but children with MR were not identified as a special
group with particular needs. This was the situation, largely, when I joined
the staff in 1957."[77]

Thanks again to Fogarty, an amendment in 1956 to the Social Security
Act did authorize so-called "survivors' benefits" (ADC or adult disabled
child benefits) for MR children of disabled workers. The benefits were to
continue beyond the age of eighteen if the surviving children of retired,
deceased, or disabled workers themselves had a disability: about two-
thirds of the recipients of these benefits had MR.[78]

A third citadel in the sprawling HEW empire was the Office of Education (before 1939 located within the Department of the Interior and
virtually forgotten). It had been founded just after the Civil War, but
not until the 1920s did it acquire a small section dealing with MR and
otherwise handicapped children.[79] The desperate nature of the parents'
need for more special-ed teachers made the Office of Education something of a force on the MR scene. Several small acts began to enlarge
the federal role in the area of MR, but the real breakthrough came in

1955 when Fogarty, following his grilling of HEW Secretary Hobby at the appropriation hearings, started quizzing some of the other senior female administrators at HEW: Martha Eliot of the Children's Bureau and Romaine Mackie of the Exceptional Children's Branch of the Office of Education, as well as Lawrence Derthick, Commissioner of Education. Warned by Hobby's experience, they were well prepared. An impressed Fogarty suggested that the Office of Education introduce a bill for the appropriation of funds to train teachers. Mayo and Boggs worked on the legislation as well, and President Eisenhower signed it into law on September 6, 1958.[80] At this point significant amounts of money began to flow into what had been an area of extreme vexation for the parents of the mentally retarded: how to get their children educated.

Again, one must be careful not to convey more dynamism than actually existed. As Nicholas Hobbs, a Peabody College psychologist on the panel, said later, "The Office [of Education] was generally a dormant place. They had a person in mental retardation, one or two, and they had some studies and kept statistics, but it was a fairly sterile operation."[81]

The last two federal initiatives in MR before 1960 were relatively unimportant, but they also nonetheless laid the foundation for changes to come. In 1946, Congress passed a bill cosponsored by Senators Lister Hill and Harold Burton to promote hospital construction. The great postwar American hospital boom depended heavily on federal funds from this source.[82] In 1958, many MR institutions became qualified as "medical facilities" for funding under the Hill-Burton Act. By 1961 they were receiving almost $3 million a year, more money than in any other federal MR program. Yet this new money was a bit of a two-edged sword, because it was precisely these giant institutions, supported by federal funds in the 1960s and 1970s, that were part of the problem rather than part of the solution. Progress on mental retardation would entail abolishing them, rather than propping them up with more federal money.

The Public Health Service administered the Hill-Burton funds. It also ran the last of the important federal programs touching on MR: the National Institutes of Health. We have already discussed, quite out of chronological order, the establishment of the National Institute of Child Health and Human Development in 1962. Before then, the only institutes concerned with MR were the National Institute of Mental Health, founded in 1946, and the National Institute of Neurological Disease and Blindness, founded in 1950. Both had small grant programs. After Richard Masland toured the country in 1955 on behalf of the parents' groups, scientific interest in MR began to quicken. "The knowledge that we have money available sometimes helps arouse interest," commented Leonard Duhl, representing both institutes at the Nassau Tavern conference of 1956.[83] In addition, around 1955 NIMH made the decision to start funding "a doctoral curriculum in psychology with emphasis on mental retardation" at an obscure school in Nashville called Peabody College.[84] It was from Peabody that the revolution in knowledge of the social and behavioral side of MR would come.

This account of the federal government's paltry efforts on behalf of the mentally retarded before Camelot leads to two conclusions. One, the President's Panel on Mental Retardation would have to offer a vast panoply of recommendations to shift the course of such widely scattered programs. Second, the vested interests resisting these recommendations would be far-flung and already well-entrenched.

The White House Office

As the panel's work neared completion in the fall of 1962, Eunice, Sarge, and Bob Cooke all felt an urgent need to translate its paper recommendations into action. Some of the panel's suggestions involved administrative changes that the White House could impose upon the federal bureaucracy by fiat, while others involved legislation. The small group of MR loyalists wanted to move forward with both.

So complex was the handling of all this legislation and administration that the Shrivers decided they could no longer operate solely from Eunice's bedroom at Timberlawn. In 1962, after Joe Kennedy's stroke, they opened a small office in downtown Washington for the Kennedy Foundation, although its accounts would still be administered from the financier's Park Avenue office in New York (later from the Pan-Am building). But the MR loyalists would need an office in the White House itself to take central command. Because it would be unseemly for Eunice to head such an office, she needed a front man, a presidential "special assistant" for mental retardation.

Eunice later said of these events, "It was my own idea that they put somebody in President Kennedy's office to show that the President would stay interested." She went to Mike Feldman, and together they steamrollered opposition by the Bureau of the Budget, which was becoming increasingly restive about how to pay for all these new MR programs.[85] (The budget bureau had thought that Mike Feldman himself was the special assistant, and they wanted things to stay that way.[86])

"So Mike Feldman and I went into Jack's office," Eunice continued. "I said, 'Jack, I would hope that you could have a presidential assistant on that level so this interest in mental retardation would continue and things could be followed up on.'" Feldman summarized for the President the opposing arguments of the Bureau of the Budget.

The President declared, "We're going to have a presidential assistant."[87]

Eunice first asked Bob Cooke, who declined. Then she asked George Tarjan in California to draw up a list of suitable individuals. Tarjan recommended a number of big-name psychiatrists and added, as an afterthought, a sixty-six-year-old physician and administrator named Stafford Warren.[88] Tall and dignified, Warren was at the time vice chancellor for health services at UCLA.

Why they went with Warren is unclear: possibly because he was not a psychiatrist. Eunice, despite her friendship with Tarjan, shared the general loathing of the parents' group for psychiatrists. Warren had a career in internal medicine and radiology, and he had also been medical director of the Manhattan Project to develop an A-bomb. He had, for example, pioneered the study of radioactive fallout.[89] This background signified that he would make an able administrator. Warren had also just put together plans for a new medical school at UCLA.

In January 1963, Warren began commuting on the "red-eye special," the overnight flight from Los Angeles to Washington. He resigned his post at UCLA to come to Washington as a special assistant to the President to coordinate programs in mental retardation. His appointment was big enough news to warrant a front-page story in the *New York Times*.[90] He would have an office on the third floor of the Executive Office Building, within easy reach of Feldman. And that was precisely the point: at all times Warren was to be a creature of the Shriver team.

Warren turned out almost from the start not to be a "Kennedy man." For one thing, he had attitudes toward mental retardation that must have embarrassed those around him every time he opened his mouth. One example is Warren's comments about the "crib cases" in an MR asylum: "Now a crib case just lies there. Sometimes its eyes are open; sometimes they're not. . . . They have to be diapered. . . . The usual policy is to change the diapers and wash them off with a hose." Then the children are force-fed. "Well, in the old days they used to inhale the stuff as often as they swallowed it, and they used to die of pneumonia when they were fairly young. Nowadays, we unfortunately aspirate them and give them penicillin, and they don't die of pneumonia."[91] The "unfortunately" would have caused Eunice's and Bob Cooke's hair to stand on end.

The Shrivers and their allies made much of the essential human dignity of people with MR. In contrast is Warren's account of a "mongoloid" (Down Syndrome) child: "Mongoloids are quite characteristic and typical. You can recognize them. They're almost identical—as if they came out of one pattern, have these funny little slanting eyes and funny face. . . . They've got to be occupied or they're in trouble because they're curious. They're just like a monkey. The closest thing that you can compare them to is a young—what's the next one below a gibbon? —well, anyway. . . ."[92]

Warren also had a political tin ear, which is to say that he never really figured out where he was and how he was supposed to act. He thought, for example, that Sarge was president of the Kennedy Foundation and that Bobby was treasurer.[93] Neither was an officer. When introduced to John Fogarty, he immediately blurted, "Mr. Fogarty, I want you to know that I am a Republican." Patrick Doyle, who was there, wanted to sink through the floor in embarrassment.[94] And Warren once dragged a Republican congresswoman, Catherine May from Oregon, to the White House dining room, ending up across the table from Kenny O'Donnell, JFK's appointments secretary, and other intimates. The next morning Warren got a "very, very nasty" phone call from O'Donnell.[95]

After Warren made the insensitive suggestion that the mentally retarded be removed from certain states and dispersed evenly throughout the country, the Shrivers started monitoring him.[96] From August 1963 on he had to send Eunice weekly reports of his activities. These abject documents provided a virtual day-by-day account of Warren's activities.[97] The Shrivers imposed on Warren an advisory committee on which Bob Cooke and Leonard Mayo figured prominently.[98] (Warren had particularly unpleasant memories of Cooke: "Either he [Cooke] liked people or he hated them."[99]) The Shrivers also imposed several of their own people on Warren as staff. They sent Donald Stedman, the foundation's executive director, over to help Warren organize a big conference in September 1963, and they brought David Ray up from Arkansas.

Ray was from Memphis, and since 1957 he had been the director of the Arkansas Children's Colony in Conway, the state's first MR institution. The Children's Colony was based on the cottage system (small individual housing units, rather than one large building) and was making—with its bright colors and lockers for personal possessions—a genuine effort to humanize the institutional environment. Eunice Shriver met Ray rather indirectly, via the President's Panel: Mayo, as chairman of the panel, had been holding meetings around the country. Ray was supposed to attend one in Atlanta but, unable to come at the last minute, sent a paper instead. "Then I got a call from Mrs. Shriver," Ray recalled. "She was interested in some of the stuff we'd been doing, so we invited her down [to Conway]. She came down and spent a few days with us." Ray thought no more about it. Then at a meeting in Portland, Oregon, he got a phone call from Sarge. "I thought it was some guy playing a joke on me. They wanted me to come by Timberlawn on my way home from the meeting in Portland. They made hotel reservations and sent a car to pick me up and I didn't know what was going on. It turned out they wanted me to come to Washington on a leave of absence to work with Dr. Stafford Warren."[100]

Quite precisely, the Shrivers wanted Ray to take responsibility for lobbying. HEW would pay Ray's salary. Hiring someone as a government consultant for the purpose of lobbying was strictly illegal, but with one's brother as President and investigative reporting not yet a media practice, "nobody thought too much about it," as Ray said later.[101] Warren was initially somewhat put out at having this assistant imposed on him, but he soon came to like the young Southerner for his ability to deal with people. Ray, forty-one at the time, reciprocated the esteem.[102]

Ray was also a valuable commodity in Washington because he already knew well two key congressmen: Wilbur Mills from White County, Arkansas, chairman of the House Ways and Means Committee, and Oren Harris from Hempstead County, Arkansas, chairman of the House Interstate and Foreign Commerce Committee.[103] Both committees would consider aspects of the panel's forthcoming MR legislation. Ray already knew Lister Hill as well. Ray, not Warren, would have the principal responsibility within the White House office of lobbying the Congress on MR.

In theory, Warren and his staff were responsible for jockeying the panel's many recommendations through the federal government. In practice, it was the Shrivers who retained the oversight and gave Warren and his people their marching orders. Warren recalled, "Sometimes she or Sarge would—or even Mike Feldman would—report what had occurred at Hyannisport or down in Florida when the family got together, essentially something that the President had agreed to, and it was given to us ten minutes after nine on Monday morning as a kind of an instruction for the week." Then Warren would have to call Cohen up to discuss it, since many instructions had to be executed through HEW. "I could hear him grin over the phone or giggle a little. It was illegal; there wasn't legislation or authority to do this yet, might not ever be."[104] And yet the Kennedy family wanted it done.

Thus, the whole Warren episode turned out to be a rather unhappy one. Warren was not respected at the White House. O'Donnell and the Irish mafia were, according to HEW's Patrick Doyle, uncooperative and condescending, and Eunice had to keep running interference for him.[105] Doyle: "When things got rough—we tried to keep Eunice out of it, but if we got into a real bind, we would call her and then she would expedite it. And that's, of course, another euphemism. She would really expedite it."[106] Ultimately Warren was sidelined (and left office only after JFK's death), and the Shrivers and the White House staffers would simply ask Ray to get the job done.[107]

What really exasperated Eunice about the gentlemanly Warren, who perhaps was more accustomed to the leisurely style of Pacific Coast academe, was that he was not a Kennedy type—he wasn't peppy enough. She realized this on their first meeting: "He was older and less aggressive and less imaginative and rather slow moving, I thought. And then we brought him in to the President." After the interview JFK "sort of shrugged his shoulders and said, 'Well. . . .'"

"I don't know," Eunice concluded. "If we had to do it over, I'd try to get a different, younger, peppier guy."[108]

The whole story of Warren and the White House office is interesting because it demonstrates what qualities the Kennedy family felt one must possess to be a mover and shaker. The task ahead was so enormous that only a small band of those with the right energy level could qualify to carry the torch. (Cohen was astonished at HEW to find himself, in historian Edward Berkowitz's words, "in an environment where people showed how tough they were in part by how hard they worked."[109]) But maybe Eunice was right: the task ahead *was* enormous.

Seizing the Reins

Warren was so maladroit that it was fortunate Eunice and Sarge were able to rely on Wilbur Cohen. As assistant secretary at HEW and responsible for legislation, Cohen was the third most powerful person in the HEW bureaucracy, after the under secretary, and after Secretary Abe Ribicoff, who was in charge of HEW until he was elected to the Senate in 1962. (Ribicoff cared little about MR; Secretary Anthony Celebrezze, who was in office from 1962 until John Gardner took over HEW in 1965, cared even less.[110]) Unlike Warren, Cohen was a Kennedy man. When he came to Washington in 1960, he began wearing his "PT 109" tie clasp.[111] Situated in the Secretary's office, Cohen had a tiny staff—two deputies, two special assistants, and a nuts-and-bolts committee, the Secretary's Committee on Mental Retardation (SCMR) headed by Luther Stringham. It was the committee's job to ensure that the HEW agencies actually implemented the report.[112]

Cohen took some beating from the HEW bureaucracy, which resisted the panel's report just as any established bureaucracy resents change. Yet Ribicoff had given Cohen the authority to "turn HEW inside out" on behalf of MR.[113] As Bob Cooke later said, "At times I got the feeling that the report had been foisted on HEW. And there was a bit of resentment that they themselves hadn't had the opportunity to develop their own report on what ought to be done, rather than have this outside group do it. It seemed to characterize a little bit, the whole question of the established bureaucracy being short circuited by a bunch of amateurs."[114]

Mike Feldman at the White House, and Eunice behind him, were beating up on Cohen, too. Cohen was at one meeting at the White House, as Cooke recalls, "and it was essentially one of these things with grabbing people by the lapel and saying, 'Look, you've got to find some sort of money.'"[115] Eunice later told an interviewer, "Mike Feldman was the person we dealt with 90 percent of the time. . . . If we ran into a problem, I would call him. I talked to him a lot about the bureau [for the Handicapped at the Office of Education]. So I honestly used the White House because we were under pressure for time, and it was a great cause and we just couldn't sit over there forever, that kind of thing. I knew that the President was interested in this and that he would want it that way."[116] Thus, at Eunice's instigation Feldman was in constant touch with Cohen.

Sometimes Eunice grabbed Cohen's lapels herself. He was supposed to file a series of almost weekly reports to her on the progress of the panel's recommendations. In his first, on February 11, 1963, he told her that he had talked with Wilbur Mills about introducing one piece of legislation in the House, and with Senator Hill and Representative Oren Harris about introducing another. He had liaised with Surgeon General Luther Terry, with Mary Switzer, et cetera. It is remarkable that this high government official was giving an outsider, a Washington nonpolitician, an hour-by-hour account of his activities.[117]

Eunice's desires would be handed down as orders within the federal bureaucracy. "Mike Feldman knew how HEW worked," she said, "and he helped us crystallize what we thought we must have. . . . He told this to HEW, they told it to Budget, and we all agreed. HEW worked under orders from the White House, and Stringham and the others essentially followed instructions."[118]

Cohen did bridle on occasion at all this interference. Once Sarge asked John Throne, the executive director of the Kennedy Foundation, to invite HEW's eight regional directors to a meeting in Washington that Sarge was organizing. It was Throne's first week on the job. "I get a call from Wilbur Cohen," Throne recalled the story. "He said in effect, What in hell are you doing calling my people to a meeting in Washington."

Throne replied, "Mr. Shriver asked me to do this."

Cohen said, "You tell Sarge Shriver that if he wants to have a meeting of HEW directors he should talk to me about it and I'll let him know whether we are going to have it or not."[119]

Doyle attributed such malentendus with HEW to the Shrivers' "great impatience." "They were quite impatient with the slow pace, and they were both impatient with the bureaucracy as they understood it. Coming from families whose whole motif was to get things done quickly, they tried to do this. Now this led to difficulties at times. Wilbur Cohen would arch his back from time to time. . . ." But when Cohen protested, the Shrivers would respond, in essence, "Well, look, if we hadn't done this, we wouldn't have gotten the retarded anything. They've been in dungeons too long." Doyle often had to pacify both sides.[120]

Eunice's clout was not just with Cohen but reverberated throughout the HEW bureaucracy. For example, Gunnar Dybwad, then executive director of NARC, complained to her about a draft bill that seemed to conflate mental retardation with "mental illness," a red flag to the parents' organization, who too long had felt themselves in thralldom to psychiatrists.[121] Dybwad's letter sparked a memo from Sarge Shriver to Mike Feldman, "Dear Mike, Would you call me about this, please. . . ."[122] Six weeks later HEW was offering Dybwad a job; a week after that the agency issued strict instructions about how mental retardation was not to be confused with mental illness. Copies of both communications were sent to Feldman and to the Shrivers.[123]

In retrospect, it is actually quite breathtaking to see a major agency of the federal government captured in this manner by outsiders. One recalls that by 1963 the panel had been dissolved and Eunice had no official status (although she retained an office in HEW[124]). It was as though the Department of Defense had been captured by Jimmie Carter's brother Billy on behalf of a worthy cause. Yet the Shrivers captured HEW without raising so much as an eyebrow.

There are many examples in American history of entrepreneurs seizing control of executive authority—the railways, the defense companies, the oil industry. These constitute, after all, the annals of lobbying. But this was the first time that a woman had seized the reins. It changes little that the woman happened to be the President's sister. Other presidents have had sisters who remained uninvolved in government. Eunice Shriver was successful not merely because she was the President's sister, but because she had grit and determination, and the desire to show the family she was every bit a match for her brothers.

Challenging the Congress

Any major new legislative program usually begins with a presidential address to Congress. JFK's message was supposed to reflect the recommendations of the President's Panel on Mental Retardation. It got off to a rocky start. The problem was that Eunice detested the draft version of the President's MR message, which somebody at HEW had written. "I saw the final draft and thought it awful. I was home one Sunday afternoon reading it. I called up Dr. Cooke, and I called up Mike Feldman, and I called Leonard Mayo, and I said, 'You know, President Kennedy's never going to be happy with this. We won't get anyplace. Will you come out, and meet with Sargent and me?'"

The men came out to Timberlawn that Sunday. Eunice said to Cooke, "We have nothing. . . . You know, everything's just so vague and so general. We ought to put in some sort of institutional things that we can ask for."

Like what? asked Cooke.

Eunice said, "What institutions are there that would provide more training and more people in the field?"[125]

Cooke then, again, raised with Eunice an idea that the panel had buried in the body of its report. In March 1961, Cooke had mentioned to her the need for comprehensive diagnostic and treatment centers for MR, associated with universities but reaching out to the community. These so-called "university-affiliated facilities" would have the advantage of getting the universities involved in MR (previously centered in asylums), and of providing a badly needed community service to the parents who kept churning around trying to find a doctor who could tell them what was wrong with their child. Finally, these centers would be multidisciplinary —a crucial concept in the parents' world of wearisome visiting to see an endless number of professionals. The centers would bring together physicians, psychologists, educators, physical therapists, and so forth, making possible "one-stop shopping."[126] In November 1962, Cooke launched the idea in public. In a speech to the Maryland Department of Mental Hygiene he called for a teaching service "in each of our university medical schools . . . supported by the state, devoted to the retarded, just as teaching services dedicated to the mentally ill characterize each university hospital."[127]

Now, in January 1963 at Timberlawn, Cooke had the opportunity to put his idea into effect. He began rewriting the draft of the President's address so that when JFK actually presented his MR message to Congress on February 5, 1963, he announced federal funds for the construction of "inpatient clinical units as an integral part of university-associated hospitals in which specialists on mental retardation would serve." Multidisciplinary MR clinics would be attached to these hospitals, as would satellite clinics in outlying communities.[128] Thus, the university-affiliated facility, or UAF, was born. Several dozen of these would ultimately bring the comfort of reliable diagnosis and well-considered habilitation to many parents with MR children.

Eunice sent the revised draft back to Mike Feldman the next day. The UAF scheme came as a nasty surprise to Wilbur Cohen's people. The bureaucrats had incorporated many of the panel's other proposals in the draft legislation they were now forwarding to Congress, but they were caught off guard by this insertion in the presidential address—they had not budgeted for UAFs. Eunice said, "Then Wilbur Cohen got cross about that because he said that would throw the budget off. Mike then talked to Wilbur and the Budget Bureau and helped lots in keeping this item in." Eunice, too, talked to someone at the Bureau of the Budget and to Cohen.[129] Finally, an institutional construction program was raided for funds, and JFK's whole MR package, assembled in this helter-skelter manner, went to Congress.[130]

The Kennedy Administration divided its MR package into two major bills. The first, introduced by Lister Hill in the Senate on March 5, 1963, provided for eighteen UAFs, twelve mental retardation research centers, money for localized day and residential facilities, and increased funds for training teachers of the mentally retarded. The President's UAF proposal became bill S 1576 as it moved through Congress, later becoming PL 88–164 as Kennedy signed it into law on October 31, 1963. The bill's provisions dealing with MR were entirely noncontroversial, and it passed at every stage with huge majorities.[131] (Its proposal to pay the salaries of physicians in community mental health centers turned out to be highly controversial and was defeated in the House by lobbyists from the American Medical Association.[132]) The research centers and UAFs still exist today, but funding for the community MR centers disappeared after 1968.[133]

The second of the Kennedy Administration bills, introduced in the House by Wilbur Mills on July 15 (and in the Senate by Abe Ribicoff), significantly increased Social Security funds to prevent mental retardation through better care for pregnant mothers and newborn children. It also tacked on an extra $2 million to help the states better plan their MR programs.[134] Called HR 7544 while in Congress (and PL 88–156 after it was signed into law on October 24, 1963), the bill's major impact actually lay in this three-year planning provision, for it encouraged the states to start thinking seriously about up-to- date MR programs.

For each signing there was a big ceremony, and Hill, Fogarty, Vice President Lyndon Johnson, the lobbyists of the MR children's association, the panel members, and Warren's staff were all invited. "[The President] would sign part of a letter and hand the pen to some favorite," said Warren. "Mr. Cohen got a pen, Mr. Celebrezze and so on. . . . These were very important historical items to show that they were blackened by the india ink. As a matter of fact, on the side Mrs. [Evelyn] Lincoln [JFK's secretary] gave me half a dozen for members of my subcommittee who weren't present that had been dipped in the ink. . . . It was sort of a sanctified thing," continued Warren. "The pen had actually, presumably, been held by the President in signing his signature and completing the bill."[135] It was a lovely event, the signing of this historic legislation, the culmination of two years of struggle. The massive weight of the federal government had finally begun to swing on behalf of the mentally retarded.

The passage of President Kennedy's MR legislation in 1963 mattered for a second reason, however. It was a kind of training exercise for the Shrivers in lobbying. Both bills passed through Congress like a knife through butter. There was never any concern that they would fail. But the Kennedy people behaved as though they hung by a hair's breadth and hurled a full-force lobbying effort at Congress. Such efforts would be necessary in the future, and it is intriguing to see how, in the summer of 1963, Sarge, Eunice, and Bob Cooke honed their skills.

Sarge had actually been perfecting his lobbying skills since the summer of 1961, when he had to push the Peace Corps proposals through Congress. Originally, the Peace Corps was to have been subordinated to the amorphous bureaucracy of the Agency for International Development (AID), the State Department's arm for administering foreign aid. Sarge Shriver had wisely resisted this, enlisting Lyndon Johnson's help to keep the Peace Corps independent; JFK had grudgingly gone along with this. Shriver then discovered that Larry O'Brien and the congressional liaison staff of the White House were doing nothing at all in Congress on behalf of the Peace Corps. According to Harris Wofford, Sarge asked for Eunice's help with the President.

After talking with JFK, Eunice reported back to Sarge, "Jack feels that you and Lyndon Johnson demanded that the Peace Corps be separate and that therefore the two of you ought to get your damn bill through Congress by yourselves."

JFK had said that the AID bill was "going to be goddamn difficult and he didn't want to have to turn around and then go to the Congress all over again to put the Peace Corps through. . . . I left it out there by itself at their request—they wanted it that way, they didn't want me to have it in AID where I wanted it—so let them go ahead and put the son of a bitch through."[136]

His pride stung by this challenge, Sarge Shriver geared himself up for a herculean effort. He told his aide Harris Wofford, "I really went to work. The one thing I was certain of—I was going to put the goddamned Peace Corps through the House and the Senate."[137] According to *Look* magazine, he buttonholed "no less than 350 legislators in the biggest personal lobbying job of the year. With some, he talked for hours. What they saw was a 45-year-old, 175-pound six-footer, handsome, hard-muscled and trim, a man who managed to talk practical politics while bubbling with evangelical zeal for his mission."[138] The Peace Corps passed Congress by a large margin: 59 to 32 in the Senate, 288 to 97 in the House.[139] Anthony Lewis, in the *New York Times,* called it "one of the most successful lobbying campaigns in history."[140]

Having tasted the pleasure of successful advocacy, Sarge was ready for the task again in the summer of 1963 with the MR legislation, this time in tandem with Eunice, Bob Cooke, and David Ray from the White House office. For the first time in her life, Eunice started going regularly "over to the Hill." She said, "All the congressmen felt that, 'My God, this is something none of us have done anything about, and we'll do something.'"

She gave her brother five or six names to call. When she saw Wilbur Mills he said, "Oh yes, I've heard from your brother. We're certainly going to do everything we can. I think it looks very good."[141] (A good deal of JFK's other legislation didn't look so good.[142]) It was a foregone conclusion, of course, that the MR bills would pass. Congressmen kept quizzing Cooke in private, "Why aren't you asking for more?"[143]

Eunice also greased the skids by applying Kennedy Foundation money appropriately. In order to keep Fogarty onside, the foundation bent over backwards to award grants for summer camps to Rhode Island, Fogarty's home state. Francis Kelley was a member of the foundation's camp review board and assistant superintendent of the Ladd School in Exeter, Rhode Island. In April 1963 he reported to Fogarty, "After the [camp review board] meeting was over I had an opportunity to talk privately with Mrs. Eunice Shriver and explained the situation and of your intensive interest in West Warwick. She was definitely impressed. I also discussed this on four occasions with Dr. Donald J. Stedman, Executive Director of the Kennedy Foundation, who in turn discussed this with Mrs. Shriver." Eunice felt the West Warwick proposal was so awful that there could be no question of a grant, but she nonetheless found it in her heart to make one to Rhode Island's "South County project," also in Fogarty's second congressional district.[144]

Behind the scenes, just making sure, was Sarge. Ray kept in constant touch with him and also accompanied Sarge to nighttime meetings with Feldman and O'Brien.[145] On handling difficult Congressmen, such as Paul Rogers, a Democrat from Florida (Rogers later became a friend of the cause), Sarge would say to Ray, "Okay, set up a luncheon. Let's you and I go to lunch with him."[146]

Working the Congress with Sargent Shriver was a learning experience for this gang of neophytes, who had no previous familiarity with the gritty task of getting legislation passed. Warren remembered, "The first time I saw Sarge Shriver do this, I was astonished at his smoothness, his ability to make [information] into capsules and be factually and scientifically correct. . . . One of the things we learned was, we'd go and say our say in the least time possible—five minutes. It was just one, two, three."[147]

Bob Cooke also sharpened his lobbying teeth in that spring and summer of 1963, employing the tactics Sarge Shriver had laid out: breakfasts with key people, or brief to-the-point interviews with follow-up letters driving home the essentials. Thus on March 26 Cooke invited Fogarty for breakfast, the next day rocketing off a follow-up: "The specific suggestions which I feel are necessary . . . are as follows."[148] It was a classical demonstration of effective buttonholing.

In the story of how the Kennedys got going on mental retardation, this spring and summer of 1963 were crucial. Not only did they acquire a platform of legislation on which to build, they polished the political skills needed to push through much more controversial projects in the future.

"Now What Do We Do?"

One of the flaws of the panel's report was its lack of provisions for implementation. In getting the ninety-five recommendations carried out, the states were key. Care of the mentally retarded was a state responsibility, and to make a success of the federal government's new program, the states would have to be brought onside. Specifically, they would have to be encouraged to plan in order to coordinate services to the mentally retarded scattered among numerous state departments. These intricate administrative matters became highly concrete for desperate parents trying to figure out who could help them.

Getting the fifty states to plan intelligently for this wall of new money was a difficult task. If the states refused to wean themselves from the institutional system, to dismantle barriers between disciplines, or to offer special-ed programs in the schools, the innovation that the Kennedy forces were doing at the center would not filter down. As Bob Cooke said, "The big problem that developed was how do you go from a federal level to a state level."[149]

Thus, Leonard Mayo had the idea of holding a big conference that would bring representatives of the fifty states to Washington, so that the Kennedy people could brief them on the new legislation and encourage them to form sensible plans rather than just leaving MR, as before, with their "mental health" staffs (usually chaired by psychiatrists).[150] The point was, as Eunice put it, "to get the states to set up a State Department of Mental Retardation apart from State Departments of Mental Health."[151]

The conference was to take place in September 1963, before the MR legislation had actually passed but with the almost complete certainty that it would. It was slated for a conference center about fifty miles from Washington called Airlie House in Warrenton, Virginia, operated by a nonprofit corporation and designed to attract public interest groups. It was selected so that "people wouldn't go off to clubs," as Ray put it, and stay right there to concentrate on MR. The Airlie House handouts billed it as "an island of thought." The job of organizing the conference was thrown into Warren's lap; Ray was assigned to help him. An overwhelmed Warren pleaded with Sarge to help line up the HEW bureaucrats.[152]

In this "State-Federal Conference on Mental Retardation" it would have made sense to have invited the governors personally. Yet Sarge and Mike Feldman insisted this not be done because, "That would be too political."[153] Instead, each governor was to send four or five representatives. Would the government pay for it? Said Warren, "We decided this was going to cost a heck of a lot of money, and Feldman blew his top and said, 'No. Make them pay their own way. They'll do it.'"[154]

Indeed they did. Invitations to the conference turned into very hot items. One can easily see what glamour the cause of mental retardation was acquiring: by August 1963, people in statehouses across the country were avid to come to Airlie House and be briefed on the subject. One governor sent nine representatives. Michael Begab, who had been working temporarily in Warren's office on loan from HEW, recalled, "I was on the phone nearly all day long receiving long distance calls from the governors' offices. Many requested that they be allowed to send more people than we could allow. . . . It was partly a status thing; they were anxious to be part of that conference."[155] According to Warren, "Some of them actually bootlegged people who stayed in the local motels and who showed up at the conference."[156] The conference swelled from the originally anticipated 250 to 400 participants.[157]

Sarge spoke. Surgeon General Luther Terry and Mary Switzer presented papers. Many moguls from HEW and other agencies put in appearances.[158] The high point came on the afternoon of the first day, September 19, when JFK spoke to the participants via a telephone hookup from the White House. David Ray later said, "I can remember that Sarge called the White House and said, 'Put the President on.'

"And then when the President came on, [Sarge] said, 'Jack, we're all set here for you.'

"And all the people standing around there heard that. . . . I was one of them. . . . I was a professional in the field—and this is just a small point, but it kind of charged these people up."[159] It would be the last time many of them would hear Jack Kennedy's voice.

Camelot thus opened a new chapter in the history of mental retardation. Flushed with their recent victories, the Shrivers decided to put on a gala awards dinner in New York City, a way of raising the scientific profile of MR by giving deserving pioneers large cash prizes, and of raising the public profile by linking the cause to the Kennedy family name. On November 15 the *New York Times* ran the story. The President himself would attend.[160] A week later, the President was dead.

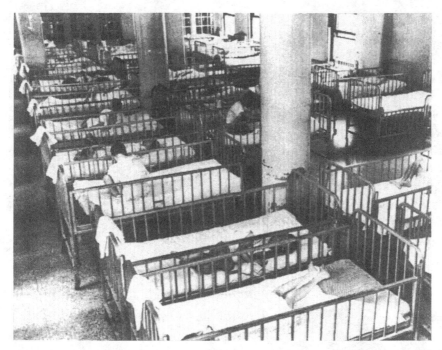

Images from a Pennsylvania institution. Courtesy of *The Philadelphia Inquirer.*

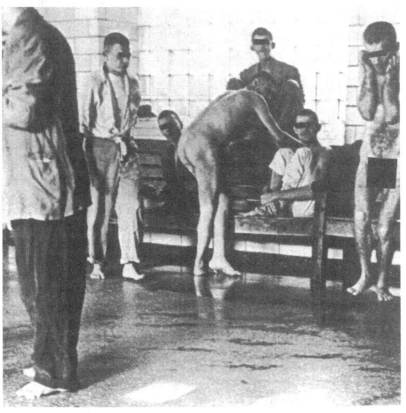

Photographs by Fred Kaplan published in Burton Blatt and Fred Kaplan, *Christmas in Purgatory* (Boston: Allyn and Bacon, 1966). Courtesy of Human Policy Press, and the National Resource Center on Supported Living and Choice of the Center on Human Policy, Syracuse University.

The Kennedy family in England (c. 1938) during Joseph Kennedy, Sr.'s term as U.S. Ambassador to Britain. Left to right: Eunice, J.F.K., Rosemary, Jean, Joseph, Sr., Edward, Rose, Joseph, Jr., Patricia, Robert, Kathleen. Photograph by Dorothy Wilding. Courtesy of The John F. Kennedy Library.

The Kennedy family attending the coronation of Pope Pius XII. Left to right: Kathleen, Patricia, Robert, J.F.K., Rose, Joseph, Sr., Edward, Eunice, Jean, Rosemary. Photograph by G. Felici, Vatican photographer. Courtesy of The John F. Kennedy Library.

President Kennedy receiving the 1962 Panel Report from the President's Commission on Mental Retardation. Chairman Leonard Mayo is standing at the President's right and Dr. Elizabeth Boggs is standing at Mayo's right. Courtesy of The John F. Kennedy Library.

President Kennedy greeting the 1963 poster child for the National Association for Retarded Children at the White House. The older child is retarded due to a metabolic condition called PKU, but the younger was saved because the condition was identified in time thanks to medical research. With the children (from left) are Eunice Kennedy Shriver; the mother of the children; Leonard Mayo, chair of the President's Panel on Mental Retardation; the President; and Vincent Fitzpatrick, president of NARC. Courtesy of The John F. Kennedy Library.

President Kennedy and his mother, Rose Fitzgerald Kennedy, at the first international awards dinner of the Joseph P. Kennedy, Jr. Foundation held at the Statler Hilton Hotel, Washington, D.C., on Dec. 6, 1962. Courtesy of The John F. Kennedy Library.

Eunice Kennedy Shriver welcomes competitors to the Fourth International Special Olympic Games, held at Central Michigan University in Mount Pleasant, Michigan, in August 1975. Some 3,200 athletes from 10 countries participated in the Games, which were broadcast nationwide on CBS's "Sports Spectacular." Courtesy of Clarke Historical Library, Central Michigan University.

Sargent Shriver at the Fourth International Special Olympic Games, Mount Pleasant, Michigan, in August 1975. Courtesy of Clarke Historical Library, Central Michigan University.

Eunice Kennedy Shriver presents medals to two competitors at the 1975 Special Olympics in Mount Pleasant, Michigan. Courtesy of Clarke Historical Library, Central Michigan University.

Celebrity images: actress Sally Struthers poses with a medallist at the 1975 Special Olympics in Michigan. Courtesy of Clarke Historical Library, Central Michigan University.

5

Special Olympics

pecial Olympics, a competitive sports program for mentally retarded people that combines daily training with an international Games once every four years, was Eunice Shriver's baby. It is her legacy to history, growing from a day camp for mentally retarded children that she began in 1962 at Timberlawn. But Special Olympics was also a product of her entire personal history, of her long development as a Kennedy and as the sister of a person with MR. And as Eunice Shriver created the Special Olympics, she herself grew in stature, from narrowly obsessing about her standing in her father's eyes to a mature, generous, and self-confident woman able to articulate a philosophically distinctive vision. It was a vision of how competitive sports can help those with mental retardation, together with their loved ones, achieve a sense of joy and meaning in life.

The Need for Play

In older photographs of the mentally retarded, it is striking to see how often they were overweight. So common was corpulence in those with MR that observers once believed it to be a biological side effect of mental retardation itself. One study in the 1960s found that mentally retarded boys were 25 percent fatter than their nonretarded peers, girls 46 percent fatter.[1] Of severely retarded adults, one-quarter to one-third were obese. "This creates a tremendous image obstacle, as well as being a health and vitality problem," said Wolf Wolfensberger.[2]

The reason they were so overweight is that they got so little exercise. "Why do retarded children have less fun than normal children?" asked Paul Benoit in 1955, a psychologist specializing in MR. Because they have fewer play opportunities, he said. Consider the plight of MR children at home. They tended to be destructive of toys because they were much stronger than children of the age group for whom the toys had been designed. As for specially-designed toys for the mentally retarded, the research director of a large toy company told Benoit, "People would not readily buy in stores materials intended for retarded children; in the majority of cases, shame would make the merchandise untouchable."[3] Also, MR children did not generally play well with children of their own mental age, aware that their nonretarded peers considered such activities baby stuff. "They have a sense of social fitness and an urge to imitate their peers," wrote Benoit. "In this situation parents can hardly do anything else than buy useless books and toys, and wonder why their children do not have as much fun as their neighbors."[4]

Thus, MR children at home typically had little to keep them busy— no friends, no suitable toys. "[A retarded child] may make friends with the children in his special class at school," said one observer in 1966. "But unlike the normal children who can play with their school chums in the neighborhood after school hours, retarded children are transported from their homes in different parts of town and have few friends in their own neighborhoods." They were "victims of enforced leisure" with a daily time-block of six to eight hours that sat empty, "during which little or no activity is available to them. Many just sit and watch television; others get restless and irritable."[5]

In institutions, the lack of play verged on the catastrophic. Even with the best of will the overwhelmed staff had little time for organizing play. Anxious about accidents and broken windows, they simply ruled out games in which balls might be hurled in all directions or poorly coordinated bodies might collide with one another. And when the budget would scarcely suffice for food, "how can a steward or business manager show interest in buying bingo sets, canceled stamps, balloons, and soap-bubble pipes?" asked Benoit rhetorically.[6] But just imagine a childhood without canceled stamps or soap-bubble pipes.

In many institutions, even a modicum of goodwill was lacking. While dedicated staffers at places like the Seaside Regional Center in Waterford, Connecticut, did attempt fun activities, most MR staff considered their little charges to be beyond fun and recreation. What would be the point of recreation rooms or occupational therapy, asked the director of New York's Gouverneur Hospital in 1965, an MR hell-hole. "They would not be able to use it."[7] Wolf Wolfensberger recalled of some of the institutions in which he had served in the 1950s, where common spaces such as hallways and dayrooms that could have served as play areas were turned into dormitories because of overcrowding. "Some people were never allowed outside the building or [were allowed] only into small fenced-in yards or, even worse, small courtyards enclosed by buildings. Even then some residents were let into these enclosures only a few times a year."[8] As late as 1961, the wheelchair-confined children at one MR asylum, when caught outside in a rain shower, "asked to stay out, because they *had never felt rain on their faces before!*"[9]

Was this deprivation owing to shortages of staff and budget, the standard response of the apologists? Not really. It was more because of a deeply ingrained institutional attitude that the mentally retarded were incapable of appreciating such pleasures. Wolfensberger attributed it "to a callousness that good things like these—small as they were—were wasted on residents. There was the idea that nice things were not what we should be doing for these individuals."[10]

For this life bereft of play, children with MR paid the price of muscular weakness and lack of physical coordination, giving rise to the myth that the mentally retarded were incapable of sports. In 1967, a national survey showed that mildly retarded children (with IQs of 50 to 75) were two to four years behind nonretarded children in the development of physical skills. Only 12 percent of the MR children did as well as the average nonretarded child.[11] In those days, when MR children were retained playless at home or confined in institutions, they were only half as strong as the nonretarded and tired 30 percent more rapidly.[12]

Another cause of obesity and poor physical development was the lack of any kind of systematic physical training. Often excluded from phys-ed programs at school, MR children failed to learn sports or to challenge their bodies. In a study commissioned by the Kennedy Foundation in 1965, Lawrence Rarick and other investigators discovered that 45 percent of MR children received no physical education at all, another 30 percent less than an hour a week. Only a quarter of the children had more than a hour of physical education a week. They also found that the level of "motor proficiency" was related to the amount of instructional time.[13]

This absence of exercise and sports was not a trivial matter. Frustrated in intellectual achievement and often scorned socially, MR children found in physical activity an opportunity to attain self-confidence. In fitness and sports they could discover that they were not worthless, because they could run and hit and jump as well as anybody. Many MR children were, of course, also physically impaired. For them, sports and athletic contests offered an opportunity to show at least that they were capable of something and were not just onlookers. As Ted Powers, head of physical education at Baylor University in Waco, Texas, said in 1974, "The process of learning through physical activity is the single most important aspect of the education of the retarded."[14]

Yet opening the lives of the mentally retarded to play and sports was not so straightforward. Many had a short attention span; some were hyperactive and required close supervision. Instructions had to be repeated again and again. As two teachers with four years' experience of offering weekly thirty-minute phys-ed classes in Jacksonville, Florida, wrote in 1965, "Discipline, due to lack of comprehension and lack of experience in responding to authority, is a primary problem. Hypersensitivity and varying degrees of social adjustment," they added euphemistically, "contribute to the problem."[15]

Clearly, then, as Sarge and Eunice contemplated the plight of the mentally retarded, their thoughts would be drawn to exercise and sports. For the children it was essential, and as things then stood, they were getting almost none of it.

A Camp at Timberlawn

We are back in the spring of 1962. The Shrivers have recently moved into their rented thirty-acre estate at Timberlawn. Sarge is frantically busy organizing the Peace Corps. Eunice has been consulting with Leonard Mayo about getting the President's Panel on Mental Retardation going. Sitting in her tiny office at HEW, she was eager that the panel's report "contain ideas and programs that would touch the lives of parents of retarded children so that when this report was issued . . . mothers and fathers could feel that something was going to happen [on behalf of] their children, they would be able to really see changes in their children's lives." It was then that she hit upon physical education and sports. "I really didn't know much about the field at that time," she said. "In fact, I knew nothing about it."[16]

Eunice was drawn to the notion of athletics for the mentally retarded because she had spent much of her own life as an athlete. Adlai Stevenson introduced her humorously at an awards dinner in 1962 as a "star touch-football player."[17] Eunice and Rosemary had played sports together. "Despite [Rosemary's] mental handicap," said Eunice, "she was able to swim, sail and play ball, and because of this she was included in the family's activity. We felt that her physical abilities were a tremendous asset for her, and kept her from being isolated."[18]

While the panel was going on, Eunice bumped into Leonard Mayo and told him that she would like to write the section of the report dealing with physical education. She went home and discussed the idea with Sarge, then "started making some phone calls to see if I could get information on what was going on in the country. And I found to my horror, I could get almost nothing." She phoned all the experts and learned that nothing was being done in recreation and physical education for the mentally retarded. "It was really pitiful, the lack of programs."[19]

So Eunice decided to set up her own camp at Timberlawn. When the Shrivers decided to do something, that usually meant that it was to happen right away. ("Nothing happens slowly around there," said Donald Stedman, the Kennedy Foundation's executive director at the time. "They think of something Friday and want to do it Monday."[20])

First, they needed a director. In 1950 Joe Senior, while visiting his neighbor Oleg Cassini in Palm Beach, had noticed a young man from Canada whom Cassini had hired to teach his kids swimming. John ("Sandy") Eiler, then twenty-three, had grown up in Welland, Ontario, moved down to Florida after the World War II, done a brief hitch in the U.S. Army, and was now looking for work. He had been a champion swimmer in Canada, prevented from joining the Olympic team only by a burst appendix. Joe Kennedy "liked the way Sandy related to the children and the rapport," in the words of Lee Eiler, Sandy Eiler's wife, "and asked him if he would be willing to take on another family." In those years, only Joe Kennedy, Ethel, and Bobby's two eldest children were around the Palm Beach mansion. (Kathleen had died in 1948.) After Eiler had worked with the Kennedys for a winter in Palm Beach, Joe Senior asked if he and his wife would move up to Hyannisport to live. The proud grandfather said there would be "quite a group." Joe put Eiler on salary and arranged for him to work during the winter with the Boston archdiocese. Eiler thus became for the next twenty-five years the Kennedy family's resident swimming and touch-football coach.

In Florida, Bobby and Maria Shriver were the next grandchildren on the scene. Eunice therefore knew Eiler well and remembered hearing that as a schoolboy in Canada, Eiler had started swimming classes for blind, mentally retarded, and deaf kids. She therefore asked him if he would be willing to take on the camp at Timberlawn.[21]

Volunteers would help Eiler out. Eunice canvassed some of the regional parochial schools such as Sacred Heart School at Stone Ridge in Bethesda and Georgetown Visitation Preparatory School, as well as private schools like Landon School and St. Alban's School, and the public schools next door to Timberlawn. "I wanted to have a large number of . . . students working as brothers and sisters to the retarded. It was going to be that kind of relationship," she said with emphasis. All of the schools were very responsive. The Shrivers selected twenty-six volunteer counselors.[22]

Eunice enlisted some special-ed teachers to come and help out, but they didn't know anything about sports. She also lined up an instructor from a riding stable as someone who would be good at teaching "very young children to ride." (Eunice herself was an avid horsewoman.) Thirty-four campers showed up, coming mainly from the Gales Child Health Center in D.C. A school bus would bring them out to Timberlawn. Camp was to begin June 7, 1962, and end in early July so that "I could go off to Cape Cod with my children," said Eunice.

Camp Shriver was to be a family affair. Bobby and Maria Shriver helped out as volunteers. This worked well until several years later Eunice discovered that Bobby, then around twelve, was going off in the woods to smoke pot with the prisoners from Lorton Reformatory in Fairfax County, Virginia, who had come to work as volunteers. "So we didn't have the prisoners back another year," she said.[23] Bobby, who had an IQ of 120, became close friends with a mentally retarded chap five years older named Raymond, whose IQ was 68. "One afternoon," Eunice remembered, "I watched Raymond fondly looking at a make-it-yourself kit. Bobby is mad about planes and I had given him the kit as a present for practicing his swimming. 'Do you like that kit, Raymond?' 'Yes,' said Raymond. 'I'll give it to you,' said Bobby, and together they ran down the hill to the house."[24] Timothy Shriver, then three, became pals with a nine-year-old named Wendell (IQ 40). Timothy and Wendell did many things "at the same speed and proficiency and loved each other. Both picked up their clothes—with some prodding—after swimming; both caught and threw a ball with the same ability, although Wendell kicked much better than Timothy. Both had the same table manners. Sometimes they would throw the food and would then have to go without dessert." The two adventurers would "hold hands and run down the hill together."[25]

Although other Kennedy family members became involved—Rose, for example, appealing to other wealthy people with estates to turn over their homes "for a couple of weeks" in the summer for MR day camps[26] —Eunice herself stood in the thick of the fray at Camp Shriver. Said Sarge, "When I'd come home from the office, there's my wife in the pool, holding this mentally retarded child in the water to see if it's possible for that child to swim. She didn't hire somebody for that. She went into that goddamn pool herself. She's a hands-on person."[27] Stedman, who along with Sandy Eiler was running the show, said of his boss, "She would actually jump in the pool and start thrashing around with them and run races. She still does that. She's hyper. She just likes hands-on direct stuff. She has never been a person to my recollection who stood in the background. She's right in the middle."[28] Throughout her life Eunice had displayed this kind of tangible enthusiasm in bringing sports to the mentally retarded and became well known for her willingness to destroy her hairdo by jumping spontaneously into the pool alongside them.[29]

The fray at Timberlawn involved not just swimming but many other physical activities, such as rope climbing and horseback riding. A mentally

Watson, John B.
   1970   [1924] *Behaviorism*. New York: Norton.
Weber, Max
   1964   [1947] *Max Weber: Theory of social and economic organization,* ed.
           T. Parsons. New York: Free Press.
White, Alan R.
   1968   Introduction. In A. R. White, ed., *The philosophy of action*. Oxford:
           Oxford University Press.
Williams, George C.
   1992   [1966] *Adaptation and natural selection: A critique of some current
           evolutionary thought*. Princeton: Princeton University Press.
Wilson, Edward, O.
   1975   *Sociobiology: New synthesis*. Cambridge: Belknap Press.
Winch, Peter
   1958   *The idea of a social science*. London: Routledge and Kegan Paul.
Wittgenstein, Ludwig
   1953   *Philosophical investigations*. Oxford: Basil Blackwell.
   1980   *Remarks on the philosophy of psychology,* vol. 1. Chicago: University of
           Chicago Press.

Index

action: authored versus caused, 38, 164,
170–72, 203; and authorship, 4, 35, 40,
74, 82–83, 87, 92–94, 98, 104, 114,
181, 189, 202; and awareness, 84; and
causation, 5, 85, 109, 112, 189, 191,
212; for the sake of pleasure, 35–36,
179; purposive-rational, 139; series versus sequence, 102, 104, 170; undecid-
ability of meaning of, 61–71; voluntary
versus involuntary, 38, 120–21, 191.
See also lifeworld; subjectivity; time;
Verstehen
action versus behavior, 10, 202–22
adaptationism, 36, 224
altruism, 160, 161–62, 164
anecdotes, 12, 40–49, 224
animal mind: agnosticism about, 139; and
anecdotal evidence, 41, 43–49; availability of, 28; avoidance of, 12, 95, 116–18,
134, 139, 150, 164, 181–82, 185, 201,
228; body-mind dualism, 23, 28, 35, 50;
complexity of, 166; and experience, 36;
implicit attribution of, 67; and language
use, 6–7, 28, 33, 100, 116, 118, 123,
149, 166, 175, 185, 202–22; and limits
of evidence, 43, 46; Machiavellian intelligence, 138–39, 151, 159; observability
and unobservability of, 22, 33–34, 35,
95, 206; open-mindedness about, 149,
164–65; reasoning, 44–46; and sexual
selection, 18; and states of being, 32–36,
142. *See also* awareness; emotion; inten-
tionality; skepticism; subjectivity
animals. *See* animal mind; behavioral
science
anthropomorphism: avoidance of, 12, 36,
134, 149, 156; Darwin's, 11–50; definition of, 7, 29, 83; and lifeworld, 83–86;
literal versus metaphorical, 12–13, 33,

53, 203; mock anthropomorphism, 150;
new anthropomorphism, 149–50; pejo-
rative connotations of, 7, 14, 53–54,
133, 149–62, 200–1, 203, 209; and
sociobiology, 133–34, 149–62, 227; and
subjectivity, 29, 49, 53, 76, 90, 185; as
supervenient effect, 31–32, 83; and tech-
nical idioms, 86, 185, 201
Arluke, Arnold, 229
Asquith, Pamela, 29, 32, 157
atomism, 96, 109, 188
Austin, J. L., 207
authorship. *See* action; *see also* animal
mind
awareness, 20, 77, 84–85, 93, 104, 114,
121, 123. *See also* animal mind

Barash, David, 126–28, 133, 164
Barlow, George W., 126, 227
Barnett, Samuel, 11, 22, 24, 28–29, 84
Beer, Colin, 223
behavior. *See* action; action versus behavior; behavioral science; vacuum behavior
behavioral ecology, 227. *See also* sociobiology
behavioral science: comparative approach
to, 2, 9, 38, 89, 143–49, 153–54, 166–
201; and experimentation, 106–16;
methodology of, 89, 143–49; and objec-
tivity, 2, 145–46, 201, 204; and statistics, 134, 147, 149; theory and theory-
laden, 88, 90–95, 107, 114, 123, 181,
203. *See also* language use; realism
behaviorism. *See* comparative psychology;
stimulus-response; Watson, J. B.
Bekoff, Marc, 226
Bennett, Jonathan, 197
Bleier, Ruth, 151
Boakes, Robert, 89, 224

retarded girl of twelve with a fear of heights came to Timberlawn to become "our champion rope climber. . . . A brain-damaged boy who had never ridden anything friskier than a Ford in his life learned to ride Pete, our little pony, with only one day of instruction."[30] This pony actually had quite a work-out, as Eunice noted in her diary: "Friday—Judy sits alone on the pony—she laughs while the pony does a slow trot and leads the next child during his turn. She hugs the animal every few minutes. An affectionate child. . . ."[31] In later years someone came from the Philippine Embassy to teach native dancing. John Palmer was seconded from the British Embassy to teach soccer; another counselor led the campers in "music, dance and rhythm."[32]

There was one counselor for every camper. Ann Hart, daughter of Michigan Senator Philip Hart and a recent graduate of Stone Ridge, became a counselor in the summer of 1965 and took on "a very autistic girl of fourteen, large, wild, and out of control. . . . I used my voice a lot to keep her connected. Lots of eye contact. I could stay unrelentingly focused on her. She was physically abusive. I'd come home black and blue. My mother was a bit concerned."[33]

In the summer of 1962, these young counselors were little more enlightened about the nature of MR than the population in general. The Kennedy family itself had not yet dared to bring Rosemary out of the closet (which would happen in the *Saturday Evening Post* article in September of that year). Counselor Ann Hammersbacher, age eighteen and a recent high school graduate, told Eunice afterwards, "We had no idea what it would be like. We'd never even met any retarded children. None of us really had any experience. . . . To tell the truth, all of us were a little afraid."[34]

A visiting businessman asked Eunice, "Aren't you afraid to work around the retarded? Won't they go berserk?"[35]

Thus, Camp Shriver represented a milestone in giving MR persons access to the experiences of normal life, such as camping. Although Eunice by no means invented MR day-camping, she helped turn it into a mass movement in the 1960s.

MR day-camping had really begun in 1950, when Kay Gould, a New Jersey NARC activist, initiated what is considered to be the first such camp. Gould influenced others after 1953, when she became chairman of NARC's subcommittee on recreational camping.[36] By 1957 enough day camps existed that NARC executives could speak of visiting "a dozen selected camps during this present summer." And NARC claimed the existence of 150 such day camps by 1959.[37] Overnight camps for MR children were slower to develop. Only in 1954 did the first Catholic MR overnight camp open, "Camp Fatima" in Gilmanton, New Hampshire.[38]

Not until 1956 was MR camping even mentioned on the agenda of the National Recreation Association.[39] After Camp Shriver, MR camping would explode.

What did these day camps have to contribute? Camp Shriver had something else to offer in addition to developing specific skills with crafts or horseback riding. These mentally retarded inner-city kids received a whole sensory experience, a bombardment of stimulation. At Timberlawn, their five senses were challenged with an intensity they had never previously encountered. Ann Hart said, "Some of these kids were developmentally disabled because of their environment. The lack of stimulation that they had experienced in their ten or twelve years was so severe that they had not had their senses and their brains ignited, so that what they got was stimulation of a wide variety—everything from water and sunlight, and touching and playing with beads, and walking and moving and jumping and archering and all the rest of it. What they got primarily was stimulation that had not been available to them ever in their lives."[40]

There was one final theme at Camp Shriver. Camp routines were filled with picnics and making little belts and dressing up like Indians. These kinds of experiences are perfectly healthy and belong to the category of activity called "recreation," the purpose of which is having fun. Camping in the United States has traditionally had a recreationist nature. The notion of physical education or physical fitness is somewhat different: developing one's cardiovascular capacity and muscle strength through the systematic training of one's body, and learning athletic skills. Finally, there is the impetus of sports: organized competition.

Timberlawn was really in the hands of recreationists. But above and beyond recreationism, the Shrivers were also very interested in physical education and sports. The campers at Timberlawn participated in tire-running to develop agility. At the Shrivers' behest, the D.C. Recreation Department set up at Timberlawn a program of "circuit training"—which means a series of exercise stations along a fixed course—with chin-up bars, old tires, balance beams, swing ropes, and so forth. At Camp Shriver this was called the "Confidence Course."[41]

There were also competitive sports. John Throne, the executive director who followed Stedman in 1964, said, "The Shrivers and the Kennedys would be constitutionally unable just to go camping. They would have to have some sort of organized competitive play."[42] So Camp Shriver also set up competitive swimming and running.

At the end of the first year of Camp Shriver in 1962, Eunice concluded, "It was clear that this was a good idea. So I went to the Foundation . . . and asked for a grant to set up camps like this across the country."[43] Because a nationwide program was a much more substantial enterprise than simply throwing open one's backyard, Eunice recruited some experts to help her out.

In particular, she sought advice from William Freeberg, head of the Recreation and Outdoor Education Department of Southern Illinois University (SIU) in Carbondale. Freeberg, forty-two in 1962, was a short, overweight, roly-poly individual whose concept of recreation was sufficiently distinct from sports that he smoked as well. Born in Chicago, he had been raised in a Swedish-Lutheran orphanage in Princeton, Illinois, then studied physical education at SIU. In 1950, he received the nation's first Ph.D. in recreation from Indiana University. Returning to SIU where he founded the Department of Recreation, Freeberg became involved around 1954 with organizing camping experiences for individuals with a wide range of handicaps, one of which was mental retardation.[44] At the SIU camp at Little Grassy Lake, Freeberg and his students put together programs in MR recreation, with "boating, swimming and hot-dogs" (as John Throne put it).[45]

Freeberg was thus a determined recreationist, dedicated to helping MR people enjoy themselves out-of-doors. He was not an uninsightful man, for he saw the ultimate mission of MR recreationism, not in perfecting the weenie roast, but in teaching leisure-time skills that the mentally retarded could use to reinsert themselves in the community.[46] But he was not oriented to sports and physical training.

Just as Eunice was getting the day camps going in 1962, she asked Freeberg to organize a one-week workshop at SIU to train MR camp directors and city recreation department staff members. The Office of Vocational Rehabilitation (Voc Rehab) would pay part of the freight: at Sarge's suggestion, Eunice had gone to see Mary Switzer at Voc Rehab, persuading her to give grants to send people to Carbondale.[47]

From 1962 until the beginning of the Special Olympics in 1968, the Shrivers would be guided by a recreation advisory group, chaired by Freeberg who took a semester's leave from SIU to come to Washington. The advisory group was composed of other like-minded types, such as Art Peavy of the Dade County Recreation Department in Florida.[48]

Thus the day-camp program was launched. In the summer of 1962, simultaneously with Camp Shriver at Timberlawn, the Kennedy Foundation supported the first of these camps, a pilot camp called the Sunny Grove Day Camp organized by the D.C. Recreation Department. The next year, President Kennedy gave $75,000 in leftover inaugural funds to the National Capitol Area in order to boost this kind of MR recreation.[49]

Sunny Grove was the beginning of a large day-camping effort. By 1963, the Kennedy Foundation was supporting eleven MR day camps, by 1965 twenty-six. In 1969, the last year of the program (because the Shrivers had gone to France where Sarge served as U.S. ambassador), the foundation was giving grants to thirty-two such day camps involving almost ten thousand children across the country. By that time, above and beyond the Shriver-supported camps, there were around 750 other MR day camps in the United States.[50]

It was in this element of sports competition and physical training for the MR campers at Timberlawn that the Special Olympics originated.

Recreation and MR

The recreation vogue had begun around the turn of the century in the United States in the form of the "playground movement." In 1892, for example, Jane Addams opened her model playground at Hull House in Chicago; in 1906 the Playground Association of America was formed, becoming in 1930 the National Recreation Association.[51]

In the world of mental retardation, this recreation movement fell like scattered raindrops upon a red-hot iron. The need was so enormous, the supply so pitiful. One thinks of the daily routine of the mildly retarded older boys at the Lincoln State School in Illinois before two women recreationists began their work in 1929: "Approximately 400 of them, inadequately provided with activity, were made to sit quietly for long periods, crowded together on uncomfortable benches around the walls of their so-called playrooms, seldom, however, used for play. . . . If the weather were good, the attendant was required to take her group walking for a half hour to an hour each day, but during these walks the patients were lined up by twos, and were forced to march with their arms folded. Talking was frequently prohibited." At Lincoln, life was even more monotonous for the six-and-under age group, who "sat all day long crowded together on benches much too high for them with nothing to do but to wiggle, pinch or bite each other." The recreationists introduced to Lincoln beanbag-throwing, croquet, group singing, and such games as "Sally Go Round the Moon." "When [the children] sing in imitation of the play leader they make sounds that resemble the words. They are able to imitate the clapping, and make an attempted jump at the proper place in the game. Evidence of the fact that this material affords the idiots [the severely retarded children] pleasure comes from the repeated requests, specific games being designated by gestures suggestive of the action, rather than by the name of the game."[52]

Without question, then, even severely retarded children profited from this kind of recreation, as was evident in the 1960s when recreation was introduced to the Woodbine State Colony in New Jersey. "Activities such as rocking, holding, and cuddling the child," wrote the dedicated recreationists, "taking him for outings (walking, carriage rides, wagon rides) . . . talking to him and playing with him—all constitute the recreation program he enjoys best." (The list suggests just how far from physical education and sports the notion of recreation was.)

The children at Woodbine learned quickly how to play. "Often, when children who did not know how to play were placed in a group with those who could, they learned how through peer example and the individual guidance of the recreation therapists." As one grateful mother wrote to the recreationists, "It was a wonderful sight to watch our lad attempt to tap a tambourine with a small soft mallet. He didn't often 'connect' because of poor coordination but when he did he smiled triumphantly."[53]

The point is that the Shrivers were not necessarily going down a blind alley in pursuit of recreation. Recreation programs held enormous potential for improving the lives of the mentally retarded. But it was not an alley that led to Special Olympics, where physical training and sports were the theme. Still, it was via recreation that the Shrivers did reach the Special Olympics, specifically through a national recreation and fitness program that Eunice and Sarge initiated in 1965 in connection with the American Association for Health, Physical Education and Recreation, or AAHPER, pronounced "eh-pher" (and, recently having added a "D" for Dance, is now pronounced "eh-pherd").

In 1956, President Eisenhower had established a President's Council on Youth Fitness. JFK, alarmed at the apparently deteriorating physical condition of the nation's youth, wanted to encourage the work of this council. One day in 1963, Eunice asked him if it would be alright "to include the retarded in the program." JFK said, "Sure. If they can do it."

Eunice wanted to make sure they could do it. She called up Jackson Anderson, AAHPER's recreation consultant, and asked him to come over to Sarge's office and talk with her and Sarge about MR recreation and fitness. Anderson, who had known Sarge since AAHPER's early work with the Peace Corps, "very enthusiastically said yes."[54]

The assassination of President Kennedy in November 1963 interrupted these events. It was not until the spring of 1964 that Freeberg, on the Shrivers' behalf, asked Anderson to get a small group of university physed types to come to Washington and talk about how university recreation programs might focus on MR. In October, in conjunction with a convention in Miami Beach of the National Recreation Congress at which Eunice was the principal speaker, this group met again.[55]

An alliance between the Shrivers and AAHPER thus came to fruition. On November 3, 1964, Sarge, Eunice, and Freeberg went to see the AAHPER board. November 3 was election day. It was a measure of the

Shrivers' commitment that these highly political members of this very political family took time off on this particular day for a lengthy meeting about recreation for the mentally retarded. At the meeting, Eunice noted how little in the way of year-round recreation was available, except for the District of Columbia public schools and the Chicago Park District (the latter of which the Kennedy Foundation was funding directly). She deplored the exclusion of the mentally retarded from phys-ed classes in public schools and said the foundation would give AAHPER money to help.

Sarge added that they wanted AAHPER to design public school programs especially for MR children who, though segregated in classes, attempted to join the nonretarded in general play at recess. MR kids needed recreation activities of their own.[56]

The AAHPER board needed no convincing. It instructed Jack Anderson to set up a recreationist task force to design specific proposals. These were formally submitted in April 1965, and on July 1 a wide-ranging collaboration began.[57] The Kennedy Foundation gave AAHPER a quarter of a million dollars, in return for which AAHPER would organize recreation clinics and help to focus community recreation programs across the country upon this hitherto ignored population of mentally retarded people. Robert ("Bob") Holland, the Ohio state supervisor of recreation and physical education, went on leave from his job for a year to become the project's first director. Holland was a recreationist.

It has been necessary to recite these developments in some detail to emphasize that, up to this point, the Shrivers, their advisers, and their AAHPER collaborators were all oriented toward recreation. The word "sports"—meaning determined physical training and competition—had scarcely fallen from anyone's lips.

All this changed late in 1965 with the arrival of two tough new men on the scene: Julian ("Buddy") Stein and Frank Hayden. I say tough not because they were mean or nasty individuals, but because they were physically taut and very fit, and because they were both resolute about implementing a notion of MR fitness that had little to do with weenie roast-style recreationism and everything to do with physically-demanding conditioning for competitive sports. Stein and Hayden represented the next generation, lighting the fuse that led to the Special Olympics.

Sports

It is not true that the MR sports scene was as empty as a vacuum before the arrival of Stein and Hayden, but it was close to that. Efforts to bring systematic physical training and competitive sports to the mentally retarded—dating back to the Seguin school in Orange, New Jersey, at the turn of the century[58]—were few in number. By the 1960s, state legislatures were slowly beginning to repeal their laws against MR children participating in organized sports. In Connecticut, for example, both the Mansfield Training School and the Seaside Center had sports teams that played in intermural competitions.[59] In St. Louis, mentally retarded boys were "playing interscholastic basketball at the junior and senior high school level."[60] But in twenty-seven other states, MR youths remained ineligible or only vaguely eligible for such sports.[61]

As for those qualified to teach phys-ed students about MR athletics, pickings were truly slim. There were a few professors—but not many. One of the few was John Friedrich, chairman of physical education at Duke University, who organized courses on "teaching sports skills to the mentally retarded."[62]

With MR sports in this piteous condition, Buddy Stein took command of the AAHPER project. Stein was determined to shift the emphasis from recreation to sports. Graduating in 1950 from George Washington University, he had spent fifteen years teaching physical education in schools of all levels in Arlington, Virginia. In 1959 he introduced a phys-ed class for the MR students at Wakefield High School that included relay races, basketball, volleyball, and touch football.[63] Then, in the early 1960s, Stein himself went back to school, enrolling in the doctoral education program at Peabody College for Teachers in Nashville. He wrote a dissertation on physical fitness for the mentally retarded in 1965, and later that same year he became chairman of AAHPER's fitness advisory committee, teaching simultaneously in the phys-ed department of the University of Rhode Island. After Bob Holland returned to Ohio in 1966, Stein himself became the director of the AAHPER program, drawing a full-time salary from the Kennedy Foundation.

"I was basically physical education and sports," said Stein later, "even though a lot of people associate me more with recreation."[64] On Stein's watch at AAHPER, sports projects began to blossom. Stein edited the project's newsletter, *Challenge,* and began to encourage phys-ed instructors to send in accounts of their work with MR. In the September 1966 issue, Dolores Geddes at the Boulder Valley School in Colorado said she had introduced a circuit-training course. "The 'reward' of moving up to a higher level has provided motivation for the students to work harder. . . ."[65] Phys-ed staff at the Western Washington State College in Bellingham had developed an MR weight-training program, in which toy black kittens were filled with seven pounds of buckshot, toy tigers with ten pounds, and toy dogs with fifteen pounds. The kids were doing two-arm curls and bench presses with their little animals.[66] This was no longer beanbag toss.

Thus, under the AAHPER-Kennedy program, physical training and competitive sports became introduced to the lives of children with MR. It was an historic achievement.

Did this mark the beginning of the Special Olympics? Not really. Buddy Stein and the AAHPER board *opposed* Special Olympics. Although willing to support competitive sports at the local level, they considered regional and national meets too adventuresome, beyond the capacities of the mentally retarded.[67] Stein did not attend the Special Olympics in July 1968 in Chicago, nor did AAHPER send a representative.[68] To Hayden's fury, the issue of *Challenge* that appeared in September—a project the Kennedy Foundation had funded—didn't even mention the Special Olympics event in Chicago. A story about MR golf received prominent play, however.[69]

AAHPER's fitness program in the years 1965 to 1968 was significant because it started people across the country thinking about competitive sports for mentally retarded children. And it was from this pool of young MR athletes that the Special Olympian stars would be drawn.

The Run-up to Special Olympics

Who created the Special Olympics? There were three major players: the Shrivers, the Canadian fitness expert Frank Hayden, and an energetic young sparkplug at the Chicago Park District named Anne McGlone-Burke. In rivalry and bickering that has not ceased to the present day, they all, together, created the Special Olympics.

The term "Special Olympics" itself was Bob Cooke's and Sarge Shriver's. Some of the members of the President's Panel on Mental Retardation were socializing one evening in the summer of 1962 at Timberlawn. Donald Stedman said, "I can remember sitting on the back porch at Timberlawn with a whole bunch of people brainstorming how to organize some kind of national effort that would get more people involved directly with mentally retarded kids, really kind of change public attitudes and also provide some service for the retarded.

"And we were talking firstly about the idea of a single event. The Olympics came up."

Was that term used?

"Yes, and I think it was Bob Cooke who said, 'I really think what we are talking about is a Special Olympics.'" Others that evening then batted the concept about. It became the Special Olympics.

"Sarge picked it up at that point. He's an incredible marketeer . . . and then he started thinking about getting outstanding athletes like Rafer Johnson and others involved, and off we went."[70]

But the idea did not long survive that brainstorming session at Timberlawn. So many ideas came and went when the Kennedys were together. It was impossible to act on them all. This one was forgotten.

Yet after JFK's death, the notion "Olympian" kept resurfacing. There had been something Olympian about the whole experience of Camelot. As friends and family thought about managing the legacy after 1963, the word would crop up spontaneously. As early as January 1964 there were intensive discussions about how best to keep the momentum going, focusing on limiting the use of JFK's name and on organizing projects that would retain the cause of mental retardation in the nation's consciousness. Eunice rejected the National Association for Mental Health's proposal to use JFK's birthday as a way of raising consciousness about mental illness. She said that the family wanted to find "ways in which the President's memory can be associated as closely as possible with the current nationwide effort to focus public attention on the problems of the mentally retarded."[71]

The John F. Kennedy Birthday Committee—which included among others Sarge, Mike Feldman, John Throne (the executive director who followed Stedman), Charles Young, and LeRoy Collins (a former governor of Florida and president of the National Association of Broadcasters) —met on January 3, 1964. As one idea, the committee proposed a series of "John F. Kennedy International Congresses on Mental Retardation —modeled after the Olympic Games." But the members seemed to be talking more about an academic seminar than a Games meet.[72] Later that week Young spun the idea a bit further, writing to Collins, "We might adopt the flame at the President's grave as our symbol. In a manner reminiscent of the Olympic Games, flames could be brought from Arlington to each state capital and from there to various towns and cities. . . . Local NARC chapters might even make 'torch light' door-to-door canvasses on behalf of mental retardation."[73] So the Olympian idea was buzzing about as Kennedy intimates discussed how best to use JFK's name in the cause of MR.

Again, however, these initiatives led to nothing. The Shrivers were pouring their apparently inexhaustible energy into MR camping and other programs, and Olympian notions went quietly back to sleep. Yet in 1964 and 1965 the Shrivers were growing increasingly unhappy with the recreation straightjacket into which advisers such as Freeberg had laced them. On June 15, 1965, when Sarge Shriver agreed definitively to go along with AAHPER's fitness program, it was with an express proviso:

"Definite physical education activities should be included in the proposed program, such as those pinpointed in the following list." Basketball, softball, and swimming were explicitly mentioned.[74]

Later in 1965, James Oliver, an MR fitness expert from the University of Birmingham in England, delivered a devastating assessment of the whole recreationist approach to MR camping. As one scholar summarized Oliver's report, "In some of the camps differentiation was not made between recreation and entertainment, with programs tending to become 'passive acceptance' of experience rather than 'active, vigorous participation' in physical experiences." Oliver urged the adoption of fitness testing in all camps and suggested an exercise program.[75]

A final nail in the coffin of recreationism was Eunice Shriver's personal experience with a Saturday recreation program at the Kennedy Institute for MR children in Washington that began in January 1965. The program involved taking the older boys to the pool at Georgetown Prep for swimming classes, the girls to Stone Ridge for exercises and games. Eunice was apparently so pleased with it that she told the nuns she was a convert to MR fitness. "It was from this time on," wrote the nuns subsequently, "that physical fitness, athletics and sports became a priority in the Kennedy Foundation programs."[76]

Clearly it was time for Freeberg and the recreationists to take a backseat. But whom could the Shrivers get instead?

The scene shifts to Toronto. The Rotary Clubs of Toronto had traditionally been active on behalf of MR, building in 1958 a school for the mentally retarded in North Toronto. In 1960, Leslie Allan, a member of one of the clubs, learned from the Toronto chapter of The Arc that no research was being done in the area of physical education and fitness for MR children, and that virtually no information existed on the subject. The five Rotary clubs of North Toronto then asked the head of the phys-ed department at the University of Toronto to conduct a research program, which the clubs would fund. To carry out this research program, in 1961 the University of Toronto hired a young Canadian named Frank Hayden, who was just about to receive his Ph.D. in exercise physiology from the University of Illinois, and who as early as 1958 had designed a physical fitness program (the 5BX Program) for the Royal Canadian Air Force. Hayden was primarily a scientist; he was not a recreationist at all.

Lean and energetic, Hayden was a "Kennedy man" without yet knowing it, combining the same mix of humorous irony and overdriven restlessness that characterized Bob Cooke, the Shrivers, and JFK himself. And like these people who played in a much faster lane—Hayden had grown up in St. Catherines, Ontario—Hayden as well intended to be a mover and shaker of events.

Hayden thus came to Toronto, read all he could find on the subject of mental retardation and fitness, and began assessing the strength, flexibility, and motor performance of the pupils at Toronto's Beverley School, an MR day school. From this work came his *Physical Fitness for the Mentally Retarded,* published by the Toronto chapter of The Arc in 1964. As the first systematic manual for MR fitness, it made something of a splash.[77] Lawrence Rarick, a noted phys-ed specialist for the mentally retarded at the University of Wisconsin and a Kennedy Foundation consultant, wrote to Freeburg in September of that year, "I located the monograph on 'Physical Fitness for the Mentally Retarded' which I mentioned. This work was done by Frank J. Hayden." Rarick said, "This looks to me like a reasonably good piece of work."[78] Rarick gave Freeburg the somewhat obscure details of the book's publication.

It was apparently Freeberg who told Sarge Shriver about Hayden.[79] In the fall of 1964, Freeberg phoned Hayden in Toronto, said the Shrivers had seen his book, and asked him to come down sometime. Hayden heard nothing more for a while. The Shrivers were only mildly interested.[80]

Around four months later, they became urgently interested. Canada was to celebrate its centennial in 1967. Already in 1963, the mills were cranking out projects. In August of that year, Harry ("Red") Foster, a Toronto broadcaster and sports figure who had a great charitable interest in MR—owing to a mentally retarded brother—told Joe Kennedy of a large MR project that Foster was going to organize for the centennial celebration. "The main idea is that as Canada celebrates her 100th Anniversary in 1967, I am going to challenge the volunteer associations— and the Federal and Provincial Governments—to start one major project on Mental Retardation NOW so that we can truly say in 1967 that Canada has really made a break-through. . . ."[81]

But what could that project be? In December of 1964, Foster held a meeting in Toronto and invited proposals for some kind of MR participation in the centennial celebration. Frank Hayden submitted a paper suggesting a "National Mental Retardation Games." It would have three components: intensive local training, followed by a provincial competition in 1966, then the national MR games in 1967.[82] "I thought in 1964 that idea was so far out," said Hayden later, "that I'd probably get a lot of static." Hayden imagined critics saying, "Jeez, these people have never been away from home. They're going to be overnight for two weeks? Their meds? What about the losers? But in our subgroup everybody said, Hey, good idea! So I myself raised all these points, what about the meds, et cetera? They were excited. They gave it a high priority."[83]

Then nothing happened. The Canadians somehow failed to pick up the ball and carry it. There were no national MR games in 1967.

However, Sarge Shriver somehow obtained a copy of Hayden's proposal. Hayden was down in New York in February 1965 for a meeting of the New York Academy of Sciences. He was summoned from the session to take a call from Freeberg. "The Shrivers want you to come over."

When?

"Tonight."

So Hayden went down to Washington the next day on the train. "Their car picked me up at the station, went to the foundation, then out to Timberlawn that evening. I spent thirty minutes talking to Eunice, then Sarge arrived."

Sarge dispensed quickly with the pleasantries. He was carrying a copy of Hayden's proposal in his hand. "Can you do this here in the U.S.?" he asked.

Hayden thanked Sarge politely for his interest but said he had other projects going. It could be done, but somebody else would have to do it. Hayden prepared to go.

Then Eunice said, "Hold on, Sarge. You aren't just going to let him walk out the door like that. What's the next step?" (As Hayden also stated in our interview, "Eunice was always asking what the next step was going to be.")

Sarge said, "Oh well, we'll just have Dr. Hayden come down."

For the next two months Hayden, who now was an associate professor at the University of Western Ontario in London, Ontario, kept getting phone calls, letters, and telegrams. "When are you coming?" By June 1965, Hayden had moved with his family to Washington, replacing Freeberg as the Kennedy Foundation's fitness director (though Freeberg and the other recreationists still formed the fitness advisory council).

Thus by the summer of 1965, the Special Olympics seems to have been a fully formed concept in Frank Hayden's mind, incorporating a competitive sports summit with a nationwide training program. Bob Holland, who had become friendly with Hayden, supports Hayden's version of these events: "In the fall of '65—it was a beautiful fall day—Frank had come over to our office in the NEA building, and he and I were working on program formats. . . . After lunch we went back to Frank's office and we were standing on the corner of 16th and something and Frank said, 'Do you think something could be organized in the nature of Olympics for these handicapped individuals?'"

Holland replied, "I personally think so but you know we have a lot of hurdles to overcome there. We have people in special-ed that are very anti-instruction and anti-activity in phys-ed."

Hayden continued, "Mrs. Shriver wants me to be thinking about some way that perhaps one or two years down the line we could have a kind of national track and field meet. And get the word out so that people could start to prepare for this." Hayden told Holland, "This is not something I'm going to do overnight. . . . I do want you to keep apprised of what's going on with the possibility of this."

Holland said later of this conversation, "That was the inception of Special Olympics because Frank was thinking about it in the fall of '65."[84]

It would be lovely to be able to wrap this story up here, saying in effect that Hayden went on to organize and stage the first Special Olympics. But that is not the way it happened. Having brought Hayden to Washington, the Shrivers discovered they had more important things than a national MR games for him to do. Hayden became involved with introducing MR fitness to the President's Council on Physical Fitness and with inserting MR into university curriculums and into park districts—in short, with the whole AAHPER agenda plus other fitness projects the Shrivers had going as well.

The national MR games was placed on the back burner. After spending a year in D.C. in 1965–66, Hayden went back to the University of Western Ontario, commuting to Washington regularly. He tried to reinvigorate his games plan. "I was aware you'd better have something in your briefcase because the Shrivers are always looking for new ideas. Eunice would call— 'Hi Frank, got anything new?' You'd get short shrift there [at the Kennedy Foundation] if you came with the same old stuff.

"So I wrote out on the plane something called 'Junior Athlete.' It was for the training arm of a games program. . . . Training would be linked in with games, in a step-by-step three-year plan." This was Hayden's attempt to revive his idea of a national MR games.

In the fall of 1967 (after Hayden was back full-time at the Kennedy Foundation), he asked the recreation advisory group—Freeberg and the other recreationists—to consider this plan. They recommended against it. The group's decision was not surprising: "There was always a little bit of tension, friendly tension" between Hayden and Freeberg on the subject of competitive sports, said John Throne.[85]

After the meeting they all walked over to Sarge's quarters at the Office of Economic Opportunity. Eunice was there. Hayden later said that given the negative report of the recreationists, "the Shrivers were lukewarm." Hayden believes that Eunice and Sarge were originally "not so excited" about the proposal because "they would have had to run it," a radical departure for people who previously had seen themselves as scientific philanthropists, sowing seed money for projects and then stepping away from them after three years. Hayden's training program was different, requiring a daunting expenditure of administrative effort to get programs going in communities across the nation. One recalls that the Kennedy Foundation at this point was being run mainly from Eunice's bedroom at Timberlawn with a couple of secretaries at an office on K street. So "Junior Athletes" was left to die. "But this was basically Special Olympics," said Hayden.[86]

Not everyone agrees with Hayden's version of events. Hayden himself refused to show me a copy of his "Junior Athletes" plan, saying he wanted to keep it for his own memoirs. Beverly Campbell, a Kennedy Foundation program officer from December 1967 on, asserts that Eunice Shriver conceived the Special Olympics and was entirely responsible for driving the concept forward. She pooh-poohs Hayden's account. "The thing that people need to realize," she said, "is that no matter who was there the vision was always Eunice Shriver's, backed up by Sargent Shriver. You can give everyone all kinds of credit but I always was aware of the Shrivers' strength and vision. They had incredible ability to surround themselves with the best people and the brightest ideas, and then to glean from those the things they would move forward to." Campbell emphasized "the tenacity and force with which they approached this. It wouldn't have happened without them."[87] And it is true that, starting in the mid-1960s, Eunice made occasional references to a national sports programs for the mentally retarded. In speaking at Dallas in 1965, for example, she called for "a national tournament of athletic contests, among teams of mentally retarded children." She envisioned elimination contests, beginning between local schools, then ending with a national games.[88] She renewed this request again the following year in a speech to the National Education Association in Washington, asking for "a national tournament of athletic contests among teams of mentally retarded children."[89] Eunice's idea represented, at least, the games arm of Hayden's two-arm proposal (games plus training). It seems clear that as the end of 1967 approached, both Eunice Shriver and Frank Hayden were pursuing various conceptions of a national MR games. To what extent each was fully aware of the other's concept, or embraced it, is unclear.

The essential point is that even before the Chicago people put in their proposal, notions of some kind of Special Olympics were circulating among the Kennedy Foundation and its advisers. The concept could not have been too subliminal. After all, in May 1967 the kids of the Kennedy Institute in D.C. had staged a field day that they called the "Kennedy Institute Olympics."[90] Thus, by the end of 1967 in Washington, Olympian plans were hot on the grill. Only an occasion for their realization was required.

Chicago '68

Why Chicago? In Illinois there was considerable interest in recreational programs for the mentally retarded because of Freeberg.[91] When the Kennedy Foundation announced in 1964 that it was giving MR grants to city park districts, the Chicago Park District applied for one. The following year, the Shrivers gave them $10,000, choosing Chicago, as Eunice put it, "because Sarge thought they could get a lot of support if we could interest Mayor Daly in this whole idea."[92] Since Sarge had almost run for governor of Illinois several times and knew Daly well from the school-board days of the 1950s, this seemed like a not unreasonable calculation. The Chicago Park District began offering recreation programs at ten different field houses throughout the city, using preexisting staff. The staff would go down to Little Grassy in Carbondale for Freeberg's standard one-week course.

For some reason, things did not go well in Chicago, at least from the Shrivers' viewpoint. "Little was happening," said Eunice.[93] At some point in 1967, Sarge flew out to Chicago and visited the president of the Park District, William McFetridge (an influential labor leader who was also vice president of the national AFL-CIO). Sarge told McFetridge of his unhappiness. McFetridge thereupon asked Daniel Shannon, a former Notre Dame football player and the Park District's vice president, to step up the MR program. Shannon got in touch with a young woman named Anne McGlone, a phys-ed major who had just graduated from George Williams University and was heading the MR program at one of the field houses.[94]

Twenty-three years old at the time, Anne McGlone (who would shortly become Anne Burke when she married Alderman Edward Burke in May 1968) was a real sparkplug. She had caught Shannon's and McFetridge's eye in the summer of 1967 when she organized at her field house a skillful production of the "Sound of Music," her hundred MR children "doing singing and dancing, making their own costumes and props."

Sometime after the show, McGlone, McFetridge, and Shannon got together. The two men asked her to put on for the MR cause "a show or some sort of competition or track and field meet." The executives wanted the program's public profile raised. For Burke, who had been organizing sports events with her kids since 1965, a track meet would be a simple matter. Thus, the Park District people themselves took the decision to stage a track-and-field event.

Sarge had suggested that the Park District use Freeberg as a consultant, so McFetridge asked Anne Burke to give Freeberg a call.[95] Freeberg, whom Burke had last seen two years previously at Little Grassy, came up to Chicago. He agreed that some kind of track-and-field competition might be a good idea, using Soldier Field in Chicago as home base.

"Why don't you call Mrs. Shriver," Freeberg suggested to Burke. Maybe Mrs. Shriver—whom Freeberg absolutely venerated—could give the Park District some money.

Eunice Shriver told Anne Burke to put her ideas in a proposal. "I went to Washington right after Christmas, in January 1968," said Burke.[96] There were meetings with Hayden and other Kennedy Foundation staff. Burke went back to Chicago and consulted with Freeberg, and the two of them submitted a plan together for a "National Olympics for the Retarded."[97] The foundation approved the plan, and Eunice flew to Chicago on March 29 to announce at a press conference with Mayor Richard Daly a grant of $20,000 to the Park District for a "Chicago Special Olympics" specifically for the mentally retarded. "Today," said Eunice, as Daly stood next to her on the podium, "by initiating the Special Olympics, the Chicago Park District once again confirms its role as a national leader in the field of recreation for the mentally retarded."[98] Hayden was to be the general director of the games.[99]

It was clear at this point that some kind of national athletic event was going to take place in Chicago on July 20. But what kind? The conceptions of the Park District and the Kennedy Foundation were miles apart. Frank Hayden told Burke and Shannon, as he put it later in an interview, that "I don't want a track meet. I want a Games." The difference? "A Games is multi-sport, not just track events. And a Games is certainly not a field day, which implies casual recreation. A Games would be track and field, swimming, and floor hockey, which is a team sport." Hayden wanted to bring the Beverley School floor hockey team from Toronto to show that athletes with MR do have the potential for team sports.[100] So Hayden was pursuing the pro-competitive sport, anti-recreationist line that he had represented since first seeing the Shrivers in 1965.

Freeberg and Anne Burke, by contrast, saw the Special Olympics as a kind of fun day. "The day was to be for clinics," said Anne Burke later. "There'd be four clinics around the field for the swimming pool, the basketball court, hockey, and touch football. It was to be a casual play day as well as competition. [Frank Hayden] envisioned it perhaps as a track meet, which was not our idea. He wanted only competition. That wasn't our goal. We wanted parents, volunteers, educators and people from Chicago to understand, to touch, feel and be part of things with persons who were retarded whom they hadn't ever seen participate before."[101]

It would be hard to imagine a more complete failure of communication than that embodied in these two views of what was to happen on July 20.

There is no agreement at all among the three principal players—the Shrivers, Frank Hayden, and the Park District people—about who gets credit for planning the Games and naming the event. Eunice said she had seen the term "special" on the wall at St. Coletta's, "depicting retarded children being special to God. So I said that 'special' be used in front of the word Olympics."[102]

Frank Hayden asserted that he had coined the term "Special Olympics" in March 1968 while making a presentation on the Games in St. Louis to a meeting of the Kennedy Foundation's recreation advisory board that coincided with a convention of Phi Epsilon Kappa, the national phys-ed fraternity. Eunice was speaking at the convention. "What to call the Chicago event?" Hayden asked the other board members. "I proposed 'Special Olympics.' The 'National Mental Retardation Games,' my Canadian title, was diplomatically not on."[103]

Hayden may indeed have coined the term, but the timing mentioned in his recollected account of events doesn't wash. The meeting in St. Louis occurred on March 28. The press conference in Chicago, at which a "Special Olympics" was announced, was March 29. The term had surely been minted more than twenty-four hours previously.

Anne Burke was adamant that the Chicago people had coined the phrase: "'Special Olympics' came from Chicago. Because we had a special recreation program, that was the name of our program."[104] Burke may be correct, yet the term mentioned in her proposal was "National Olympics," not "Special Olympics." And in the working documents of the Chicago people in January and February it's "Olympics" full stop.[105] Are these disputes petty? Not really. People want to claim their place in history, and the creation of the Special Olympics was an historic event.

But there's more. Even in regard to who drew up the list of events and designed the rules, the parties disagree completely. "I spoke to Sarge," said Eunice, "and we thought it a good idea for Frank to go out there and talk and see if more sports could be added, especially swimming, as I'd seen my sister Rosemary do so well in swimming."[106]

As far as Frank Hayden is concerned, he himself structured the entire Special Olympics from A to Z. "I selected the sports, wrote the rules, conceived the divisioning system for ability grouping, helped train volunteers, ran the operation at the La Salle Hotel [the headquarters hotel], and worked out the whole format for the day. . . . It was a very, very stressful time for me."[107]

Anne Burke was proud of the contribution of the highly professional Park District sports staff, who had long-term experience in organizing such events. "The seeds for every event came from the Chicago Park District. . . . The evolution of what the Games were on July 20, 1968, started from the Park District employees and their professional staff. Then the specifics of every event and what the rules would be were a combination of Park District people and the Kennedy Foundation people."[108]

Untangling the origins of the Special Olympics is a bit like unraveling the causes of World War I, what with the participants—embodying the principle that victory has a thousand fathers—all claiming the lion's share of credit for themselves individually. And perhaps each is right as these subjective recollections go, for we know how selective human memory is.

It was July 19. The Shrivers had left for Paris in the spring. Eunice was now on her way back for the opening of the Games on July 20. Hayden had been getting "about two hours of sleep a night." He, Beverly Campbell, and Mrs. Shriver's speech writer, an advertising executive named Herb Kramer, were all crafting the speech she was to deliver at the opening ceremonies the next morning. This speech was to be crucial in the evolution of Special Olympics, for she was to announce that they would be a regular event, and that the Kennedy Foundation was going to fund a training program for them, which was exactly what Frank Hayden recalled in our interview.

"At the time of the Games, there was only one person in the world who knew this was the beginning of something else, and that was me."[109] According to Hayden, he himself had dictated to Herb Kramer the remarks that Eunice was to read in her speech at the opening ceremonies.[110]

Beverly Campbell disagrees completely with Hayden's version, saying that Eunice Shriver—not Hayden—determined that the Games would be a regular event and that the Kennedy Foundation would fund them. "If you know Eunice, you know that [Hayden] didn't 'determine' at all. It was a recommendation. He had spent time with her in Paris. We had talked about the possibility of what could happen. . . ." Campbell allowed, however, that Eunice Shriver might not have committed herself to supporting a nationwide Special Olympics until she saw what was happening there at Soldier Field.[111]

It was, in fact, only when Eunice arrived in Chicago and saw these hundreds of mentally retarded youngsters from all over the country milling about the lobby of the La Salle, overflowing with the enthusiasm of doing something that no child with mental retardation had ever done before, that she resolved to take on the Special Olympics as her personal cause. She later said, "I decided out there in Chicago that we should have every state do this sort of sports event each year. I discussed it with Sarge and Herb in the hotel room. I thought otherwise all this time and effort (literally months) seemed far too much for too little. . . . I figured if the Kennedy Foundation couldn't do this, I could go out and raise that kind of money."[112]

The nine hundred Special Olympians who had gathered for the Games—in eighty-five groups from twenty-five states and Canada—breakfasted that Saturday morning from 6:30 to 8:30 at the "training table" in the hotel. But already at eight, buses for the Silver Competition were leaving the hotel for Soldier Field (the more than two hundred events had been structured on the basis of ability, or level of handicap, so that the Silver Competition represented the younger and more seriously handicapped).

The day began with an opening parade, led by a U.S. Navy band. Rafer Johnson, who was the Olympic gold-medal decathlon winner in 1960 (and later a member of the Black Athletes Hall of Fame) marched with the participants wearing his Olympic medal.

The Johnson gold medal had been a nightmare. "We were up all night," said Beverly Campbell, "because we had lost Rafer Johnson's Olympic medal. He had sent it by airplane. It was the time of the post office strike in Chicago and everything was just piled high, and Mayor Daly had everyone go there, pull everything out, put it on a huge loading dock and go through every package. A week's worth of mail. Literally minutes before the ceremony started, Rafer said to me, 'You can't replace an Olympic medal. I hope you understand that, Beverly.'

"Then we heard the siren and they came rushing in with it in a police car. He got it around his neck just seconds before the parade started."[113]

The day began nightmarishly for Frank Hayden, too, though for a different reason. Having exactly choreographed the events, allocating each to its own bit of turf and plotting exactly the location of the announcer's table—"I detailed who sat at the table, how many mikes there would be"—Hayden arrived at Soldier Field to find complete disorder. "When I walked out on the field there was chaos. There were no flags up. I couldn't realize why I couldn't find anything. Then I realized they had reversed the map. I was on a razor's edge with two hours sleep. I ran into the office of the superintendent, Pleasant Amick. Pleasant was one of those people who took great pride in his work, loved his job."

"Pleasant, I'm in trouble," said Hayden.

Hayden and a human chain of volunteers joined hands, swept the field, and tried to restore order. "Someone runs over. A kid is hurt. No first aid! Finally I get a mike, things are getting organized. [He lifted the microphone to his lips to speak] No power!"

"Sorry, doc. The noise is disturbing the press conference."

The press conference! While Hayden was struggling to get events started on the field, Eunice and the Park District people were holding a press conference. It was here that the day began nightmarishly for Anne Burke, Bill McFetridge, and Dan Shannon.

"I wish to announce a national Special Olympics training program for all mentally retarded children everywhere," said Eunice. "I also announce that in 1969 the Kennedy Foundation will pledge sufficient funds to underwrite five regional Olympic tryouts. . . . The winners of these trial meets, and of hundreds of others like them, will participate in another International Special Olympics in 1970 and every two years thereafter."[114]

It was as though a bomb had exploded in front of the members of the Park District. They had thought this was their little show, their idea over which they would exercise ultimate control. Until that moment, they had no hint that the Kennedys would take the Special Olympics away from them. "The first time we had any inkling that the Kennedy Foundation was going to proceed with a national program was on the podium July 20," said Anne Burke, "coming from Mrs. Shriver's speech. We were absolutely in shock. I should have foreseen that, but no one mentioned it, no one talked about it. In retrospect, they used us. Everything we did, our expertise, they just used it to conceive and develop their program. This was a trial run for them, which we didn't know."[115]

All this infighting was lost on the joyous participants, however. Seventeen-year-old Philip Weber "carried the Special Olympic Flame into the stadium and lit a 40-foot high John F. Kennedy Flame of Hope. As the flag bearing the newly-designed Special Olympic symbol reached the top of the flagpole, 2,000 yellow and blue balloons were released. Each carried a postcard bearing the name and address of one of the competitors, in the hope that the person finding the balloon would write to him."[116] Out there on the ground, people were having a super time.

Celebrity athletes were in attendance to run clinics. This was a theme that would become steadily more magnified in subsequent Special Olympics. Among the coaching staff at the event that day, Barbara Ann Scott, a Canadian ice skater who in 1948 had won the Olympic women's figure-skating championship, was teaching Special Olympians how to skate—on a special plastic surface. Joey Giardello, a former middleweight boxing champion who himself had a mentally retarded son, taught the Special Olympians how to jump rope. They could line up with former Green Bay Packers halfback Paul Hornung, Notre Dame halfback Johnny Lattner, and other football greats against a team of Notre Dame sophomores. Astronaut Jim Lovell was on hand to run the fitness clinic, and the MR floor hockey team from Toronto faced off against the Chicago Black Hawks, coached by Hawk ace Stan Mikita (who, like Hayden, was from St. Catherines, Ontario).[117] These events were more in line with the goals of the Park District, which was not at all alarmed at the "chaos" that had so upset Hayden.

There was one sad note. In the sparsely populated stands (the vast stadium was largely empty), few parents had shown up to cheer on the Special Olympians. As Herb Kramer later said, "If there were twenty parents there, that's generous. Parents had not yet learned that they could be proud of their mentally retarded kids."[118] In 1968, MR still counted as shameful, and the parents who had banned their children to institutions—from which most of these Special Olympians were drawn —had banished them for life.

A happy note, however, and one that would be steadily augmented in the future, was the spontaneous outpouring of generosity on the part of all those whom Special Olympics touched. The Olympians, of course, were staying at the La Salle Hotel, owned by Avery Brundage, president of the International Olympic Committee. "We were having trouble raising money," reminisced Hayden. "I wrote Avery Brundage. Could he contribute a meal? Brundage had a reputation of being a tough guy, an autocrat." Hayden went up from his hotel suite to Brundage's office.

Brundage was slumped over his desk. "You Hayden?"

"Yeah," Hayden answered.

"I understand you want a meal."

"Yassuh."

"The hotel can't give you a meal, but" said Brundage with a smile, "the Brundage Foundation can."

The dinner that Saturday evening cost $15,000. "By the time I got back down to my suite," said Hayden, "the hotel public relations officer was on the phone. Up to then the hotel PR had been stuffy. They didn't want to make a piano available in the lobby for a band from the Mansfield Training School. The kids had been practicing for months. They were supposed to greet the guests as they came into the lobby. But now it was, 'Frank, I just got a call from Mr. B. A dinner Saturday night?' Brundage wants balloons, clowns, decorations. The works. For dinner that night, the dining room was beautiful, cascades of balloons flooding out in our blue and yellow colors."[119]

It was clear that Special Olympics was the future way of fitness and sports for mentally retarded children. "We all saw after that day the potential," said Beverly Campbell. "Always from my discussions with Eunice Shriver it had been the fact that if this succeeded, this is the direction she wanted to go."[120]

Eunice's Vision

In 1968, Eunice Shriver was forty-seven years old. Her father had ceased to exercise tutelage over her since his stroke seven years earlier. Her husband, a willing partner in all her enterprises, had turned his intense energy on other goals, and it was Eunice herself who now called the shots at the Kennedy Foundation. Ever since the President's Panel in 1962, she had acquired a sovereign presence on the national stage and, even though she herself was a poor administrator, she felt comfortable in evoking grand designs and directing their execution. One sign of this new maturity was her soft-pedaling of the insistence that she herself had originated everything. She grew generous in sharing credit with Sarge Shriver. "To put it bluntly," she later said, in acknowledging the contribution he had made, "Sarge's presence here . . . has been absolutely crucial to the growth and stability of the Special Olympics program worldwide. . . . His international experience and vision, and his executive capacity" had been especially important in ripening the organization.[121]

In short, Eunice came into her own with the Special Olympics. It is not grandiose to speak of her as articulating a distinctive vision of the role of athletics in the lives of MR children, because she had the wisdom and maturity to formulate such a vision.

Yet a barrier to breaking through to Eunice's true thoughts in these years was the silver pen of Herb Kramer. Kramer had done public relations for Sargent Shriver in the mid-1960s at the Office of Economic Opportunity and in 1968 was hired part-time by the Kennedy Foundation to conduct its public relations. Around forty-six years old at the time, he had a background in advertising and lived with his wife and seven children in Hartford.[122] Herb Kramer was not really a "Kennedy man" in the way that he looked or presented himself, being rather a "very low-key and very haven't-been-pressed-for-five-days man," as one participant on the scene described him.[123] Yet over the years, he was tremendously loyal to the Shrivers and literally made himself available night and day. The point is, however, that he wrote beautifully, and when we encounter elegant and impassioned declarations in Eunice's public utterances, we never know if they came from her or from Herb Kramer.

Still, the ideas, the essence of the vision, came from Eunice. First of all, why was she so drawn to the Special Olympics, as opposed to any of the other vehicles for helping the mentally retarded that came along? It was partly because of her own tropism toward athletics. As Sarge said, "If Eunice hadn't been a sportswoman, she wouldn't have thought of the Special Olympics."[124] Also, she was more at ease with athletes than with scientists. According to Donald Stedman, "She felt very uncertain standing up there talking about chromosomes. [Sports] was something she felt that she could talk about and feel comfortable. She was very uncomfortable with neurologists, psychiatrists, and the rest, although she knew she needed them. She would tell me that. I could tell. I'm a psychologist. I could see how pained she was."

Why did she admire athletes so much? As Stedman said, "She admired them for their endurance. She's a long-distance runner herself in a metaphorical sense. She liked gutting it out, excellence of that type. She's not anti-intellectual, but she put a big premium on performance."[125]

It does seem to be true that Eunice felt a physical resonance with athletics, with events that challenged the body, an inheritance of decades of swimming and sailing at the Cape and of touch football on the back meadow at Timberlawn.

But Eunice had one more deep psychological wellspring. It was a quality that knocks awry the vicious media image of the Kennedy family as elitist and patrician. Eunice Shriver was very much a democrat. Having no patience with the voluptuousness of the rich, she herself lived almost ascetically and brought up her children in a materially rather tightfisted household. (Anthony and Bobby Shriver, at least, believed themselves continually short of cash. Anthony, circa age eleven, once reproached the much older Bobby: "I feel . . . that you place too much emphasis on money. I do realize that neither one of us have very much money. . . . I suppose I should not entertain myself in the same manner you do, because I am so much younger and have less money."[126])

Thus Eunice made the Shriver home a household like all the others (except for being a little larger), shunning the imperial aura with which her father had surrounded himself. "Eunice had this kind of common touch," said Stedman. "It's an interesting contrast. On the one side she's a Brahmin, a very high-toned person, but she had this populist sense that the Olympics allowed her to play out. . . . It would be something that everybody could have and everybody could participate in."[127] As Eunice said at one point, Special Olympics teaches "that all human beings are created equal in the sense that each has the capacity and a hunger for moral excellence, for courage, for friendship and for love. Whatever the speed of our feet or the power of our arms, each of us is capable of these highest virtues. Intelligence does not limit love, nor does wealth produce friendship."[128]

It was this quality of populism that led Eunice to the core of her vision of the Special Olympics—that through sports not only do we help the mentally retarded, but they also help us. She constantly emphasized growth: we grow as we help those with mental retardation grow. Only somebody intently attuned to the lives of the parents and their suffering would have understood that the Special Olympics was not just a classical act of noblesse oblige, handing something down patronizingly to the suffering poor, but of self-help as well. She brought this out in praising, for example, Pittsburgh Steelers running back Robert (Rockey) Bleier "who overcame," as she said, "crippling war wounds to become a professional football superstar. [In Vietnam a grenade had destroyed part of Bleier's right foot, for which he received a Purple Heart in 1969.] He said that he discovered new sources of strength himself through helping the retarded . . . overcome *their* disabilities." This was a distinctive Eunice touch; the comment was not present in Herb Kramer's original draft of the speech.[129]

Ethel Kennedy had a slightly different perspective on her sister-in-law's motivation. She believed it was because of Rosemary that Eunice was so sensitive to the moral and psychological benefits of helping the mentally retarded. From Rosemary, said Ethel, "They learned a great deal about love. That is why Eunice is so forceful in arguing for programs for the retarded. She knows that you're not only helping *them,* they're helping *you!*"[130]

The insight that moral growth may flow from the experience of philanthropy did not, of course, originate with Eunice Shriver. Yet she articulated it as a compelling justification for parents participating in the Special Olympics; working with their children in sports helped parents reattach themselves psychologically to these kids who once had been relegated to the outer darkness as "imbeciles."

What psychological benefits did the Special Olympics in particular confer? From 1968 onward, "hope and joy" were the themes that ran like a scarlet banner from the local Games to the international meets. Eunice's perspectives on these matters were buoyed by the scientific finding that systematic fitness programs do increase the IQs of mentally retarded children. As early as 1958, James Oliver had discovered that mentally retarded boys who participated in a "ten-week course of systematic and progressive physical conditioning" increased their IQs, most likely from the exhilarating effect of success and the pleasure of feeling in shape.[131] In 1966, another researcher showed that eight mentally retarded boys who were given an intensive twenty-day program of physical education "made significant IQ gain scores" over a control group.[132] Physical fitness and sports did indeed offer hope—a fact not lost on Eunice, whose scientific advisers kept her abreast of research in this field.

Two years before the Special Olympics in Chicago, Eunice captivated an audience with stories of mentally retarded youngsters whom sports had helped to develop. She cited, for example, "a fourteen-year-old retarded boy in Toronto who could not read a word until he learned to play hockey. Now he reads the sports pages and can tell you the standing of every team and almost every player in the National Hockey League."[133]

In March 1968, on the eve of the Special Olympics, Eunice appeared on the "Mike Douglas Show," accompanied by a gymnastics team from the Laurel Training School in Washington, D.C. "The star of the team was a boy named Robert. When Robert first came to Laurel, he was poorly coordinated, accident prone, lacked confidence to do the simplest exercise, and his IQ tested at 62." Helped by a dedicated phys-ed teacher, Robert made the tumbling team and eventually became "the star of the basketball team as well.

"His IQ now tests at 78, a gain of 16 points!" Indeed his actual, everyday performance made Robert equivalent to a person with an IQ of 90, which is within the normal range.[134] Thus, sports participation had actually "cured" Robert of his MR (though in reality "cures" of such nature are unusual with persons whose MR has an organic or genetic basis). Yet one can see why Eunice spoke of "growth" and "hope" in connection with the Special Olympics. There was in fact hope.

Thus when Eunice said at the Soldier Field press conference on the morning of July 20 that "through sports they can realize their potential for growth," she was enunciating a vision that had a solid scientific basis. Many scientists were aware of the relationship between psychological development and sports. Yet no one except Eunice Shriver acted on that knowledge to benefit the lives of the mentally retarded.

Over the years Eunice and Herb Kramer kneaded these intuitions and insights into a virtual Special Olympics creed: the creed of "skill, sharing, and joy." This kind of prose was hammered out in a relationship between patroness and craftsman not unfree of tension. On August 18, 1980— a day that saw Eunice at her virtual worst in human relationships—she reached, at an organizational meeting in Smugglers' Notch, Vermont, her virtual best in the lyrical evocation of the Special Olympics. Behind the scenes, she had castigated Kramer as an incompetent dullard for an inadequate earlier draft of the speech she was to give. "The speech came. I thought it was awful—a disgrace! It has no themes. It is barren of ideas. . . . I wouldn't give this at a High School session! Herb better come back and work on the speech 48 hours if it takes that long. It would be a disgrace for a President of any organization to give this speech I have. I have torn it up!"[135]

Spurred on by this tongue-lashing, Kramer went on to give her a brilliant speech that defined the Special Olympics, first of all, as skill: not just sports skills but preparation for life. "[It is] an exercise of the spirit as well as the body, a struggle to achieve, through which mentally-retarded people demonstrate their right to be numbered among all the rest of us. Our equals in skill. Our associates in humanity."[136] When one thinks of the long decades of isolation and neglect that the mentally retarded had suffered, these words were a balm to the Special Olympians themselves and their assembled families.

Second, she said, the Special Olympics were an occasion for sharing. It was the energy of the by then enormous volunteer program that was being shared. "If we did not share a strong sense of common humanity with the mentally retarded we would not be here."[137]

Finally, the Special Olympics was a celebration of joy, for both the Special Olympians and their parents, who by 1980 were attending events in the tens of thousands. Eunice said that the late President Kennedy "could not imagine a day when the parents of the mentally retarded would be proud of their children and show them to the world with pride."[138] Now the parents brought their MR children with pride to Games featured on network television and visited by famous athletes and celebrities. One of the most striking sights at the Special Olympics is the parents themselves, so moved by the achievements of their children that tears alternate with radiant joy.

Eunice was an intensely serious, even dour individual. Yet her face would invariably light up as she attended MR sports events, hopping into the pool with the Olympians or hugging them as they finished their races. She experienced at a profound personal level this joy that she articulated as a vision, and she choreographed the Special Olympics to make sure that each event mirrored this joy and celebration of achievement, for in the sports events each participant was a winner.

Too Good to Let Go

There was no chance that the 1968 Special Olympics in Chicago would be just a one-time event, regardless of what the Chicago people thought. "It was just too good to let go," said Hayden.[139] The first step was to wrest it definitively from the control of the Chicago Park District, and this could only be done through incorporating the concept so that the Kennedys would have exclusive control over it.

Unfortunately, the term "Olympics" in the United States was already copyright by the U.S. Olympic Committee (USOC). Hayden had an advance inkling there would be trouble when he went to see Brundage in Chicago.

Brundage asked, "Who told you you could use the word 'Olympic'?"

Hayden thought to himself, "Oh Christ," but said, "Actually, Mr. Brundage, I'm aware that the Committee has exclusive use. I wrote them asking permission to use it."

"Yeah?"

Hayden continued, "They never answered the letter. They figured it was just some little retarded event."

Brundage shook his head about the USOC, "Those assholes."

Hayden went back to Washington. Beverly Campbell, who had a great deal of experience in the corporate world, told him in August that he should talk to her husband Pierce, an investment banker, about safeguarding the title to prevent the Chicago people from keeping the Special Olympics there permanently, as they were now planning to do. The three of them had lunch. Pierce Campbell suggested incorporating the Special Olympics in the District of Columbia.

"Incorporation," said Hayden. "What's that?"

Pierce Campbell told him, "It's small potatoes right now. But if you're successful over the next year, this is going to be big. There may be TV rights. So you want to capture that name."

That very afternoon Hayden was in a lawyer's office. They worked until 4 a.m. fleshing out the details. It was 9 a.m. in Paris. Hayden got on the phone to Sarge Shriver and told Sarge what he had done. Sarge suggested a couple more names for the board of directors, and by 4 p.m. that afternoon, the Special Olympics was incorporated in the District of Columbia.

The composition of the board of directors shows who belonged to the little band of loyalists at the very beginning. There were Eunice and Frank Hayden, of course, plus Bob Cooke. Only one sports figure—Rafer Johnson—was included. James Lovell, the astronaut, was on the list, as was Lawrence Rarick in order to have someone from the scientific side. Finally, perhaps to make a bow to Chicago yet keep the board of directors among insiders, there was Thomas King, manager of the Merchandise Mart. King was married to Barbara Ann Scott. Hayden was the executive director of the Special Olympics, Campbell the director of community relations.[140]

In the following months there were angry communications with the U.S. Olympic Committee. Hayden's basic tactic was to stall them with circumlocutions. "I hoped they'd just forget about it. All the while we're building momentum. All they can do is take us to court. What the hell are they going to do? Sue the retarded?"

Hayden had also blackmailed Brundage into putting in a good word with the USOC. Early in January 1968, it had seemed possible that South Africa might be admitted to the international Olympic Games scheduled for that September in Mexico City. A group of black American athletes had mobilized against this eventuality, threatening to boycott the Olympics if South Africa was present. By the summer of 1968, this boycott was endangering the participation of the U.S. team. According to Hayden, "They [the USOC] didn't need any more bad publicity. Rafer Johnson was there [with me] at some meeting with Brundage. Brundage asked Rafer if he would help to diffuse the black boycott thing at the '68 Games. Brundage became more malleable after Rafer said yes."[141] According to Hayden, Brundage struck a deal in which Rafer Johnson, who had been a fence-sitter in the dispute, would agree to intervene with the dissident black athletes if the Kennedy Foundation were permitted to use the term "Special Olympics."

To further claim the public relations high ground—thus undermining the cases of both the Chicago people and the USOC—the Shrivers planned a grand announcement on December 2, 1968, of the incorporation of the Special Olympics. There would be a cross-country hookup involving, in Washington, Ted Kennedy and Bob Mathias, a representative from California who had won the Olympic decathlon in 1948 and 1952, and Rafer Johnson in California. The actor Don Adams, who had starred in the television series "Get Smart," would be the "Head Coach."

This press conference and the Kennedys' accompanying public relations efforts attracted an enormous amount of attention. By January 1969, around 560 letters, coming from 132 communities and representing more than fifty thousand children, had arrived at the offices of the Kennedy Foundation. Seventeen cities had requested permission to hold regional meets in 1969.[142]

Interest was snowballing. The foundation made a film of the 1968 Special Olympics titled "A Dream to Grow On." It was to be shown the evening of March 11, 1969, to an audience of three hundred prominent Washingtonians at the Pan-Am building in D.C. The following day there would be a meeting of the directors of the regional meets at Airlie House.

That evening Ted Kennedy came and introduced the seven regional program directors. He gave them checks from the Kennedy Foundation before the assembled group. One of Fred MacMurray's TV sons (from "My Three Sons") came and was supposed to sing. But just before the song, Ted had to leave. As his limo was rounding the block in front of the building, he saw the candlelight dinner that the women volunteers had arranged in the lobby. He stopped the car, ran in and thanked the ladies, and then moved on.

The song was "Has Anybody Here Seen My Old Friend John." This was just five years after JFK's death and eight months after Robert Kennedy's death.

Hayden said to himself, "Thank God Teddy left."

The Special Olympics had been launched.

6

Power

etween the 1960s and the end of the century, the lives of people with mental retardation were completely transformed. For the first time in history, the mentally retarded were able to attend school, find jobs, marry, settle into proper homes, and live "normally," to use the movement's great rallying cry. These changes occurred in part because of a fervor sweeping the social service professions for "deinstitutionalization," or "normalization," meaning the integration of those with MR into community life. This was not really a Kennedy story. The great shift in MR was made possible in part by a more welcoming social climate. It was also made possible by federal legislation that directed billions of public dollars toward aid for those with mental retardation—which is a Kennedy story that took a quite unexpected direction once the Kennedys lost the White House.

After JFK's assassination, the Kennedy family has never again been able to deploy the executive authority of the U.S. government. Instead, they chose two separate tactics: one, using the media—which is very resistant to being used in this way—in order to inculcate more favorable public attitudes toward MR, and influencing Congress.

Two, using power. In the three decades from the 1960s to the 1990s, Ted Kennedy, Eunice Shriver, and Sargent Shriver made a major commitment to changing the lives of the mentally retarded. They did so with the exercise of power: of the power that accrues from celebrity, from effectiveness in the Senate, and from systematic and determined lobbying. The story is an interesting example of how to convert good inten-

143

tions into concrete political action that has real implications for the lives of millions of people.

Managing the Legacy

JFK's death in November 1963 represented for the Shrivers not merely a personal tragedy but a serious political setback: they had lost control of the command center of the federal government, the White House. "It was a mess," recalled Donald Stedman. "There was a recognition that the bully pulpit was not nearly as high up in the air as it used to be."[1]

What to do? Public attachment to Jack Kennedy became much more intense after his death than before. This vast national reservoir of sadness and memory constituted a legacy that could be managed. Here Eunice fell back upon an insight developed in long association with her father, her three elected brothers, and her high-energy husband: the secret to change lay in public opinion, and the secret to public opinion lay in the media. Said Stedman, "Eunice had an instinct that public attitudes were a major barrier, and one way to pierce them was to get people cheek to jowl with people who looked funny and who were retarded. She was right."[2]

The Kennedy family, one recalls, had many years of experience in managing the media. At Bobby Kennedy's funeral requiem mass in 1968, five hundred of the twenty-one hundred invited guests were journalists, "considered friends of the family."[3] Old Joe Kennedy had always talked about "placing" stories, as though he actually controlled the products of the press. Perhaps he did, at least to some extent, given his intimacy with the great press lords. (He addressed the wife of William Randolph Hearst as "Dear Bootsie."[4]) On another occasion, to get PR for a movie of his, he simply instructed the editors of *Look* magazine (via Sarge) to insert material on the movie in a story they were doing on a related subject.[5]

Sarge learned his lessons well and became a master at placing favorable stories. He once wrote to his father-in-law about an editorial in the *Chicago Tribune* on the need for an international trade fair in Chicago: "I thought this editorial would interest you. The basic idea came from us, but we didn't plant this edit."[6] By this Sarge meant that they had inspired it, but for once hadn't planted it.

As Sarge struck out on his own in the 1960s, he became bolder about planting stories, even false ones. The *New Yorker* "Talk of the Town" column claimed in 1962 that Sargent Shriver was such a man of the people that he had worked out a way of sleeping while stretched out in the tourist class of airplanes, a considerable feat as those who travel tourist class know. You do it as follows, he told the *New Yorker* writer, "Crouching, first, in the foot space in front of your assigned seat, you wriggle down until you have your head under the seat in front of you and your legs straight out under your own seat."[7] The entire story, as it turned out, was made up and planted in the *New Yorker* to achieve some publicity. "The whole trip was first class," said Edwin Bayley, who at the time was Shriver's press chief at the Peace Corps and knew exactly what was going on. "And that poor Sarge had to sleep on the floor. Well, he slept on the floor, it was the best place you could sleep. They'd give him that section about a yard wide back of the last seat in the first class section and fix it up with pillows and blankets, and he was very comfortable. All this hardship was completely phony."[8]

Sarge, one of the most principled men in American politics, was not being particularly wicked in misleading the press in this manner. It was merely that he was contemptuous of the press and didn't consider it wrong to use journalists: "You tell them one thing today and the next thing tomorrow," he said. "They'll forget."[9]

The entire milieu in which the Kennedys functioned reflected this contempt for journalism, not unpardonable in view of how much the Kennedy family has suffered from the media. Give lunch to the press. As Ted Kennedy would say, "It's a small price to be 'safe' not 'sorry.'" The view was that the media could be bought off with sandwiches.[10]

When Robert Kennedy was a senator from New York, his family routinely assumed that he would be able to place material in the New York press. "We have learned," wrote Kennedy Foundation executive Fred McDonald, "that it takes a contact by a top person with the publishers to draw their attention to the [Advertising Council] material. . . ."[11] On another occasion McDonald pleaded with Kennedy brother-in-law Stephen Smith to do his best with the *New York Times*.[12] Often the family would ask favored writers to ghostwrite magazine and newspaper pieces. As Pat Lawford wrote to Stephen Smith in 1980 on the subject of "Mother's article on 90th birthday": "Bobby Shriver does not have the time to finish mother's article so I think we should get ahold of [a prominent Kennedy biographer] to do the job.

"Do we offer any payment or just the ticket to Florida?"[13]

It was simply assumed that journalists and writers would do what was bidden. Clearly, these were people accustomed to dealing with journalists as, in a sense, servants.

These skills were passed on even to the third generation. Disappointed on one occasion at some untrustworthy journalists who had omitted the part on Ted's character from a newspaper article about him and his mother Rose, Eunice complained to her son Bobby, "Dad says the only answer would be to have had you here to handle the editor. They gave me their word that would be left in."[14] Bobby Shriver evidently would have horsewhipped the editor.

In managing JFK's legacy, the first opportunity for demonstrating these media-handling skills came two months after the assassination. On January 3, 1964, a small group calling itself the "John F. Kennedy Birthday Committee" met in Washington to decide how Camelot should be memorialized. The committee devised many plans, such as a folk song to be written by Carl Sandburg, or a "John F. Kennedy School of Medicine with a special emphasis on the functioning of the human brain." But what really caught the Shrivers' eyes was a plan for some kind of national "public education in mental retardation, utilizing all media. . . ."[15] Many of the other proposals went by the wayside. But the Shrivers picked up this national "public education" notion and made it the basis of their own efforts for the next five years.

LeRoy Collins, president of the National Association of Broadcasters and former governor of Florida, was made the coordinator of the committee. Prompted by Sarge, Collins then involved the Advertising Council, a Madison Avenue-based organization founded to get public service advertising into the media. (The choice seemed logical to Sarge because the Ad Council had just finished a big campaign on mental illness.[16]) The Ad Council resisted any focus as narrow as mental retardation: "It seems too bad and somehow unfitting to tie his [JFK's] memory in only with mental retardation," wrote one of their officers.[17] Yet the Shrivers persisted. On January 13, Collins held a meeting of the committee at his home in Georgetown. Eunice attended. The following day Collins wrote Sarge that MR would in fact provide the theme of the campaign: "While Ted Repplier [of the Ad Council] . . . and others have made good arguments for associating a memorial event with a broad spectrum of causes in which the President was interested, it has been our feeling that over the range of time the advancement of a good MR program would give to a memorial event a sharp focus of great humanitarian appeal."[18]

Dave Ray, who had done so well lobbying Congress during Camelot, was summoned back from Conway, Arkansas, where he had gone after the passage of President Kennedy's MR legislation in October 1963. Ray devised a detailed proposal for a national publicity campaign on behalf of MR that would involve close cooperation with the parents' group, NARC.[19] This proposal became the basis of the "Ad Council campaign," which ran officially from 1965 to 1969 and involved the investment of $250,000 from HEW and the Kennedy Foundation, in exchange for newspaper, magazine, radio, and TV ads that would have cost $30 million had they been purchased commercially.[20] NARC paid for a million copies of a give-away booklet, "How to Bring New Hope to the Mentally Retarded," that was distributed nationally.[21]

The Shrivers devised the campaign's themes and guided its day-by-day course. Getting editors to pay attention to the material was a major struggle. Sarge would write letters such as the following to Randolph Hearst, inheritor of the Hearst newspaper empire: "Dear Randy, I hate to ask you for another favor but this one is also vital. . . ." Sarge explained how the lives of the mentally retarded were being changed: "Ten years ago there was absolutely no hope for the youngster who was retarded. Today many retarded people, young and old, are made whole again. Many, many more are made from human vegetables to human beings who live, work, and even marry." But there was a problem: "We can't seem to bring home to the newspapers of the San Francisco area the importance of bringing retardation's message to the Bay area people." Could Hearst not call the attention of his papers to the Ad Council material?[22]

Sarge monitored even the "California Food Mart News," entreating its editor to use the Ad Council material. It worked. "You know," the editor told Sarge, "from where I sit, it sometimes becomes very difficult to select the various causes espoused by the Advertising Council. Yet I feel very good about having run that particular ad in lieu of any of the others forwarded to me."[23]

In April 1964, Ray began working as publicity director of the Kennedy Foundation, overseeing the nuts and bolts of the campaign. What had to be done for the second year? A new TV kit had to be mailed out featuring Dr. Benjamin Spock. Special "How to Do It" manuals were dispatched to over thirty-five hundred individual volunteers, telling them how to organize publicity in their local communities. The superintendents of all 140 state MR institutions got letters and posters. Personal letters went out to the MR coordinators in all fifty states. All local chapters of The Arc received the manual, as did, for example, the Woman's Auxiliary to the Medical Association of Georgia (two hundred manuals) and the Maryland Jaycees (twenty thousand manuals).

The Shrivers' campaign achieved what ten years of NARC's efforts had failed to accomplish: an initial, glacial shift in public attitudes toward MR. The agency at HEW responsible for MR, the President's Committee on Mental Retardation (PCMR), received over two million letters.[24] Local media outlets all over the country—including such "outlets" as the monthly bills of the San Francisco Water Department—used Ad Council material.[25] For the first time, the message that there was hope in MR was brought home to the common person.

The Corridors of Power

With the force of the White House no longer behind them, all the Shrivers had going on Capitol Hill was Eunice's younger brother Ted, who had been elected to the Senate only in November 1962 (and who had been seriously injured in a plane crash in 1964). This seemed unpromising as a strategy. With one or two minor exceptions, Eunice and Sarge did not use Ted for heavy MR lifting before 1970. Their strategy instead was to try to maintain a privileged post at the White House from which they could chivy HEW. The ultimate failure of this strategy made it necessary to turn up the heat on Ted, thereby driving his office staff crazy but ultimately producing dividends.

Having a special assistant to the President for MR under Camelot, headed by the compliant Stafford Warren, had been almost too good to be true. The Shrivers had been able to bypass Warren and bang away directly at the federal bureaucracy, in alliance with Wilbur Cohen and Mike Feldman. After JFK's death, Cohen and Feldman remained on the scene, Cohen moving up to undersecretary at HEW (just one notch beneath secretary) and Feldman staying in the White House as LBJ's Deputy Special Counsel (and Counsel in 1964–65). Yet things were not the same.

For one thing, LBJ saw a much reduced role for Warren (who stayed on until May 1965) and the White House office. Although LBJ was personally well disposed to Sarge, making him head of the War on Poverty, he evidently felt the Kennedys had achieved entirely too much influence in the federal government. (LBJ was probably also using Sarge as a way of solving his "Bobby Kennedy" problem, and Sarge evidently consented to be used as a foil against Bobby.[26]) LBJ disliked all the lobbying that people like Ray had been doing and brought it to an end, telling Ray later, "Leave the lobbying to me."[27] Feldman's constant badgering of Cohen came to an end.

Cohen himself suddenly became much more resistant to outside influence. Even as early as October 1963, Cohen snapped at Feldman that Warren's office had gotten entirely out of hand. The Warren people were to have no role in implementing the new Camelot legislation on MR: "I believe that it will be very confusing if Dr. Warren's office begins to take an active role in the administrative implementation of the legislation. This will set up conflicting lines of responsibility. . . .

"I think that we should have a frank and full discussion of this matter so that later on there will be no difficulties."[28] In federal administrative talk, this is equivalent to drawing a line in the sand.

On another occasion after JFK's death, Cohen turned venomously upon Sarge about the interfering role of the White House office (the

Shrivers' main means of control): "If Dr. Warren's office had been abolished three and one-half months ago and there weren't so darn many meetings on mental retardation, we might have been able to settle this matter [a point about funding the UAFs] three and one-half months ago. In the meantime all I want to say is that I am discouraged also by the vast number of people who are involved in these mental retardation activities outside of the Department. . . . I think the present situation is very discouraging."[29]

Thus, despite his personal friendship with the Shrivers, Wilbur Cohen would be the last person in the world to advocate perpetuating their influence within the federal government—at least from a base in the White House. Under the Johnson Administration, Cohen moved swiftly to cut back Warren's staff, sending Thomas Murphy back to the parents' organization (where he had been NARC's PR officer) and Michael Begab back to the Children's Bureau of HEW (where he was in the permanent civil service).[30]

The Shrivers could see the handwriting on the wall: they were about to lose their White House command post. Johnson made no move against the Kennedy clan until he won the presidency in his own right in the election of November 1964. It was then that he apparently felt psychologically more capable of dismantling the old regime. Early in January 1965, Johnson said to Cohen that he had decided to move MR from the White House into HEW.[31]

At this point the Shrivers realized that they desperately needed something they had always denied to Warren: a "Presidential Committee," a blue-ribbon panel to oversee the implementation of the growing body of MR legislation. For Warren it had always been a source of bitterness that he had never been permitted to establish such a committee. He had been expressly denied one in order to keep attention focused on the Kennedy family as the benefactors of MR. "You don't need a committee," Feldman had told him. Warren said, "They didn't want to have anybody not a Kennedy come in to develop an image in mental retardation. This was a Kennedy show, Kennedy Foundation show, presidential show, and a Shriver show. . . ."[32]

As the Shrivers saw the loss of the White House looming, they began pushing for a committee, something more modest perhaps than Warren's well-staffed office of "special assistant to the President," but an organization that nonetheless would be run from the White House. It was the White House cachet that they sought. "I think it would be a fatal mistake to let mental retardation activities fall into the HEW with its present organization," Bob Cooke warned Sarge in March 1965. Cooke tried to think up angles that would appeal to the White House, some kind of a "National Council" perhaps.[33] Cro Duplantier, a Kennedy ally then in Warren's office, tried to convince Vice President Hubert Humphrey that an evident concern with MR could have big political payoffs. The six million citizens with MR had about thirty million relatives, the implication being that all would vote Republican if LBJ tried to mess around with the mentally retarded.[34]

These efforts were to no avail. In the late spring of 1965, Hubert Humphrey invited Cohen, Sarge, and some of the other principals to his office to carve up the cadaver of Warren's White House office.[35] It had been decided that HEW would hire three new assistant secretaries, one of them concerned with mental retardation.[36] Evidently as a concession to Sarge, it was determined that the assistant secretary for MR would probably be David Ray.

Thus the demolition of the White House command post unfolded. Staff Warren bowed out on May 30, 1965, and the *New York Times* announced that MR would be leaving the White House for HEW.[37] Hours later a furious Eunice was on the phone to Wilbur Cohen. "Mrs. Shriver called me Sunday morning after reading in the *New York Times* that Dr. Warren has resigned and that his responsibilities would be assigned to an Assistant Secretary in H.E.W.," Cohen told HEW chief John Gardner. "Mrs. Shriver indicated extreme annoyance that she had not been consulted on these developments in view of the fact that she had asked various people what was going to happen and couldn't find out anything definite. She was so upset I wasn't able to complete a sentence in the conversation. She said she was going to talk with President Johnson about the situation."[38] The conversation is highly interesting as evidence of the extent to which the Kennedys (but not Sargent Shriver) had been marginalized under the new regime. Sarge knew well in advance of the change but for whatever reason didn't tell his wife, and none of her former friends instructed her either. One does get a sense that for Eunice the going was getting tougher.

The new bunch in the White House and at HEW were able to take only so much heat from Eunice Kennedy, who ultimately had enough political savvy to make things very uncomfortable for Johnson and Cohen if she felt she had been crossed. So the Johnson Administration came up with quite a cynical compromise: they would call this new coordinating body the President's Committee on Mental Retardation, but there would be nothing presidential about it, no ties to the White House of any kind. It would be entirely situated within HEW, thus insulated from outside meddling. As Bill Moyers, LBJ's chief of staff, told another White House aide later in June, "There is so much activity on behalf of the mental retardation people that I now worry about the repercussions of *not* working something out satisfactory to Eunice, Sarge, et al.

"Why not—with appropriate folderol—set up the President's Advisory Committee which has been recommended, let the Vice President be Chairman, and let all operational matters be handled, as we have already done, at HEW?"[39]

This cynical proposal found great favor at HEW. A week later Wallace Babington, the second-in-command of HEW's own internal MR committee, told Cohen, "I like Bill Moyer's suggestion. . . . The only question would be the necessity of having someone called 'Special Assistant to the President for Mental Retardation' actually sitting in the Executive Office Building. I would hope that we could get by without this. . . ."[40]

Many years later Babington bristled when it was suggested to him that the entire idea of a "President's Committee" had been "a sop to the Shrivers."[41] Long out of government, he had forgotten how urgent the imperatives of power actually appear to insiders. And there is no doubt that power was being taken away from the Shrivers and Kennedys in the struggle to control the multibillion-dollar MR budget now being spent on what a decade previously had been an orphan cause.

The Shrivers' fears turned out to be fully justified. Over the years, the PCMR demonstrated itself to be ineffectual in the complex task of actually getting federal funds to help the mentally retarded, Eunice's original agenda. Dave Ray headed the PCMR until Richard Nixon's victory in the election of 1968. But even Ray was backing away from the Shrivers. For example, in May 1965 as it became clear that Ray would be coming to HEW, Sarge Shriver asked him to lobby forcefully with Congressman Oren Harris, the Arkansan head of the House Interstate Commerce Committee (through which all MR legislation passed). Ray reported the conversation to Babington. Babington asked Ray not to lobby Harris, and Ray abstained from doing so.[42] When in 1966 the twenty-seven-member PCMR was actually constituted, Sarge observed unhappily to Fogarty that both of Fogarty's candidates had gotten on but none of the Kennedys' candidates.[43] (Fogarty's candidates were apparently Dr. Robert Kugel, an internist at Brown University in Providence and medical consultant for the Ladd School for MR children in Exeter, Rhode Island, and, at Georgetown University, Dr. Patrick Doyle, who made no secret of his admiration for Staff Warren and John Fogarty.[44])

With the Nixon victory, the PCMR went rapidly downhill. By the mid-1970s, the Shrivers no longer had any working relationship with the organization.[45] Kennedy Foundation executive Robert Montague opined in 1978 that the PCMR had "outlived its usefulness and may actually be a liability." He recommended that Mrs. Shriver not accept an appointment to it.[46] Elizabeth Boggs was equally emphatic about the PCMR's lack of impact: "The committee did not then, nor has it since represented a major or active and visible force outside of the executive branch."[47]

As a force for getting things done, the PCMR was virtually useless.[48] It might issue reports and was supposed to coordinate government activities outside of HEW (though it usually did not).[49] But HEW was the main game in town, and the PCMR, as later generations of Washingtonians would say, was "outside the loop" of power. Not only could the Shrivers not control it, it had no influence. In order to gain political heft within the federal government, the Shrivers would have to try other means.

The Senator

In 1965, Ted Kennedy was thirty-three years old, eleven years younger than his big sister Eunice. "He is the most handsome of the Kennedys," wrote journalist Nan Robertson, "and the biggest—6 feet 2 inches tall, 200 pounds—with a perfect set of teeth, piercing, deeply set blue eyes and a kind of bandbox air."[50] In the Senate only three years, Ted was just beginning to establish independence from his two dominating brothers and his bossy sister. President Kennedy had once joked that the new senator from Massachusetts seemed to be striking off on his own: "Instead of being Teddy Kennedy, now he is changing his name to Teddy Roosevelt."[51]

Ted Kennedy would have a meteoric career in the Senate, balancing an ideological liberalism almost as pure as the driven snow with a pragmatic clubbishness in which archconservatives such as Senator James Eastland of Mississippi felt perfectly comfortable asking him for favors.[52] As early as 1969, Ted displaced Louisiana's Russell Long as majority whip—assistant to the Senate majority leader and responsible for mustering votes. In the summer of that year, his upward trajectory received the only interruption it has ever sustained: the tragedy of Chappaquiddick, which caused his colleagues to depose him as whip in 1971. But so punctilious were Ted's relations with other senators—such "extraordinarily careful manners" did he have in one biographer's phrase[53]—that the Senate did not hold his past against him for long. In 1978, Eastland retired and Ted moved up to head the Judiciary Committee, a post he would hold only for two years. In the Reagan revolution of 1980, the Democrats lost the Senate and Ted lost the headship of three strategic committees and subcommittees: the Judiciary Committee, the health subcommittee of the Senate Labor and Public Welfare Committee as it then was (after 1977 "Labor and Human Resources"), and an energy subcommittee. He was, however, minority leader of the Judiciary Committee.

Intent upon "defending classic liberal programs, with large Democratic constituencies, against the onslaught of the Reagan Republicans," in 1981 he exchanged his status as minority leader of the Judiciary committee for minority leader of the Labor Committee—which of course is responsible for health legislation.[54] He was now aptly placed to influence all health legislation—including MR—in the Senate. In the elections of 1986, the Democrats regained control of the Senate and the following January Ted Kennedy decided to become chairman of the Labor Committee rather than the Judiciary Committee. (A Senator can chair only one full committee.) Reforming American health care was now his number one goal.

By 1987, Ted Kennedy had served in the Senate for twenty-five years. "Today," announced family friend and *Newsweek* columnist George Will, "Kennedy is a substantial component of the Senate's, and the government's, institutional memory."[55] *U.S. News & World Report* lauded him a year later as "the King of the Congress." "He is on his way to becoming one of the greatest senators of this century," said Norman Ornstein, a congressional scholar at the American Enterprise Institute, who had been interviewed for the story.[56]

These are not trivial accomplishments. Ted Kennedy established himself as one of the great progressive legislators of the twentieth century. How did MR fit into all this? It makes more sense to ask, how did Ted's relations with his sister Eunice fit into the story? For she, of course, was the wellspring of his interest. Shining forth from Eunice's private correspondence is great affection for her younger brother, despite their differences of opinion on abortion—he was in favor, she opposed. She called him "Teddy." He by contrast signed his notes to her "Eddy."

It was almost certainly at Eunice's urging that Ted became the president of the Kennedy Foundation in 1961 (although no doubt with the consent of his father, who had his stroke only in December of that year). "My family wanted to make sure I was president of something," Ted cracked, "so they elected me to this."[57]

What Ted and Eunice had in common was a commitment to public service. This is something Eunice Shriver was deadly serious about: she saw the point of her own life as public service and assumed that her brother shared this dedication. She once wrote to him in a personal communication not at all intended to impress others, "Dear Teddy, You were great at the Trustees meeting [of the foundation] today. I appreciate very much your personal effort to force us to think of ways to cut the Kennedy Foundation contribution to the [JFK Presidential] Library. . . . It is the retarded who will be benefited and, of course, most appreciative —even if they don't know the force of their joy."[58] The force of their joy.

Just imagine a line like this in a private conversation: it would normally come across as stilted and pompous, unless one were absolutely serious. The line is a warranty of Eunice's belief that she and Ted lived in a world of shared assumptions about the purpose of the family's celebrity and about the purpose of life. We have no way of knowing Ted's private thoughts on the matter, but in public he agreed with his sister. In 1985, he told *Time* magazine that he would not be a contender in the next presidential race. "I know that this decision means that I may never be President," he said. "The pursuit of the presidency is not my life. Public service is."[59]

From the mid-1960s on, Ted and Eunice played the government in a kind of cross-ruff, to borrow a bridge term, each leading to the other's strongest suit in a way that gave them extraordinary influence. Ted's strong suit was his ability to initiate legislation, and over his thirty-plus years in the Senate he has sponsored hundreds of bills, many of which have gone on to become important laws. Eunice's strong suit was the moral force with which she could invest a cause, along with her ability to give it a public profile. Hidden from the public eye for fear that the Kennedy clan would seem too influential, this cross-ruff was responsible for a substantial amount of the executive and legislative progress made on MR in the 1960s and 1970s.

There was the measles vaccine. Measles and particularly German measles (rubella) were once an important cause of MR. In 1964–65, for example, a rubella epidemic in the United States caused approximately eighteen hundred cases of MR, twenty-two hundred deaths, and sixty-three hundred miscarriages; the epidemic also left twelve thousand children deaf, blind, or both.[60] (If a mother contracts rubella within a month before pregnancy or three months after, the virus may damage the development of the child's nervous system.) In 1963 a vaccine had been developed for measles, and in 1969 for German measles. That is the background for a letter that Eunice received in April 1966 from James Bowes, a forty-six-year-old obstetrician in Portsmouth, Rhode Island, whose specialty was conducting mass vaccinations.

In 1957, two years after the polio vaccine was introduced, Bowes had carried out a mass polio immunization in Salt Lake City. After moving to Rhode Island, in 1960 he conducted a state-wide immunization program, and another in 1963, that was determined to stamp out polio "once and for all" in that state. (On a single day his campaign immunized over six hundred thousand Rhode Islanders.) Bowes had been all over the country conducting measles vaccination drives. In 1966, he became medical director of the Pitman-Moore Division of the Dow Chemical Company, maker of one of the most often used measles vaccines, although he did not mention an association with Pitman-Moore to Eunice when he wrote to her.

In his letter he told her of Pitman-Moore's highly effective measles vaccine and said that the price could be made competitive if enough units were purchased at a single time. Did Mrs. Shriver have any idea how the funds necessary for such a purchase could be obtained?[61] We don't know what became of this proposal, but we do know that Eunice was sufficiently enthralled with Dr. Bowes to make him the Kennedy Foundation's adviser on vaccines. (She also wanted him to be the chief physician at the Chicago Special Olympics in 1968, which he declined.) In this capacity she introduced him to her brother Ted.

Back in 1962, Senator Lister Hill had championed the Vaccination Assistance Act. Yet millions of children remained unprotected against measles. Resolved to do something about this preventable cause of MR, Eunice began writing legislators all over the country and asked them to step up their eradication programs. In February 1968, Bowes was summoned to Washington to help with this task, specifically to advise Ted on drafting a bill to extend Hill's Vaccination Assistance Act.[62] Ted introduced the bill two weeks later.[63] To strengthen the case for such an act, Eunice had a questionnaire drawn up, which Ted's office then sent to big-city and state health department directors all over the country. Did they think an extension of the Vaccination Assistance Act necessary? Unsurprisingly, ninety-five percent of them thought so.[64] Nonetheless, the bill died in the Senate Labor Committee. Their first efforts failed, but that is beside the point. This particular segment of the story shows how smooth was the cross-ruff in which Eunice and Ted maneuvered: Eunice prodding Ted to get going on a measles bill, Ted drawing from the Kennedy Foundation's expertise to make the case for it. Bowes continued to function as vaccine adviser to the Shrivers and to Ted Kennedy, ghostwriting, for example, an article on measles vaccination that appeared in 1969 under Ted's signature in the Ladies' Home Journal.[65]

Eunice might use Ted's glamour as a resource for promotional purposes, sending him places in order to present checks—or to accept them—in the name of mental retardation. Thus when Milton-Bradley, the Springfield, Massachusetts, game-maker went public in 1966, its PR people had the idea that company president James Shea might present the first hundred shares of stock to the Kennedy Foundation on the floor of the "big board," the New York Stock Exchange. On such occasions it was customary for the president of a company to appear on the floor and watch the company's stock move first across the ticker that day. Could Senator Kennedy be on hand to accept the check? This one Ted took a pass on, and Joe Kennedy's executives James Fayne and Thomas Walsh turned up to accept the check instead.[66] On another occasion Ted was asked to present the check when the Kennedy Foundation wanted to give the Boston Recreation Department $15,000 for "a year-round program of recreation for the mentally retarded." This apparently was not to his liking, and things were reconfigured into Ted speaking at a luncheon in Boston that kicked off the Ad Council campaign featuring six-year-old Dickie Bach, NARC's national poster boy for 1965.[67]

Even though the young Senator Kennedy could refuse his importunate sister on occasion, some occasions just couldn't be refused. Ted's sister Jean Kennedy Smith had organized a substantial art program for the mentally retarded, with the Kennedy Foundation and HEW jointly funding arts and other workshops. In 1974, they were to have a spectacular six-session workshop at the Kennedy Center in D.C. The whole family would be there. Ted, of course, spoke at the opening.[68]

Much of this negotiation involved Ted's staff rather than the senator himself, for he had a thumb in many pies and could not possibly be expected to follow every development in MR. At one point, Ted Kennedy had over a hundred people working directly under his supervision, either on his personal staff or on his various Senate committees (the line between personal and committee staff so thin as to be virtually invisible).[69]

Eunice found dealing with this large staff, in constant turnover, often highly vexing, and she made herself notorious for her imperious behavior with her brother's aides, many of whom were distinguished professionals in their own right. Elizabeth Boggs, who had an insider's knowledge of relations between the Shrivers and the Senate office buildings, said simply, "The Kennedy staff found Eunice impossible."[70]

Because of the difficulty of gaining a purchase on Ted's giant office, the Shriver people demanded that he hire an MR specialist among the many other specialists present on his staff. "This is the only way," said Beverly Rowan, the Kennedy Foundation's legislative specialist in the mid-1970s, "his office is going to begin to understand all the problems and issues involved. . . . At the present time the Senator has no one in his office who can spot and deal with these issues."[71]

As far as Ted was concerned, however, it was the responsibility of Eunice and her people "to spot and deal with the issues." That was how he organized the rest of his staff, encouraging them to be legislative entrepreneurs who would lock onto and pursue their own targets, seeing him periodically for consultation. He would act when his sister suggested that he do so, but he was otherwise not "proactive" on MR—unless it benefited his own interests or his staff believed that it would.

There were occasions when it did. Norman Knight, an aide in the senator's Boston office, was "very explicit that the family did not want to use the achievements of the Foundation as direct political propaganda."[72] But there were shades of gray. Knight, for example, suggested that Ted might well accept an invitation of the American Association on Mental Deficiency to speak at its banquet in May 1968 in Boston. "Fred [McDonald—executive director of the Foundation] and I have discussed this at some length," Knight told Kennedy, "and I am convinced that you should accept this for the following reasons." One such reason: "It's the *National* meeting on our home ground and it definitely will result in AP, UPI and possibly TV network coverage." The AAMD might present the award, Knight continued, "on behalf of your total concern and commitment to the relief of human suffering in many forms."[73] So we are, in fact, dealing with politicians and not with plaster saints.

But in fairness to Ted Kennedy, while I have not had access to his private archives, I can report that very little material of the above nature is to be found in the Kennedy Foundation's archives. Kennedy would not deliberately have exploited MR for political purposes, if only because such a move would backfire, as it had with Tom Mboya in 1960 (see chapter 2). Although on occasion the senator's lifestyle and personal staff made his pocketbook wheeze, he nonetheless donated his speaking fees to MR-related causes.[74]

Eunice, by contrast, had a passion to influence her brother. On one occasion she reminded him, in essence: You have a meeting coming up with President Carter, Teddy. Here are some points for you to mention. The points included raising the budget of the child health institute. Also, "Please congratulate President Carter on his stand on abortion."[75] When Eunice wanted Ted to act on the problem of teenage pregnancy (teenage mothers tend to have less prenatal counseling and more toxemia and placental insufficiency, which can cause mental retardation in the baby), she simply drafted the legislation and sent it over for him to submit.[76] She commanded two of his staffers to help her with the drafting: "Please let me know when you are available, the sooner the better." Then, as events progressed, she instructed her brother about what amendments were and were not acceptable.[77]

These examples could be multiplied many-fold. There is nothing wrong here: no illicit lobbying, no abuse of power. Eunice Shriver was merely trying to use her younger brother as a command post to replace the lost position at the White House. For her, the cause counted far more than not being burdensome to other family members or the bruised sensitivities of staffers. It is emblematic of her dedication to mental retardation that when her brother Bobby was assassinated in June 1968, she was quite desirous of using the "RFK funeral list" to shore up the support of celebrities and others who could be useful to the Kennedy

Foundation in its projects. As she told the staffer at the RFK-for-President headquarters who was organizing invitations to the funeral, "I've included a lot of celebrities etc with whom the Foundation has been working on projects—you probably already have them on your other lists. If not—be sure to add them."[78] Among the names starred for special emphasis were the baseball player Stan Musial; Francis Kelley, by this time superintendent of the Mansfield State Training School in Connecticut; and the members of the President's Committee on Mental Retardation. Some of these people knew RFK in other connections, but they were on Eunice's list because they could help the foundation with MR. How could her surviving brother have resisted such determination?

Sarge and His "Buzz Bomb"

As Eunice was tugging at the ear of her brother in the mid-1960s and the 1970s, we catch Sarge on the backstretch of a lifetime in public service. He had entered Camelot as "the brother-in-law" and emerged from it with a reputation as a dynamic executive and politician in his own right, considered as a potential Democratic nominee for President or Vice President in every election from 1964 to 1976, nominated only in 1972 for Vice President, and elected in none of them. It was heartbreaking that his idealism made him so unlikely to be chosen for political office. Pollster Patrick Caddell, speaking of Sarge Shriver, once said that he had "seldom seen a candidate with so much potential that was so unlikely to be used."[79]

With his failure to beat out Jimmy Carter for the presidential nomination in 1976, Sarge retired to the privacy of a Washington law practice and dedicated himself to advocacy on behalf of MR and to the Special Olympics. But in the 1960s and 1970s, as we find him jabbing the federal bureaucracy into action on MR, he was the very mirror of manic energy— a man at the height of his career. At the Office of Economic Opportunity he would agitate his "buzz bomb"—the telephone console on his desk that permitted him to "push a button and speak to Columbia, South America, and then push another button and speak to Columbia University in New York."[80] One aide said that he might "pick up the phone and call anyone who strikes his fancy, somebody in the news or the author of a book which interested him."[81] He was, in the words of those who knew him well, a "very able man."

Sarge's energy seemed inexhaustible. Not only did he run the Peace Corps starting between 1961 and 1996, in 1964 he took on the Office of Economic Opportunity as well, called the "War on Poverty," relinquishing it in 1968 only to go to Paris for two years as U.S. ambassador. "I remember especially going with Shriver on a speechmaking trip that took us from Washington to St. Louis and back," wrote his biographer Robert Liston. "Before leaving his office Shriver filled three attaché cases with papers to be worked on en route." He had gone through one case by the time they reached Andrews Air Force Base. He handed this case to his driver Richard Ragsdale to be brought back to the office. "Throughout the plane ride to St. Louis, Shriver continued working. . . . Before retiring in St. Louis that night, he pushed a pile of memos into the hands of one of his public information aides, William Sanzski. Sanzski spent much of the night carrying out the instructions on these memos, with the result that another package of material went off to Shrivers' secretaries the next morning. This was the program on every night of the journey."[82] Frank Hayden, in charge of the Kennedy Foundation's sports program, remembered what lengths were necessary to buttonhole Shriver. "The best way was to wait in his limo until he would come out of his office at the end of the day. His secretary was friendly with me. She'd call and say he's about to leave. I'd be sitting there with his chauffeur Rags. From the Peace Corps to Timberlawn was about forty minutes. Rags would drive me back into Washington."[83]

Sarge believed that "it was better to try 50 things and succeed in 30 of them than to try ten and succeed in ten."[84] As he said of his own style in contrast with Eunice's, "I know how to organize things so that 10,000 people can teach 100,000 to swim, but I might never get in the pool. My wife might not be able to organize the numbers—but she is in the pool."[85] These were the skills that Shriver now unleashed in lobbying Congress and the government bureaucracy.

One example of Sarge in action in the late 1970s involves the problem of getting the budget for a clinical building at the NICHD approved. He wanted Wilbur Cohen, at the time the dean of the School of Education at the University of Michigan, to help him. (Remember that Sarge was now just a private citizen.)

There had been a problem on the Senate side. "The [Appropriations] Subcommittee got confused. That shouldn't have happened, but it did happen." Warren Magnuson ("Maggie"), the Democratic senator from Washington State, had just been chosen chairman of the subcommittee. Perhaps some of the threads had been lost.

How to sort out this imbroglio? Magnuson was willing to let Tom Eagleton of Missouri, also on the subcommittee, have a shot at raising the NICHD budget again in full committee. Said Sarge, "Tom Eagleton is ready, willing and able, but we have to make sure that when Tom gives his speech he will be backed up by the other Subcommittee Members."

Sitting in Sarge's shoes, how does one pressure the other committee and subcommittee members to support Eagleton and thus turn about the subcommittee's unfortunate decision? "We need to convince Lawton Chiles of Florida [another committee member]," Sarge continued. How? "We need influential Floridians to write, telephone Lawton Chiles urging him to support the building and the research." We need the same tactics with Republican Richard Schweiker of Pennsylvania and Republican Edward Brooke of Massachusetts, said Sarge, and he mentioned another three senators on the appropriations committee as well, Democrats and Republicans alike, who could be brought about for the sake of child health.

"Basically, the men on this list are for the NICHD building," Sarge said. They simply need to be encouraged to overcome their qualms about busting the budget by telephone calls from the grassroots.

"Most of all," he told Cohen, "we need your help with Maggie. At the Subcommittee meeting, Maggie had eight proxies. He could have approved the Basic Research Building by himself." But no, the Carter Administration was pressuring Magnuson to "hold the line." "You know better than anyone that the line is always held most effectively when women and children are concerned."

Sarge concluded the letter by asking Cohen how best to get to "Maggie."[86]

There were many similar occasions. Sarge might, for example, be trying to save the University Affiliated Facilities, the diagnostic centers of such benefit to the parents, from cutbacks—a constant threat. His staff assembled for him a whole briefing book, outlining various strategies (for example, renewing existing legislation versus some kind of block financing), listing the key staffers in the offices of each member of the Senate Labor and Human Resources Committee (Robinsue Srohboese, for example, was the key staffer on these matters in Ted's office), and containing detailed backup material.[87] It was classic inside-the-Beltway lobbying, conducted by a master. (The Kennedy Foundation had a horror of the term "lobbying" and preferred the expression "advocacy." When Beverly Rowan was taken on as the legislative coordinator in 1974, she was instructed to make absolutely sure not to get the foundation in trouble around "tax- exempt organization and lobbying. Most important as it is a sensitive area."[88])

To help Sarge coordinate the enormously complex MR legislation (and to run the mushrooming Special Olympics), in 1974 the Kennedy Foundation hired a retired army general named Robert Montague. Montague, fifty at the time, had left the army when he found his further advancement at the Pentagon blocked for political reasons. General

Maxwell Taylor had called him "one of the smartest, most capable officers in the military service."[89] Rather than trekking to the corporate world as many others did, Montague decided to try his hand at Kennedy Foundation-style philanthropy. (He said in his resumé that he had wanted to "involv[e] myself in the political processes in the United States."[90]) He had done well at many other tasks in life, graduating first in his class at West Point in 1947, and had the kind of disciplined mind required to give some follow-through to Eunice Shriver's many ongoing campaigns.[91]

Montague helped focus the foundation's lobbying efforts. He might, for example, assist Eunice in "guiding" a series of witnesses through testimony on behalf of a bill to reduce the number of adolescent pregnancies.[92] Or he might help Sarge orchestrate a campaign to increase funds for the adolescent pregnancy legislation in the House appropriations subcommittee. In this latter case it was Montague's job to stake out the positions of each member of the subcommittee. He wrote of Joseph Early, a Democratic congressman from Massachusetts: "Quite supportive and probably would accept Administration's request [for full funding]." And of Louise Stokes, a Democrat from Ohio: "Considers program is poorly designed."

As Montague told Sarge, "Calls to Early, [George] O'Brien and [David] Obey would be very helpful. In them you or Mrs. Shriver should support full funding for Fy [financial year] 80 and sufficient start-up money. . . ."[93]

Bob Cooke often joined Montague and Sarge Shriver in these ventures, sometimes appearing himself as a witness at committee hearings, sometimes bearding individual congressmen in private. Although Cooke left Johns Hopkins in 1973 for the University of Wisconsin medical school (going in 1977 to the Medical College of Pennsylvania in Philadelphia), he remained in constant touch with the Shrivers, functioning on occasion as a paid part-time consultant and head of their scientific advisory board. Having acquired his advocacy skills during Camelot, by the late 1970s Cooke was an old hand at seeking congressmen and senators out in their offices for five minutes of talk.[94] Or Cooke himself might seize the initiative on an issue—for example, why rates of mental retardation in Sweden seemed to be so much lower than in the United States—and put the wheels into motion. As he said to Sarge in 1980, "The final product should be a plan of action for Congress—especially Senator Kennedy—to reduce mild mental retardation in the United States downward toward levels in Sweden." Eunice had already approved the plan. Cooke simply wanted Sarge's final okay.[95]

These were four highly energetic and motivated individuals: Eunice, Sarge, Bob Cooke, and Bob Montague. With Sarge Shriver's understanding of tactics, Eunice's sense of public relations, Montague's administrative skills, and Cooke's massive scientific authority, they made a formidable force on the Hill and in the government bureaucracy. But they were such an unlikely team. On the face of it, who were these people anyway? A former President's sister? Many other former Presidents have had sisters. A Washington lawyer? There are masses of them. An obscure army officer unknown outside the Pentagon? A white-haired pediatrician familiar only to a few scientists? Again, not unique. But together these four individuals present a story of determination—and of what determined people can set out to accomplish, together with the power of the Kennedy name, once they put their minds and wills to it.

From MR to Developmental Disabilities

In the eighteen months from January 1967 to May 1968, three key events happened. John Fogarty died of a heart attack in January 1967. The standard bearer for MR in the House was thus swept from the scene. "The great problem at the present time," wrote Bob Cooke to Fran Kelley in July 1968, "is that there is no one in the House who is really dedicated to the cause of the retarded."[96]

Second, in 1968 Lister Hill, the Alabama Democrat with a thirty-year tenure in the Senate who was chairman of one powerful committee and of another influential subcommittee related to MR, decided not to run again. Given that Ted Kennedy up to this point had been scarcely visible on the scene, the Senate thus lost its champion on behalf of MR.

Third, in May of 1968 the Shrivers moved to Paris as Sarge became the American ambassador.

A huge vacuum suddenly opened in MR leadership in Washington. Simply for family honor, Ted would have to fill it. He told Boggs he felt that he "had an obligation to perpetuate the MR legislation."[97]

Crystallizing in the late 1960s more slowly than the above events—but nonetheless of equal historic force—was a decision of the parents' movement to no longer provide services but instead to demand them. Tired of organizing sheltered workshops and private special-ed classes, the parents began to insist that the state provide the services needed to help their children develop and realize their full potential as citizens. Mindful that during Camelot the big increases in federal funding had all gone to building things, in 1965 NARC began to demand action on the broad "band of services" entailed in the social habilitation of those with MR.[98] From 1968 on, "We stopped talking about promoting welfare and started talking about implementing rights," said Boggs.[99] This was tough talk.

Ted Kennedy and a number of parents' groups made a start with the developmental disabilities act of 1970. But it was not just the parents of mentally retarded children. All the advocates for the developmentally disabled were involved.

In the panoply of disabilities that begin before eighteen—and thus are considered "developmental" in nature—MR is statistically the most important.[100] In 1967, the mentally retarded represented the majority of adults receiving social security because of a disability arising in childhood. If you include individuals with other disabilities—such as cerebral palsy and severe epilepsy—who also are mentally retarded, the proportion rises to about two-thirds. Other disorders such as childhood schizophrenia account for the remainder.[101] Historically, however, the advocates of those with other disabilities had never been eager to associate their clients with mental retardation. For years, the cerebral palsy people made a big deal of keeping CP separate from MR in the public mind, not wanting to be dragged down by the stigma. ("Help the cerebral palsied because they are not mentally retarded" was the watchword of the early 1950s.) Yet a majority of persons with cerebral palsy are in fact mentally retarded as well.[102]

These other childhood disabilities had parents' groups of their own— the Epilepsy Foundation of America, for example, having been founded in 1939 (originally named the Laymen's League Against Epilepsy), and the United Cerebral Palsy Association founded in 1949.[103] Elsie Helsel, director of the cerebral palsy association and herself a Ph.D. scientist, had a child with both MR and CP, and just as Elizabeth Boggs commuted to Washington from New Jersey, Helsel commuted from Athens, Ohio.[104]

At the outset, however, these groups were suspicious of each other and resisted any common identification. In 1950, the National Society for Crippled Children and Adults, founded in 1921, opposed including the mentally retarded in a bill on federal aid to handicapped children. In fund-raising drives in the early 1950s, the cerebral palsy people squabbled openly with the adult branch of the National Society for Crippled Children. "Let us learn from these things," wrote Boggs to Alan Sampson, chairman of NARC.[105]

Indeed, people did learn from these early histories of internecine conflict. A kind of umbrella organization for disabled children had constituted itself in 1922. Called the Council for Exceptional Children (CEC), it was composed of professionals—mainly in special education —rather than of parents.[106] It was the CEC that launched the parents toward unity. In 1964, its "Interagency Committee" under the leadership of William Geer convened a meeting in Washington, D.C., of the various parents' groups for the purpose of lobbying on behalf of handicapped children generally. The meeting was clearly sailing in the wind of Camelot, a wind blown up by MR. Those attending the meeting were an honor roll of the incipient developmental-disabilities lobby, among them Leonard Mayo from the Association for the Aid of Crippled Children in New York; a whole squadron from the lobby for the blind; representatives for cerebral palsy, polio, and the deaf; and Luther Stringham, himself a recent HEW bureaucrat, who had just come to NARC to replace Gunnar Dybwad as executive director.[107] This represented the first push toward a parents' coalition.

The second step came in April 1969 as Eleanor Elkin, president of NARC, convened a meeting in Washington of all the disability constituencies. From this meeting an "ad hoc coalition" emerged. Harry Schnibbe, head of the association of state mental health program directors, made office space available for the mental retardation and cerebral palsy groups amid his own people on the top floor of Dodge House on Connecticut Avenue. (Schnibbe's organization had the tongue-twisting acronym NASMHPD, or National Society of State Mental Health Program Directors. He had been an active disabilities lobbyist during Camelot.[108]) Cynthia Sturdevant was taken on as NARC's first full-time Washington lobbyist, while Elsie Helsel continued to carry the ball for cerebral palsy.[109] Boggs hovered as NARC's parent-volunteer and the guiding light of the entire developmental disabilities lobby.

This coalition came into being only because of NARC's willingness to build bridges to other groups, for the MR parents' group had been there first. Indeed under Camelot, local chapters of The Arc had sometimes rejected alliances with groups for other disabilities. They felt, in the words of Michael Begab, "sometimes with justification, that if they joined forces with other groups, they would tend to be relegated to the low priority position they had occupied in the past. They were kind of gun-shy."[110]

But the late 1960s were a different ball game. Other groups had now mobilized, and it would have been unseemly to compete against them in lobbying. Also, Dave Ray at PCMR had warned Boggs and her people to hook up with other groups. The Kennedy exclusive focus on MR was too much.[111] Boggs took the question to Eleanor Elkin, then president of NARC, and to the legislative committee. "We just felt it was a calculated risk that was desirable to take."[112] NARC thus took the initiative in cutting its own throat, so to speak. From NARC went the signal that "MR" was now out and "developmental disabilities" was now in.

By the beginning of 1970, there were a number of players on the disabilities scene in the Washington. Some were great regional barons— for example, Lloyd Rader, director of Oklahoma's social services department (which included MR), who came often to Washington to lobby such powerful members of Oklahoma's delegation as House majority leader Carl Albert or John Jarman of the Interstate Commerce Committee.

Others, such as Robert Gettings who in 1970 had just been appointed head of the society of state MR directors, had already settled in as old Washington hands in one MR connection or another.[113] A long list of acronyms was now onside for the disabled.

The point is that by 1970 a great army of people interested in disabilities had emerged. In contrast to NARC's meager band in 1960, ten years later an entire network of organizations now represented "developmental disabilities," a term that avoided fracturing the movement into categories. This network had been spawned in part by burgeoning parents' movements in other disabilities, in part by professionals who owed their jobs to the flood of social service legislation coming between 1964 and 1968 out of Lyndon Johnson's "Great Society." This network now wanted action.

In the early days of 1969, as the new Nixon people streamed into Washington, there was a power vacuum at HEW.[114] The Nixonites were suspicious of the Great Society-style liberal bureaucracy they believed they were inheriting (falsely suspicious; the great majority of bureaucrats were more interested in successfully accomplishing their mission than in any particular political agenda). And there had been a long delay in Senate confirmation of the assistant secretary. So all the legislation that Wilbur Cohen as previous secretary had drafted just sat there on Secretary Robert Finch's desk, including legislation to renew the MR laws of Camelot.

This hiatus created a wonderful opportunity for Elizabeth Boggs and Elsie Helsel, who were leading the disabilities show and could shape the renewals rather than reacting to the Administration's proposals. So they sat down with the staffers of the Senate health subcommittee, working out a deal in which Ralph Yarborough (from Texas), chairman of the Senate Labor Committee, would draft both the mental health and the mental retardation bills. Yarborough needed the visibility because he was coming up for reelection. But Yarborough's mental health bill failed in the House.

Then Ted Kennedy decided that he wanted to sponsor the MR bill. Yarborough agreed, and Boggs and her people began working on the details with Kennedy's staff, especially with a bright young aide named Carey Parker, a lawyer just fresh from a Supreme Court clerkship. "I spent quite a bit of time with Carey Parker," said Boggs later. "It was clear to me that Carey had been told by the senator to give this priority attention."[115] In consultation with Kennedy's people, Boggs and her group agreed that the bill's thrust would be on "developmental disabilities," not on MR. (Eunice was "not a little annoyed" with her brother when she returned from Paris in the spring of 1970 and learned that MR had vanished as a legislative concept.[116])

But who would be included as developmentally disabled? Certainly those with cerebral palsy, who had been in at the beginning. It didn't seem fair to leave epilepsy out, even though the epilepsy lobby was disorganized at that point. (They were amazed to learn in August 1970 that they had been included when Congressman Paul Rogers, who took responsibility for getting the bill through the public health subcommittee of the House, spoke at the epilepsy lobby's annual convention.[117]) The drafters had to be careful not to clip the turf of the National Institute for Mental Health, whose feelings were already bruised from having MR removed during Camelot. It was therefore agreed to leave childhood schizophrenia and autism out of "DD." (Autism would come in only later, after a huge struggle, in the 1975 DD amendment act.[118]) In the end, the official list included mental retardation, cerebral palsy, epilepsy, and other neurological conditions "closely related to mental retardation."[119] What constituted a "developmental disability" therefore was highly political. "Various organizations working with various disability groups jockeyed to move their groups in or out of the definition," Boggs later said.[120]

But the DD concept was driven by need as well. Up to that point, the money available for MR had been limited to voc rehab for the mildly retarded, meaning people who might work, and to training teachers for special education as a result of some legislation in 1965–66. This benefited only the "educable" retarded. There had been nothing for the severely retarded. But at the beginning the Boggs group insisted on the widest possible definition. They wanted "zero reject," a novel idea then. Although they later had to make compromises, the committee originally demanded that nobody was too handicapped to be excluded from aid as long as the handicap originated in childhood.

We are now into July 1969. At this point a big delay occurred, as Ted Kennedy became involved in the turmoil of Chappaquiddick. The bill was dropped into the Senate hopper only on August 13. Rogers introduced a revised version of the Senate bill in the House early in October, coinciding with the NARC convention in Miami. (Rogers' home was in West Palm Beach.) There was a great deal of interest in the bill in the House. Senate hearings began in November.

The Nixon Administration opposed the bill: the expanded notion of disabilities would cost too much and they preferred, they said, to concentrate on "prevention." Seeing a chance to boost funding for his UAFs, Bob Cooke appeared at the Senate hearings and showed a video of several DD children who had been treated at the UAF at Johns Hopkins. In December, Ted Kennedy and Creed Black, HEW's assistant secretary for legislation (Wilbur Cohen's job under Camelot) had a meeting. The

Administration agreed to accept the DD concept. Finally in the spring of 1970, the Senate Labor Committee "reported," or passed, the DD bill.

The bill was hugely popular. On April 13, the Senate accepted it 69 to 0. The House approved a slightly different version on July 30 by 338 to 0. As time passed, waiting for a conference to reconcile the Senate and House versions, Ted Kennedy did some preliminary lobbying with Magnuson and got him to slot an extra $4 million in appropriations. The Senate accepted the conference report on October 14, the same day as the dedication of the Eunice Kennedy Shriver Center on the grounds of the Fernald State School in Waltham, Massachusetts. Ted spoke at the luncheon. "We have come a long distance together since the early days of President Kennedy's administration," he said. "The prospects are bright for the future."[121] Two weeks later Nixon signed the DD act into law.[122]

The services mandated by the act were actually quite long in arriving. But that was not the main significance of the first DD act (the "Developmental Disabilities Services and Facilities Act of 1970"). It opened the way to the habilitation of those with chronic handicaps of any nature, a forerunner of the Americans with Disabilities Act of 1990. As Boggs put it, the act was intended to grant "developmental potential, 'habilitation,' and the right to optimal remediation" to a group that in the past had been relegated to a static diagnosis requiring "custodial" care.[123] This was an epochal historic achievement.

Given that federal spending on mental retardation rose from around $100 million a year in 1962 to $7.8 billion yearly in 1985, the DD Act was an important milestone.[124] For the first time money flowed not just to MR but to a range of disabilities, and the states set up special councils to vacuum funds out of Washington in a formula based on population. After 1970, spending on services, so ardently desired by parents, would soar.[125] The story of the DD act is a classic example of the use of power, as an alliance between parents and Kennedys succeeding in obtaining large amounts of money in order to relieve a terrible social injustice.

This is what making a difference is all about. Ted Kennedy used to tell a story that makes this point:

An old man walking along a beach at dawn saw a young man picking up starfish and throwing them out to sea.

"Why are you doing that?" the old man inquired.

The young man explained that the starfish had been stranded by the tide on the beach, and would soon die in the morning sun.

"But the beach goes on for miles," the old man said, "and there are so many starfish. How can your effort make any difference?"

The young man looked at the starfish in his hand, and then threw it to safety in the sea. "It makes a difference to that one," he said.[126]

1

Image

B y the time of the Special Olympics Summer Games in the Triangle area of North Carolina in June 1999, Eunice had ceased her hands-on involvement. The Special Olympics had grown to include seven thousand athletes with MR from 150 countries: there were chapters all over the world. In contrast to the empty stands at Soldier Field in 1968, by 1999 over fifteen thousand family members (roughly two per athlete) and three hundred thousand spectators would be present. Over a million kids all over the world were involved in training, and of those, only the best competed in North Carolina. In the world of mental retardation, by 1999 the Special Olympics had acquired a very special resonance.

The organizers of the Special Olympics—the Kennedy family at the top—emphasized time and again media coverage. In the early years: When would ABC feature the Games? Or, in later years after the number of reporters at the various venues had increased over the years: Why this media emphasis?

A principal obstacle to the integration of the mentally retarded in community life lay in image: their negative images of themselves, others' negative images of them. Bettering these images represented a contribution to change as material as the group homes that began sprouting after the 1970s. The Kennedys were singularly well placed to attract press and celebrities.

Celebrity Images

The major problem in promoting the Special Olympics was spreading the word. The concept itself was path breaking:

168

periodic Games at the state and national level, combined with a year-round local training effort. This had the real ability to change the lives of children with MR. It also had the potential of changing the image of mentally retarded people in the public eye, if Special Olympics could only be brought to the public eye. But reaching the vast public, convincing them that the Special Olympics was something more than a glorified track meet, was a challenge. As Dick Sargent, a family friend and actor (Samantha's husband in "Bewitched"), mused to Eunice in 1978, "The other night I was watching a television show (The Captain and Tennille in Hawaii) and I was struck with the fact that a musical format contains easily-palatable information, color, sweep, etc. in an entertaining package. It suddenly seemed analogous to what you and I know has been an almost unreachable goal—getting the public to realize the Special Olympics as a source of achievement, joy, and love. By the public, I mean that large television mass who don't want to watch a straight-forward documentary about the retarded, who just want to be entertained."[1]

How did one reach such a "mass"? Here is where celebrities came in handy.

Although celebrities were recruited for all levels of Special Olympics competitions, the periodic International Games provided the main focus for celebrity power. There had been four international Games between 1968 and 1975, after which Special Olympics split into summer and winter Games, each occurring in four-year intervals, so that every two years an international Special Olympics of some kind would be brought before the public.

Generally speaking, the American media considered athletics for the retarded a nonstory. At the 1975 D.C. premiere of the movie "Funny Lady," starring Barbra Streisand, ABC was said to have scorned the live TV special that the Kennedy Foundation had put together as "all Special Olympics and not enough entertainment . . . a big bore."[2] (The foundation, by contrast, believed too little had been seen of the mentally retarded rather than too much. As General Montague complained of the spectacle, "All we're getting is a lot of publicity about Barbra Streisand."[3])

Eunice was very frank in dangling the celebrity hook before editors and producers. "Good Morning America" should cover the Winter Games in 1981 at Smugglers' Notch in Vermont, she told the producer, because (1) Olympic speed-skating gold-medalists Eric Heiden and Beth Heiden "will be at the Games the whole time," and (2) because "celebrities like John Denver, Goldie Hawn, Billy Kidd . . . will be there. Members of my family will also attend."[4] Such bait was needed because only large numbers of celebrities would magnetize media attention, affording the

MR athletes their momentary turn in the spotlight. Thus the Kennedys embarked on a policy of drawing in the Hollywood glitterati as massively as possible.

This is a story that has its roots in the 1920s, when Joe Kennedy was a Hollywood movie mogul. As Rose Kennedy later reminisced of those years, "I knew a number of the stars, some of whom visited us at Bronxville or Hyannisport." Gloria Swanson often visited the Kennedy family at the Cape or in New York, somewhat surprisingly because Joe Kennedy was having an affair with her. Pat and Eunice had early memories of Gloria kissing them goodnight or of wishing to emulate her perfume or her style.[5] The Swanson business gave the Kennedy children early familiarity with the world of celebrities and made having recourse to them a natural reflex.

In the 1950s, using Pat Kennedy Lawford's Hollywood connections, the family started systematically bringing in celebrities to help with Jack's campaigns for the Senate and for President.[6] In the spring of 1960, Eunice asked her father if she should get the Lennon Sisters, a musical group, to sing on behalf of her brother. ("I can't imagine that I would have any use for them," Joe Senior witheringly replied).[7]

After Jack Kennedy was elected President, contacts became frequent among the family, the White House, and the glitterati. Celebrities became almost a kind of commodity, a form of stock on the shelves that could be traded upon when needed. When in 1961 John Fogarty's friend Arthur Trudeau wanted Danny Kaye to perform at a benefit put on by the Rhode Island chapter of The Arc, Trudeau turned to the Kennedys. Trudeau phoned Fogarty, asking Fogarty to phone someone at the White House, who in turn should phone Peter Lawford in California. Could Lawford possibly "arrange with Kaye to accept"? The request never got beyond Fogarty's desk, his staffers somewhat embarrassed at Trudeau's naiveté.[8] Nonetheless, the perception was that the Kennedys controlled the pathway to the stars.

The budget of the 1999 North Carolina Special Olympics was $36 million. A good share of this money was raised from corporations, and again, celebrities were the bait that got corporations to bite. In 1979, an executive of a large insurance company that had a history of helping the Special Olympics told Sarge that the company was going to provide a big send-off for Olympians from the D.C. area to the Summer Games in Brockport, New York. Could a Kennedy not attend the party? "Perhaps you might also be able to arrange for a celebrity speaker who could deliver a brief inspirational 'charge' to the athletes," the executive suggested.[9] Underlying the request was the idea that celebrities were interchangeable commodities, and that the Kennedy family had a store of them they could dole out at will.

Things were not that simple. Hollywood was another world, not automatically attracted to the gray bureaucrats of the capitol even if wrapped in Kennedy allure. "There's the big time, and then there's the big time," said the *Washington Post* when Hollywood and Washington collided in 1975 at the Streisand special in D.C.

At that event a PR lackey for Columbia Pictures was trying to herd guests from the foyer of the Kennedy Center into their seats so the special could begin.

" 'Will you people please move into the theater,' she shouted at the black-tie crowd in general and the gray-haired man in particular.

"He smiled and pulled out his two gold VIP tickets. . . .'Could you tell me where these seats are?' he said.

" 'Inside,' said the woman abruptly.

"Behind her a Washingtonian gaped at the faux pas. 'That's Lloyd Bentsen,' the Washingtonian explained [Bentsen was then Senator from Texas]. 'He's running for President.'

" 'I'm with Columbia Pictures,' the woman replied. 'I have my job, he has his.' "[10]

So the world of Hollywood did not automatically come when summoned. They had to be wooed. One mechanism for wooing them was to create a kind of irresistible honeypot, a mixture of big-time influence and glamour to convey the feeling of being at the absolute epicenter of the American power elite. Sarge was trying to invite one celebrity (whom we'll call Celebrity X) in 1987 to participate in the opening ceremonies of the Special Olympics at Notre Dame in South Bend, Indiana. Why should Celebrity X, this big-time personality, take the time to journey to some obscure spot in Indiana? George Shultz, the Secretary of State, would be hosting a dinner the night before in Washington. "A few of our Washington friends" will be there, said Sarge. ("A few of our friends" usually meant Supreme Court justices and columnists with the national punch of someone like George Will.) The following morning Celebrity X and his wife would be flown in a private plane along with the Special Olympics board of directors from Washington's National Airport to South Bend.

In South Bend the Celebrity X couple would find Whitney Houston, for example, who would be singing at the event. "John Williams of the Boston Pops is conducting the band." (Indeed Williams had written the theme song "We're Lookin' Good" for that Special Olympics event.) ABC would broadcast the opening ceremonies on prime time. "We'd really love to have you come and be part of this occasion scheduled for late Sunday afternoon," said Sarge. In fact, "It would be great fun to have you with us for the entire weekend."[11] This was powerful bait.

Because celebrities love to be flown around in private planes, the procuring of such aircraft was a high priority. The Shrivers would borrow them from corporations, then dangle them in front of big names. Sarge tried to line up Henry Fonda and his family for the celebration of Rose's ninetieth birthday, which was simultaneously to serve as a Special Olympics fund-raiser. "If you and Jane [Fonda] and . . . Katharine Hepburn could all come down together [to Hyannisport], we wouldn't have to look any further for charismatic talent to heighten interest in my Mother-in-law's celebration.

"I have arranged for private jet air transportation for you, Jane, and for Katharine Hepburn, if all of you can accept our invitation."[12]

The Fondas apparently did not attend at this occasion. Massachusetts Senator Paul Tsongas did, however, as did influential Congressman Claude Pepper. Sports broadcaster Curt Gowdy was master of ceremonies.[13]

The Shrivers, knowing Warner Communications chairman Steve Ross well, would often borrow the corporation's private plane. On one occasion Eunice thanked him for his cooperation, going even beyond the bounds of the hyperbole customary in such letters: "Without your plane, the stars just would not have come [to South Bend] and there would not have been a show *period*!" She sent a copy of her Ross letter to Bobby Shriver, who was organizing the celebrity participation for the Special Olympics, and added, "I went a little overboard, but then I gathered from you, you need planes and planes, and they are very hard to get—yet so essential."[14]

Indeed, it was increasingly Bobby Shriver, thirty years old in 1984, who played the role as manager of the celebrity patrol. Bobby had graduated from Yale with a degree in American studies, hacked around as a journalist, earned a degree from Yale Law School, and after a stint in the financial world drifted into movie production in Los Angeles, drawn to that vocation perhaps by his sister Maria and his brother-in-law Arnold Schwarzenegger. Bobby was therefore well situated to line up stars for a "sports luncheon" that Eunice was hosting in May 1984 in Los Angeles.

At this luncheon, as at all such luncheons, the ostensible purpose was giving out awards for support of the Special Olympics. The real purpose was attracting press coverage of glamour gatherings, and thus harvesting donations. Hence, it was important that prominent stars attend. Who should be invited? Bobby sent his mother a list. Tom Cruise was on it, identified for Eunice as "young" and starring in "Risky Business." Also Heather Locklear, "young, t.v. show that I can't remember." (The show was "T. J. Hooker," a cop show in which Locklear played "Stacy," the captain's daughter.) Jane Fonda and Tom Selleck each had a "good sports image." And Lou Ferrigno was a "body-builder, friend of Arnold's [Schwarzenegger]." Another prominent actress was classed as "a blonde bombshell type," and Warren Beatty was included for the simple reason of "glamour."[15]

On a number of other occasions as well Bobby Shriver served as contact person to the stars. But where he rendered his parents and the Special Olympics greatest service was in arranging for the best-selling album "A Very Special Christmas," released in October 1987. The album went back to the idea of doing a Christmas record that producer James Iovine had been pursuing since the early 1980s. In 1983, Iovine had even made a demo, with Stevie Nicks (of the group Fleetwood Mack) singing "Silent Night." After Iovine's father died in 1985, he decided definitely to go ahead with the project. Iovine's wife Vicki had worked for the Special Olympics for a few years, and the Iovines thought that the Shriver organization "seemed like the obvious place" for such an album. Bobby Shriver was supposed to represent the Kennedy Foundation in the co-production, forming his own company—"Special Olympics Records" —in order to release the album in October 1987. (Up to this point Bobby had been involved in making Special Olympics promo films.) The proceeds would go to the Special Olympics.

Shriver and Iovine lined up a number of prominent artists. Through the intervention of John F. Kennedy, Jr., they were, for example, able to get Madonna. "Now that we have gained Madonna," Eunice told her nephew, "people are fighting to record. . . ."[16] Bruce Springsteen, John Cougar Mellencamp, Whitney Houston, Sting, Run D.M.C., and eight other performers, many of whom had previously worked with Iovine, were brought on board—all singing Yuletide songs.[17] Two months after the album's release many of the performers appeared in a CBS television special about very special Christmases on December 23, 1987.[18]

The synergism between the TV special and the album's star cast caused "A Very Special Christmas" to take off like a rocket. By March 1988, the record had sold nearly three million copies worldwide, going gold (more than half a million sold) in the United Kingdom, platinum (more than a million sold) in the United States, and double platinum (more than two million sold) in Canada. At a press conference on March 12, 1988, during the convention in Los Angeles of the National Association of Recording Merchandisers, the distributor, A&M records, handed Eunice and Sarge a check for $5 million.[19] Further millions were to come.

Because the record and TV special had done so well, in February 1988 ABC approached Bobby Shriver about producing a further TV special along the lines of "A Very Special Christmas." "They explained," Bobby told the family, "that once you have successfully established a television idea, it's important to revisit that idea regularly." Shriver and Iovine sat down to think about what kind of TV special they might do for round two. How about a Christmas party, held in somebody's living room, at which Madonna-rank singers would appear along with Special Olympians and superstar athletes? He explained somewhat abashedly to such furious Kennedy family members as Pat that because notice was so short, Rose's living room at the Cape seemed like the best idea. (None of the other family had been informed.) Bobby concluded his apologia: "I believe that each of you will be pleased with the result. The Special Olympics [sic] sing a song, lift weights, tell their stories and make toasts. . . . I hope everyone will see the value of these images."[20]

The show, "A Very Special Christmas Party," starring Arnold Schwarzenegger, Maria Shriver, Barbara Mandrell, Susan Saint James, Mike Tyson, and other stars, was filmed in one November week of 1988 and aired on ABC December 22. The special in turn reinforced the sale of the album, and by 1993 "A Very Special Christmas" had earned over $17 million for the Special Olympics.[21] More important, it exposed a vast TV public to quite a new image of people with MR.

At the Games, the image of the MR athletes was profiled against that of the celebrities. Games pyrotechnics were programmed to produce this juxtaposing of images. One example is Sarge trying to line up singer Neil Diamond for the closing ceremonies of the Games in July 1983 at Baton Rouge:

> During Closing Ceremonies, the athletes from every state and 40 countries will join hands in a "Friendship Circle," filling the entire floor of Tiger Stadium at Louisiana State University. The Special Olympics flag will be lowered, the torch will be extinguished. . . . Then, when the field is in semi-darkness, it would be incredibly moving if you were to sing your beautiful "Heartlight."
>
> Over 4,300 athletes and thousands of parents and volunteers could join you in a chorus, if you thought that was right. Then, the lights in the stadium will go out completely and as you sing, all the athletes on the field will wave glowing sticks as a gesture of love and farewell.[22]

Talk about images. The scene Sarge described would have been overwhelming on TV. (Diamond couldn't come. As things turned out no one sang because the closing ceremonies were cut short due to the intense heat.)

Other times the play of images occurred in the sweat of the boxing ring. Joey Giardello, world middleweight boxing champion in the mid-1960s, had a mentally retarded son who was eleven in 1965. Giardello had painstakingly taught the boy to hit a ball on a fly "seven times out of ten." "You should have seen him the first time I rolled a ball to him. What a disappointment!" said Giardello at a press conference the Kennedy Foundation had arranged to announce its new fitness program. But having helped his son develop, Giardello pledged, "I will do all within my power to help this new program to become the greatest thing that ever happened for the retarded."[23]

Giardello's personal joy became a beacon of light for others when in May 1965 at the behest of Eunice Shriver he appeared as a celebrity at the Mansfield Training School to referee a boxing match between two of the residents.[24] News photographs show the boys crowding around him, the very figure of hope and achievement. It was not just a play of mirrors. The celebrity images projected into the media had the ability to reflect people with MR in a new light.

Moving Images

The Kennedys made great use of movies in boosting the image of the mentally retarded, not in making movies but in premiering them. Few profile-raising stunts better capture editors' attention than a celebrity-studded opening of a celebrity-packed film. This became the Kennedy family's number one technique for putting the cause of MR in the public eye.

It was actually the other Kennedy sisters who, in the 1960s, experimented with the premiering techniques that Eunice and Sarge would later perfect. In order to raise money for two of the family's charities founded in the 1950s—the Kennedy Child Study Center in New York and the Kennedy Institute in Washington—the family put on a series of benefits. Jean Kennedy Smith organized the fourth benefit in the series, a premiere of Stanley Kramer's "It's a Mad, Mad, Mad, Mad World" in November 1963 in New York, five days before the President's death. But unlike the later Shriver premieres, in which a central specially-staged event was telecast—and the movie itself shown only to a select audience—the 1963 premiere began with a dispersed series of private cocktail parties, ending with a public showing of the Stanley Kramer's film. Also, Jean had been unable to persuade her brother the President, who remained in Palm Beach, to attend. So the event lacked regal class despite the presence of cabinet members, New York's two U.S. senators, and Milton Berle and Eva Gabor. (A journalist noted that the Kennedy brothers received almost as much applause as the entertainers.) It was covered on page thirty-six of the *New York Times*.[25] Surely one could do better.

One problem with "It's a Mad, Mad, Mad, Mad World" was the Jonathan Winters-style highbrow comedy: many in Middle America had never heard of it. But everyone had heard of Barbra Streisand. In 1974, she made "Funny Lady," a sequel to her earlier hit "Funny Girl." In the autumn of that year officials of Columbia Pictures and Rastar Productions (named after Barbra's friend Ray Stark who produced the movie) consulted about the launching of "Funny Lady." Mort Engelberg, vice president of Rastar, had worked with Sargent Shriver in the Peace Corps. Engelberg wondered if some kind of TV special, built around "Funny Lady" and emphasizing the Special Olympics, could be put together to promote the movie. They approached ABC. ABC still had ashes in its mouth about the low ratings of a recent Sinatra live special but was said to have liked the media play the special had received.[26] So all the ingredients started to come together: Streisand would get press, and the entire venture would be ennobled by the connection to the Special Olympics.

Scheduled for March 9, 1975, at the Eisenhower Theater of the Kennedy Center in Washington, the TV special "From Funny Girl to Funny Lady" represented Streisand's first live special. She was said to be terribly nervous and went off to a retreat to lose weight. A premiere showing of the film "Funny Lady" for invited guests in the Eisenhower Theater would follow the special. From the outset there were tensions between Rastar Productions and the Kennedy people. "The problem," said a Columbia Pictures source, "came down to a matter of: Are Ray's guests more important or are Eunice and Sarge's friends more important?" Eunice, under pressure, began "acting like a drill sergeant," as the *Washington Post* reported. "Some of the local [arrangements] committee members were admiring, some scared to death of her, some furious, some literally in tears," revealed Sally Quinn, ace gossip specialist.[27]

Given the level of disorganization (throughout the years organizers of these events would lament "constant interference by Family members"[28]), it was no surprise that the live special went off schedule and the nation did not get a chance to see Barbra Streisand singing "People." But after ABC slammed the lid at 8:30 sharp, Streisand went on to sing it anyway for what was probably "the most glamour-laden [audience] she had ever sung for [up to that time]," including President Ford in the presidential box with Rose Kennedy as his guest.[29]

From the viewpoint of sharpening the focus of Special Olympics, the "Funny Lady" premiere improved upon that for "It's a Mad, Mad, Mad, Mad World" in two other ways. There was a central party the night before at the opulent Iranian Embassy—still in the era of the Shah—that simply cried out for media coverage. In addition to the presence of numerous Kennedys and of Streisand herself, the 350 guests included such inside-the-Beltway heavies as Secretary of the Treasury William Simon as well as showbiz types like Barbra's co-star James Caan; Dick

Cavett, who would host the special the following evening; and Barbra's boyfriend, hairdresser Jon Peters.[30]

The event at the Iranian Embassy was thus a media honeypot and attracted wide coverage. *Women's Wear Daily* quoted Cavett to the effect that, "Howard Cosell knocked an entire glass of wine onto the lady next to him and then blamed it on his wife."[31] This is the kind of information people like, and this time they were reading it in connection with mental retardation rather than cancer, heart disease, or any other of the mainline causes.

The "Funny Lady" special also improved upon previous efforts by prominently featuring mentally retarded people—to ABC's dismay. Visibly different individuals were shown to a national TV audience to be persons of accomplishment. In fact, Streisand was having an animated conversation on air with Marie Chillemi, age fourteen, and Tony Wright, age thirteen—both Special Olympics gold-medalists—when ABC pulled the plug, a voice from the wings calling, "Thank you, Barbra."[32]

The "Funny Lady" premiere had been such a huge success that a series of other premieres followed, the only modifications being that they were now labeled "presidential premieres," because the President or Vice President could be prevailed upon to attend. Some were premiered simultaneously in Washington and New York, to maximize the number of celebrities recruited. Thus on December 10, 1978, "Superman" was premiered in Washington, the following night in New York. Barbara Walters attended in Washington, declaring, "There's almost nothing I wouldn't do for Eunice and Sarge." A dinner dance was held at the Shrivers' estate Timberlawn (called "Timberland" in the *New York Times*), attended by the standard mix of showbiz types (Christopher Reeve who played Superman), politicians (the Kissingers), and clanspersons (Arnold Schwarzenegger dating the twenty-three-year-old Maria Shriver). There was more of the same in New York, and, later, in Boston and Chicago.[33]

The Special Olympics premiered "Superman II" in 1981, "Superman III" in 1983, and several other films as well. The family had found a vehicle that superbly profiled positive images of MR in the public eye.

But in all the annals of using cinema images to promote social causes, nothing trumps the success the Kennedys achieved with producer Stephen Spielberg's 1982 film "E.T. the Extra-Terrestrial" in raising public consciousness about mental retardation. Probably the most winning of the various images created by Spielberg, a cinematic genius then thirty-five, E.T. was a little creature from outer space who comforts a ten-year-old lad whose father has just walked out. E.T., desperately lonely himself, becomes the boy's best friend. "He's fat and he's not pretty," said Spielberg of his creation. "I really wanted E.T. to sneak up on you—not in the easy way of an F. A. O. Schwarz doll on the shelf. The story is the beauty of his character."[34]

Let's see, ugly outside, beautiful inside. Where have we heard that before? The parallel to the situation of the mentally retarded was breathtaking. Soon after the movie was released, Spielberg began getting letters from families of children with MR. The letters "related such astonishing stories," as Bobby Shriver summed up what Spielberg had told him, "that Spielberg was apparently alerted to the identification of E.T.'s spiritual qualities with the spiritual qualities of the retarded."[35]

Nor was the parallel lost on Eunice, either. In August 1982 she wrote Spielberg, "Today I saw your movie, 'E.T.' What an extraordinary achievement! It certainly appeals to the best in every person.

"An aspect of the film was deeply moving to me. You took the little creature from outer space—who is ugly, scary and physically awkward and who speaks fewer than 20 words during the 2-hour film—and made him into a marvelous hero. When he started to die, it broke nearly everyone's heart." Eunice said that the good in E.T. had lived on in the young boy. "This transformation, which you handled so beautifully, resembles the Christian concept of the good Lord living on in men."

Then Eunice posed a question to Spielberg. "I head a program called Special Olympics," she said, deferentially assuming that he'd never heard of it. Could Spielberg advise them on how to produce the next international Games? "You were able to take the little creature from outer space and move the hearts of millions of moviegoers. Couldn't you show the world through the International Special Olympics Games that mentally retarded individuals have the same indomitable spirit?"[36]

Spielberg expressed interest. In November 1982, Bobby Shriver went to see him. Could Spielberg advise them "on making the TV coverage of the Games [forthcoming in Baton Rouge in July 1983] exciting and appealing"? "How would you make the mentally retarded participants who are limited in intellect, who may lack beauty and who are not as skillful as regular Olympians, as lovable as E.T. is in your marvelous film?"[37]

Spielberg bit on the idea of making E.T. a "special friend" of the Special Olympics, in December 1983 authorizing his executives to explore ways of making this happen: a special costume so that E.T. could appear at state Special Olympics meets ("Chapter Games"); a special showing of the movie "E.T. the Extra-Terrestrial" at the forthcoming winter Games at Park City, Utah; and re-releasing the movie itself.[38]

From the correspondence it is evident that the more Spielberg thought about this link, the more enthusiastic he became. By the spring of 1984, as Bobby Shriver again saw him at the offices of Universal Studios, Spielberg was ready to create "a symbolic identification between E.T. and Special

Olympics," letting the little alien promote the cause of MR through a whole series of "public service spots, film trailers, a special electronic press kit, etc."[39] This was now big business. Just preparing such promotions would cost millions of dollars. Spielberg was ready to pay for the promotions as well. Bobby told his mother, "In my opinion, this opportunity represents potentially the most significant financial possibility to ever come into Special Olympics."[40] It had fallen into their laps because Spielberg had thought about forming his own foundation to help children, then discarded the idea as "too complicated."[41] Given that truly making a difference had required someone like Eunice Shriver to dedicate her life to it, one can understand the wisdom of Spielberg's decision. He would funnel his charitable activities toward the Special Olympics.

The Kennedys pushed ahead with the E.T. promotion in a number of areas: there might be a "Phone E.T. from Home" program involving AT&T, licensing the E.T. image to fast food companies, and hooking up with the "E.T. Cereal" that General Mills was introducing.[42] But of all these campaigns, none would reach the public more directly than a thirty-second TV spot featuring E.T. and Chuck Cross, a mentally retarded child in San Diego. Such spots, aired again and again, have the ability to reach into the public consciousness in a way that cereal boxes do not.

In July 1984, Eunice asked Richard O'Brien, secretary of the Special Olympics (and also a senior vice president of Dancer, Fitzgerald and Sample, a New York advertising agency), to help develop a spot "showing a warm relationship between E.T. and a Special Olympian."[43] The agency people all volunteered their time, and Spielberg paid for the production costs along with the McDonald's Corporation (of hamburger chain fame). In the commercial, the child was shown trying hard but failing to clear a high-jump bar while E.T. watched from behind a tree. As *New York Times* advertising columnist Philip Dougherty summed it up, "Watching the child's constant failure, a tear comes to the alien's eye about the same time the voice-over says, 'All they need is a little help from a friend.'" In a final scene at a Special Olympics meet, the boy clears the bar as E.T. cheers him on from the stands. "It's heart-tugging advertising at its best," said Dougherty.[44]

Released in May 1985, the spot was a tremendous hit. In October, Eunice told Joe Pytka, who had donated three days of his time directing the commercial, "More than 300 television stations in every state are running the spot. Their comments have been incredibly complimentary. They love it so much that most are broadcasting it with the McDonald's logo." The major networks and cable stations were also running it.[45]

The image of E.T. helping the mentally retarded retained its power across the years. The Special Olympics would borrow the film for various occasions, such as an awards luncheon, or a convention of the Independent Grocers' Alliance (IGA), one of the Special Olympics' major sponsors.[46] Eunice had wanted Spielberg to direct "A Very Special Christmas" that ABC aired in 1986, but he was too busy to do so.[47] When in 1988 Spielberg released "E.T. the Extra-Terrestrial" in videocassette form, it was with a Special Olympics tie-in. By April 1989, cassette sales had yielded a donation of a million dollars, with twenty-five cents per tape going to the Special Olympics.[48]

In retrospect, of all the ways in which Eunice and her allies attempted to improve the lot of the mentally retarded, none stirred popular consciousness more than the presidential premieres and the E.T. promotion. What NARC in the 1950s and the Ad Council in the 1960s had unsuccessfully attempted was achieved in the 1980s by the little alien.

Sharpening the Image

In 1968, when the Games began, Eunice Shriver was forty-seven. In 1990, when she stepped down as chairman of the board of the Special Olympics, she was sixty-nine. Although she had been involved in other matters relating to MR in the 1970s and 1980s, her main interest over those years had been the Games. She knew exactly the image of the mentally retarded that she wanted the Games to project, and the image that MR athletes had of themselves that she wanted to reinforce. The question was, how to sharpen these images, how to hone events so they would project overwhelmingly the messages of joy and hope. She spent much effort on this.

These matters may strike readers as trivial. Yet the devil is often in the details, and success lay in getting them right. Running a multimillion dollar organization, she agonized endlessly about things like chalk lines. She had, for example, attended the New Hampshire state Games in 1986. "I know it is very difficult to run games when the weather is bad," she told the state director later, but there had been a problem with the softball throw. "As you will remember at the softball throw, held outside, the chalk line disappeared in the rain and when the athletes were ready to throw there was no clear line for them to stand on." Also there weren't enough signs. People had come up to her asking for directions, and Eunice couldn't find the signs to direct them. "I know all of this is more difficult in the rain."[49]

A person of lesser energy would have crumbled at the onslaught of detail, for staging these events was an immense effort. Take the example of ribbons. The winners of each "heat," or event, must have ribbons, but because they take these ribbons back home with them and cherish them, the ribbons must be exactly right. The ribbons at South Bend had been "fouled up," as director Bill Bankhead admitted. Eunice noted that they didn't have the words "Kennedy Foundation" on the card on the back. Also, they were too small and "not the quality we have come to expect at International Games." The supplier was replacing them free of charge and the head office would send replacement ribbons with a note to all ribbon winners. "I cannot allow items of this importance to slip through the cracks," Bankhead confessed manfully.[50]

The ribbons were in fact important because they affected the image that the Games transmitted to the kids. The matter of "even heats" similarly preoccupied Eunice. Events were staged on the basis of contestants' ability so that no child would be humiliated running a distant last behind much abler competitors. Many of the contestants were physically quite handicapped, and also sometimes not inclined to focus on the competitive aspects of the event—for example, stopping in the middle of the race to help a fallen teammate. Therefore, making the proper ability groupings was of capital importance.

"Heats very uneven," Eunice noted with dismay of the state Games in South Carolina in 1978. A girl came in at fourteen minutes for a mile run. "She stopped three times. Severely handicapped. Cannot understand how she was ever put in mile run. Had to be urged on. Should not there be some minimum speed before someone goes in a mile run?" Eunice deplored that the local officials had not understood "our ideas about divisions—doing the lowest children first and have a cut-off time regardless—or eliminating children when their time is grossly wrong."[51] In 1980, she berated the state directors at a meeting at Smugglers' Notch, Vermont, saying that the Special Olympics wanted its athletes to improve and develop their skills, yet so many "have had *no* training or so little training that they are not prepared for their events. I have seen swimmers who could not swim even the length of a pool. How humiliated and discouraged they must be. How humiliated and discouraged their parents must be."[52] That was the toned-down message for public consumption. In private Eunice was even more emphatic: "I have been to races this year and I thought I was back in 1968! Don't we understand that when children lose they are saddened? That when they run last if they are not saddened then they have lost hope, and that is the worst."[53]

Why was this so important? Why not just let them paddle about and pat them on the head? It was crucial, in Eunice's overall scheme, for these kids to develop pride in themselves at the skills they had so courageously acquired. "We must not have *any* event in which Special Olympians, no matter how severely handicapped, are not demonstrating *some* skill acquired through training."[54]

How else to sharpen the Olympians' image? The various ceremonies of the Special Olympics were central in image-projecting. "We have never had a satisfactory Victory Dance at an International Games," executive director Montague informed Bankhead in 1983, Eunice having found the dance at Baton Rouge to be "like a high school prom." A proper Victory Dance should have "attractive lights on the tables. Votive light candles are nice."

There should be a Master of Ceremonies at a Victory Dance. "Think of ways to introduce Special Olympians from different groups to one another. Example: Boys form in circle outside circle of girls. Master of Ceremonies says, 'All boys go to the right. . . .'" And so on.[55] These details sound prosaic enough, until one recalls that these were kids who until recently had been smearing the walls in institutions with excrement. None of them had ever attended a Victory Dance of any kind. The votive candles and a band that played "a variety of music" would be like Woodstock to them.

Aware that awards ceremonies had both the capacity for great tedium and great joy on the recipients' part, Eunice fiddled endlessly with their format. She found the ceremonies at all the state Games she had attended in 1988 "uninspiring." Medal winners were rushed through ceremonies and then whisked off. "I ask you, is this the type of award ceremony befitting an Olympian? I think you will agree, it is not!"

What would befit an Olympian?

- Make sure there's a Special Olympics banner as a backdrop.
- "Have volunteers instruct all athletes in awards staging—what to do on the awards stand so that athletes are not jumping down before the ceremony is completed." (One can only imagine some of the nightmarish ceremonies Eunice must have witnessed.)
- "Play some sort of Olympic fanfare music just before the athletes are given awards." This would draw everyone's attention "and really adds to the ceremony."[56]

As for the opening ceremonies, often empty "except for a few parents," Eunice had a Kennedy-style solution: bring in some "first-class entertainment." In New Jersey, thousands attended when the band "Blood, Sweat and Tears" played at the opening.[57]

This attentiveness to detail paid off. The athletes were made to feel good about themselves, and the parents were tearful with pleasure and relief. In girls' figure skating, for example, it's important to have on hand hairdressers and makeup artists for the elaborate self-presentations of the contestants. As one grateful parent from Arizona wrote in 1989, "Our daughter, Holly, competed in the recent Winter Games. It was a wonderful time for our whole family. . . .

"One of the nicest things for me," said Holly's mother, "was the hair-dressers and make-up artists for the figure skaters. That had been a big concern of mine—that Holly might not look her best with me not being with her to help with hair and make-up. That was a matter of great importance to me, and whoever handled that area should be commended. Holly looked so pretty every day, and I was so proud of her."[58]

So it was not in vain that Eunice Shriver spent so much time sharpening the images of the Olympians.

In the Eyes of Others

Both Kennedys and people with MR have done well in the story of mental retardation. Each has lent luster to the other. The Shrivers became celebrated as the "gurus of the games,"[59] a plus in an era when the tabloid press hummed with Kennedy gossip. But the family had something to offer in exchange. As Herb Kramer, the publicist for the Kennedy Foundation, once bragged of the success of the Special Olympics, "We have something nobody else has. . . . We have the association with the most glamorous, controversial, but in a way, well known, famous family of our century, and I don't know if, without this affiliation Special Olympics could have achieved the quick standing and status they have."[60]

Eunice the drill sergeant dispatched her family about the country on behalf of the Special Olympics. In 1979, Bobby Shriver was instructed to take his fifteen-year-old brother Mark to state Games in Texas, Kentucky, and West Virginia. Meanwhile, Timothy Shriver was to drag the fourteen-year-old Anthony to the Florida games.[61] On other occasions, Maria Shriver would try to get NBC to run Special Olympics clips.[62] Arnold Schwarzenegger created a ten-hour training curriculum for the Special Olympians.[63] Jackie Onassis periodically loaned Eunice her blue-and-white tablecloths for events such as Special Olympics sports luncheons. ("Anything possible that can be done to improve the dining room at the UN," said Eunice, "is a major contribution to the luncheon."[64]) The Kennedys have worked hard at Special Olympics and are entitled to whatever image-bolstering may have come their way.

Yet the essential point is not that the Special Olympics has improved the image of the Kennedys, but rather of the mentally retarded. The family's commitment to change did make a difference. Special Olympics has transformed many young lives—lives that in an earlier generation would have been consigned to barrenness in some high-walled backyard or MR institution.

The image of mentally retarded children in the eyes of their parents and families has been raised as well. While virtually no parents attended the Chicago Special Olympics in 1968, the stands would later be jammed with families who were proud of their children and were glad to be raising them at home. For example, when Jimmy, son of former Dodger pitcher Carl Erskine, finished his race in the Los Angeles Games in 1975, Erskine was reported as weeping so hard he could scarcely take Jimmy's picture. Erskine said, "There is no way of describing the satisfaction of seeing Jimmy just finish the race."[65] A sample of parents interviewed in 1978 strongly agreed that the Special Olympics constituted "one of the finest experiences the child has had."[66] Sixty-five percent of forty parents polled at random in 1993 had gone beyond being spectators to serving as "coaches, fundraisers, chaperones, and [in] other volunteer positions."[67] This stands in stark contrast to the familial uninvolvement of yore.

A letter from the mother of Jeffrey M. to Eunice Shriver perhaps best describes how the Special Olympics affects a family's image of their MR child. In 1987, Mrs. M. and her nonretarded son Rich took Jeffrey, a gold medalist in the state Games, to the International Games at South Bend. Mrs. M. adored the Special Olympics. She would look at her son and say, "Jeff, I love you. If it wasn't for you, Rich and I could never have attended . . . these Olympics." When they got home, Mrs. M. put together three scrapbooks of memories—"two of mementoes and one 100 page photo album of our trip." Moreover Jeffrey's green ribbon "is framed and proudly displayed in our living room along with roses and streamers that each athlete received. We look at them all often."[68]

Success at sports also buffed up the images of the MR athletes in the eyes of their classmates at school. Tom Songster, who in the early 1970s was the director of the Indiana State Games (and later the Kennedy Foundation's sports director), remembered the forty-six children with MR from an Indianapolis inner-city school whom a dedicated teacher brought to the state Games in Terre Haute. "As luck would have it, two of her children happened to be in the first race of the 50-yard dash. There were those forty-four other kids standing there watching those two run the first race of the games for them, and the two kids came in first and second. Well, the enthusiasm in that group, from that time on, was unbelievable. On Monday morning, back at school, they were the honored guests at a special school assembly. They were no longer mentally retarded kids but the winners at Special Olympics."[69] In 1989, Eunice was thrilled to learn that three high schools in Milwaukee had started giving Special Olympians athletic letters. "Think what it must mean to the special student who receives a school athletic letter after long hours of training and competition!" She told the Games executives that it wasn't just Milwaukee: 165 schools across the country were now awarding such letters.[70]

Thus the image of mental retardation in the eyes of the community changed. People became accepting of these young athletes—of these mentally retarded citizens in general—whose often distinctive appearances had once consigned them to the dustbin. In 1990, Christi Todd, of Shadow Mountain High School in Paradise Valley, Arizona, became "the first Special Olympian in the nation to give a high school commencement address." She told the graduating class, "Thank you for making me feel at home here. . . . I challenge each of you to strive for the best and make a difference in your life and in the lives of others."[71]

Think what a long way people with MR have come. Not so long ago labeled merely "morons," "imbeciles," and "idiots," and cast out to the margins of social life, by the end of the twentieth century they were giving high school commencement addresses and going off to work, as Christi did at the local "ABCO market near her home." This is a wonderful story, involving many dedicated people. And if mentioning the Kennedy name helps us remember it, so much the better.

Dynasty

The story of Eunice Shriver is also the story of the Kennedy dynasty, an imperial American family conscious of roots going far back in time and intent upon projecting its influence far into the future. The family crystallized its public presence in the Kennedy Foundation. One might think that the real purpose of such a foundation would be to protect and enhance the family name. No doubt some of the Kennedy brothers and sisters believed this. But Eunice Shriver did not.

For her, the purpose of the Kennedy Foundation—and of the exalted position the Kennedys had gained in American public life—was not family interest but public service. For Eunice that meant the cause of mental retardation. It's impossible to understand Eunice Shriver without grasping that for her, being a Kennedy, whatever that means, was secondary. Her chief loyalty was to this cause that her father had chosen and that she had initially embraced in an effort to convince him that she was every bit a match for her brothers.

Nowhere in Eunice Shriver's voluminous papers have I encountered concerns about "the family image" or "the family name." Although she could not have been indifferent to the misadventures in which her male relatives entangled the family name over the years, there is no evidence that she saw the Kennedy Foundation as somehow putting a good front on a backdrop of recklessness and high-living. If anything, later in life she seems to have washed her hands of much of the Kennedy brood, deciding that she would be buried in the Shriver family plot in a cemetery in Maryland rather than in the Kennedy plot in the Holyhood Cemetery in Brookline, Massachusetts.[1]

Eunice dedicated herself to the cause of mental retardation with the single-mindedness of a medieval saint. A former executive director of the foundation declared, "It was extremely exhausting to work for the Shrivers. You were on call twenty-four hours a day seven days a week. That's the way they work. I would get calls at two a.m. from Mrs. Shriver who would say, 'John, did I get you up?'

"I would lie and say, 'No, no, I was just sitting here thinking of going to bed.' Kennedys never rest. Nobody around them rests."[2]

This manic energy was a not sign of illness but of total earnestness. In politicians, the projection of earnestness plays well with voters. In Eunice Shriver it ran throughout her private life, for example, through her communications with her children. One summer her son Anthony, age fifteen, was staying on a ranch out west. Some mothers might have cautioned their boys about rattlesnakes or those chilly mountain evenings. Not Eunice. One letter began, "Dear Anthony, I am so thrilled that you are getting a picture of the west. It is so different from the east where you have lived. How people talk and dress . . . [she gave further examples of the difference]. It makes the west like a completely different country from the east.

"I have enclosed a little note pad for you. I hope you are keeping a journal. Maybe you could write about the differences between children in the east and west. You could answer some of the questions that I mentioned." She concluded the letter, "Learn all you can, see all you can. You may never get another chance like this. Love." (The office copy was unsigned; it had been typed by a secretary.)[3]

Four days later, mother wrote to son again. After a preliminary injunction to do "some reading," Eunice launched into the subject of Indians. "Do you ever see any Indians out there. I am very much interested in Indians. . . . Not only because all my brothers worked hard to put more money into reservations [via legislation], but Dad started many programs on reservations. . . . As you know, Indians have the highest infant death rate in America—four times White babies, and twice Black babies. They die younger, they commit more suicide. . . ." Further statistics followed. The letter concluded by mentioning the rather dismal news about Anthony's report card, which had just arrived.[4]

What is striking in such letters from Eunice to her sons is not the note of impersonality but of total and utter seriousness. The Shriver children were not for one moment to forget that they were to dedicate themselves to causes, to public service. A letter to Bobby, Maria, and Timmy in 1981 began, without further ado, "Enclosed is an excellent speech on violence which I heard Teddy give this morning." Eunice asked her children to put themselves in their uncle's shoes. What would they do in his place?

Should Ted give an anti-gun speech at the risk of arousing the gun control lobby? "If you do this, you must remember that if you decide to run for president again in four years, the western states will be even angrier. The gun control lobby is very strong and Reagan is against gun control.

"What is your political judgment?" Signed, "Mother."

Mark Shriver later said of the experience of growing up in this household that his mother and father had never exerted any "overt pressure" to go into public service but had placed a "heavy emphasis upon contributing."[5] In this relentless pressure to be mindful of public problems, Eunice wanted her children not foremost to be proud of "being Kennedys" but to realize that they were destined to contribute to the nation's public welfare, that making a difference was the point of the family's privileged status.

Even as the Kennedy family lay embattled in politics, Eunice urged upon her children that making a difference, not family loyalty, was the primary desideratum. As Ted was trying to decide in 1980 whether to contest the Democratic nomination, Eunice telegraphed Bobby Shriver:

> Teddy's career as politician at absolute crucial stage next two weeks. Friends prove their friendship by helping now. Everybody making sacrifices. Some of time, others money, jobs, careers, even family. Teddy's record of helping Dad [Sarge] politically is inadequate but in other ways very good. Letter explains. Consider all this in planning your vacation. One year from now I don't want you to look back and say, "I wish I had done something at the crucial period." Churchill said, "These are the years—nineteen to twenty-six." You can change things! Love, Mother.[6]

In this most critical moment of her brother Ted's political life, Eunice's message to her children was not to help their uncle become President, but the more altruistic message that they could make a difference.

Eunice's decision to make a difference in MR, as opposed to maintaining clan loyalty, appeared most starkly in a family revolt that took place against her rule of the Kennedy Foundation. The origin of this revolt was her insistence, in a crisis that arose in the fall of 1983, that back in 1977 the entire family had approved a decision to back mental retardation as the exclusive Kennedy cause. Eunice claimed that in 1977 all four siblings, the "trustees" of the foundation—herself, Ted, Jean, and Pat—had agreed that the Kennedy Foundation was to spend $2.3 million on MR annually, regardless of whatever other commitments the family might want to make.[7] (This was close to, if not in excess of, the foundation's annual income in the 1980s.)

But the other siblings favored a number of family-related causes having nothing to do with mental retardation. For example, over the years the

John F. Kennedy Library had continually requested support. While Ted and the two other sisters wished to provide the needed money, Eunice herself became increasingly exasperated at these incursions into funds she wanted to spend on MR.

At this meeting in 1977 at the Cape, the three other siblings rather tentatively accepted Eunice's proposal that non-MR projects such as the Kennedy Library would be supported by taking money from the foundation's endowment rather than from its annual income. After this provisional accord, Eunice dashed from the Smiths' house, where the meeting was taking place, over to Rose's house to confer with her mother. "She [Rose] reaffirmed very strongly that she felt that the Foundation had been started for the retarded and that the money should be spent for that purpose and not for other purposes. I spent considerable time with her, explaining what we were trying to do [depleting the endowment], and how we would be able to continue to work for the mentally retarded under this arrangement. She did not seem convinced. I left and returned to the Smiths' house and we reached an agreement that $2.3 million would continue to be spent [from annual income] for the mentally retarded."

The grumbling first heard in 1977 became louder as time went on. Sarge's and Eunice's enthusiasm for bioethics, especially for supporting the Kennedy Institute of Ethics—founded in 1971 at Georgetown University as the last of the family's research institutes—became a particular bone of contention. The original idea had been that the ethics institute would do research on ethical questions relating to MR. But the bioethicists and philosophers assembled there during the 1970s had evidenced virtually no interest in MR, to the growing consternation of the family and the foundation's advisers.[8] Finally in November 1981, Jean Kennedy Smith wrote to Sarge (not to Eunice): "I have no doubt that the Institute is doing an outstanding job. My concern is whether the Trustees [of the Foundation, meaning herself, Pat, and Ted] given their own involvements with various family activities are as enthusiastic as you are and wish to continue funding the Institute at present level.

"As you know, the Joseph P. Kennedy, Jr. Foundation is relatively a small Foundation and a sizeable amount of money is going to the Institute. I think at the next meeting the Trustees should reassess the direction of the Foundation for the next few years."[9]

Therewith the first sparks of revolt were struck, but against the Kennedy Institute at Georgetown and not against the cause of MR as such. Eunice and Sarge cooled down the angry relatives and hit the brakes on funding for bioethics.

Eunice may have overplayed her hand at this point. She was so keen to press ahead with MR that in September 1983, as it looked as though the foundation's endowment would not produce the needed $2.3 million, she again suggested dipping into capital. We can't stop now, she apostrophized her ring of loyalists, including Sarge, Bob Cooke, General Montague, and Bobby Shriver. "At the present time, the Kennedy Foundation is engaged in a number of extremely important projects. . . . Even if during the first two or three years we had to go down to $16 million [the endowment, or corpus, was then $18 million], that is still a substantial amount to have in the Foundation for people to work with."[10]

Dipping into the corpus is seen in the foundation world generally as something to be avoided if one wishes a foundation to remain effective. Eunice's proposal seems finally to have exhausted the patience of the other members of the family.

Although her brother and sisters had never before challenged any of Eunice's decisions,[11] this time discontent flared into open revolt. Ted, Pat, and Jean somehow made their unhappiness known to Eunice, proposing projects of their own that would have involved dipping into capital, such as restoration work on the family home in Hyannisport.[12]

This kind of a raid on the endowment was entirely unacceptable to Eunice. Reminding her relatives of the decisions taken six years earlier, she pointed out, "Whenever assets of the Foundation are siphoned off for other purposes, even laudable family purposes, such grants reduce the capacity of the Foundation to fulfill its primary function."[13]

So there it was in black and white: in Eunice's view, the cause of MR came before family. The single-mindedness of her position seems to have exasperated her brother and sisters. We can only speculate about who refused to talk to whom. We know only that it was Bobby Shriver and not Sarge who early in October 1983 went to see Ted for a powwow. They agreed that the trustees—Eunice, Ted, Pat, and Jean—would have a special meeting later that month.[14]

One contentious issue concerned the exact intentions of Joseph P. Kennedy, Sr. toward the MR cause. At the forthcoming meeting, as Bobby told his mother, Sarge was to produce evidence backing Sarge's and Eunice's contention about "J. P. Kennedy's assent to the Kennedy Foundation's being focused exclusively on mental retardation issues."[15]

The financier's will had stipulated merely that his fortune go to the Kennedy Foundation "to fulfill its dedicated purpose."[16] It is unknown what additional evidence Sarge had.

At the meeting, the family was also to consider the fate of other family foundations beset by squabbling among the successor generations, such as the Mellon Foundation. (The foundation world generally considers fighting among the heirs of a founder to be a great source of instability.)

Apparently all the data that Ted and Bobby Shriver considered relevant to the meeting couldn't be gathered in the next several weeks, and the special meeting was adjourned to April 1984.

Eunice couldn't wait until April. Already in December 1983, she was peppering her siblings with arguments about why the foundation should stay the course on MR. "Mental retardation is still, by far, the largest disability affecting children worldwide." She recited familiar statistics about the gravity of the problem.

"Despite these facts, no other Foundation or private agency contributes in any significant way to meeting the problems of mentally retarded children and adults." For this reason, she emphatically urged no change. "The objectives of the Joseph P. Kennedy, Jr. Foundation for the next 10 years should remain fixed as they have been for the past twenty years."

She concluded on a rather interesting note. Forgetting completely the origins of the Kennedy Foundation in the postwar hurly-burly of recycling profits from the Merchandise Mart and of supporting her brother Jack's political campaigns, she said, "These proposals for the Foundation over the next 10 years honor a commitment made to mentally retarded individuals when the Foundation was established."[17] Either Eunice had forgotten the early history, or she assumed that her siblings had forgotten it (or didn't know it in the first place). What she really meant was that her proposals for the future honored the commitment that she herself made when she and Sarge took over in 1960.

In January 1984, Eunice's brother and sisters responded to her letter with an ultimatum, telling her there must be changes in the way the foundation was run. "Our first and principal conclusion is that the Foundation should be a family enterprise and support all of the areas of charitable interest held by family members, with a special emphasis on mental retardation."[18] That was it: "special emphasis" on MR but nothing more.

What other causes should the Kennedy Foundation be supporting? The rebellious siblings would accept any others that "bear the Kennedy name and have family members on their boards." That meant the Kennedy Library in Boston, the memorial established for Bobby Kennedy (which was chronically in financial trouble), and the Kennedy Center in Washington. The siblings also plumped for a special archive for the family's papers, which they deemed mismanaged at the Kennedy Library: "They [the papers] have not been carefully controlled nor exploited due to the lack of family control over that institution."[19]

Thus a perspective was being forced upon Eunice that she had strenuously resisted all her life: letting dynastic considerations take precedence over altruistic ones. Her brother and sisters wanted foundation money for the purpose of safeguarding the family's image, for example, to keep out preying historians, who had been receiving access to papers at the Kennedy Library too easily for the family's comfort. (The disaster in 1992 surrounding historian Nigel Hamilton's treatment of their father confirmed their fears.[20])

The siblings further demanded that the corpus not be violated, that an investment adviser be appointed, and that "long term planning" be implemented, which they deemed hitherto "nonexistent" for the foundation. It may be that the siblings also resented their sister's monopolizing of the charity limelight, while their own efforts (such as Jean's Very Special Arts) had not enjoyed the same public profile,[21] or because (as in the senator's case), his sister's identification with the foundation left the media free to focus upon "Bad-Ted" stories. In any event they had had enough of what they perceived to be Eunice's obsession with mental retardation: "Because it has always been the policy of the family to generally limit the Foundation to funding mental retardation programs, the family's other efforts have suffered for it."

The four surviving children of Joe Senior confronted one another on April 9, 1984, at Ted's house on Chain Bridge Road in McLean, Virginia. Sarge, Bobby Shriver, Bob Cooke, and the family's financial adviser Joe Hakim were also in attendance. The agenda included all the non-MR projects for which the rival siblings had been pressing, such as restoration of Rose's house and a repository for their father's papers.[22]

But there was one other point as well. In their protest letter of January 1984, the mutinous siblings had also mentioned the problem of "the next generation." Concerned for the future, Ted, Jean and Pat had been thinking about how the grandchildren of Joe Kennedy could be brought into the family tradition of charity. "If one believes in charity and family, the role of the grandchildren should be part of any long term strategy and mission," they urged upon Eunice.[23]

Indeed they had reason to be concerned about the wild behavior of some of the grandchildren, for five months later Bobby Kennedy's son David would be found dead of a drug overdose in a Palm Beach hotel, and in the years ahead, in 1997, Bobby's son Michael would die in a skiing accident. In July 1999, John F. Kennedy, Jr. would perish along with his wife and sister-in-law in a reckless night-flight attempt over water.[24]

Eunice herself had not been unmindful of the problem of the "third generation." Already in September 1983 she had told her inner circle, "It is, of course, enormously beneficial to have some people in the family active in the field of mental retardation. Hopefully, the grandchildren will take an interest, but that will take 5–10 years to develop."[25]

We do not know what happened at this April 9 meeting at Ted's house, but apparently an agreement was reached: the family foundation would continue to focus upon MR if in return the twenty-nine grandchildren were brought into the picture, not five to ten years from now, but immediately. In time, then, the grandchildren would make their own decision about the Kennedy Foundation's charitable course. From that meeting in April 1984 on, Eunice made a concerted effort to get someone other than her own children—her numerous nieces and nephews—to pick up the torch of Camelot.

Did she succeed? Did the grandchildren rise to the challenge of the grand cause of mental retardation that their grandfather had begun, or to any grand cause? That remains to be seen. Eunice Shriver's ironclad dedication to public service may well have been a peculiar twist in her own personality, reinforced by her husband Sarge, rather than a familial tradition capable of being passed from generation to generation.

It had been the famous uncle, John F. Kennedy, who had tried to make the family name synonymous in the public eye with disinterested service. Of the nine children of Joseph P. Kennedy, it had been Eunice who had tried hardest in private to make that image a reality. In her metallic Boston accent she urged those around her forward, unremittingly, unceasingly, telling the weary executives of the Special Olympics at a meeting at Smugglers' Notch, just before herself collapsing of fatigue, "Let us redouble our efforts to make certain that 'the work still goes on, the cause endures, the hope still lives, and the dream shall never die.'"[26]

Those were the words of her brother John F. Kennedy.

Postscript

This story is a bit like a triangle. One angle is the history of the Kennedy family, already hugely investigated yet still mysterious. Another angle is the story of the children themselves with mental retardation, a story by and large so sad that few investigators save those with afflicted family members have the courage to take it on. The final angle, one little explored in the current book but of great importance, is the history of the parents' movement, because the parents and their organizations were instrumental in several key aspects such as the move to deinstitutionalize children with MR beginning in the 1970s. No comprehensive picture will emerge of the whole unless all three angles are studied.

The Kennedy family has been highly secretive about its record, some might argue with good cause given the shabby treatment the Kennedys have received at the hands of "gotcha" journalists whose main interest is sniffing out sexual scandal involving the male members. The family has been burned several times by writers who claimed blue-eyed to have the best of intentions and then savagely put the boots to their prey. As a result, key collections of papers, such as those of Joseph P. Kennedy, Sr., in the John F. Kennedy Presidential Library in Boston have been difficult to access. The papers of Senator Edward Kennedy will some day be a scholarly goldmine. One hopes the family might become more forthcoming as the Kennedy scholars themselves become more professional. This book relied heavily, of course, on the Kennedy papers in the Presidential Library and those held by the Joseph P. Kennedy, Jr. Foundation in Washington, D.C.

Of the many books about the Kennedys, few shed much light on the activities of the Kennedy women or the family's behind-the-scenes charitable activities. A must read is Laurence Leamer's *The Kennedy Women: The Saga of an American Family* (New York: Villard, 1994), which gives a relatively sympathetic picture of Eunice Kennedy Shriver. The several biographies of Joe Senior are mainly hatchet jobs. Ted Kennedy has yet to find a knowledgeable biographer.

The story of mental retardation itself is probably hardest to put together. It really has two sides: efforts to relieve it, centering on the activities of the professionals, and the story of the children and adults themselves with MR. Probably the best place to begin the professionals' story is R. C. Scheerenberger, *A History of Mental Retardation* (Baltimore: Brookes, 1983), now somewhat dated. Among current historians writing about MR, the most comprehensive introduction is David Wright and Anne Digby, eds., *From Idiocy to Mental Deficiency: Historical Perspectives on People with Learning Disabilities* (New York: Routledge, 1996). For indispensable background reading, see Edward Berkowitz, *Disabled Policy: America's Programs for the Handicapped* (New York: Cambridge University Press, 1987) and *America's Welfare State: from Roosevelt to Reagan* (Baltimore: Johns Hopkins University Press, 1991).

As for individuals with MR themselves, those wishing a good introduction to the condition should consult Mark L. Batshaw and Yvonne M. Perret, *Children with Disabilities: A Medical Primer,* 3d ed. (Baltimore: Brookes, 1992). The story of children with MR who were institutionalized may be reconstituted from the records of MR institutions, many of whose case files have been preserved.

A fundamental aspect of the MR story is the parents' movement, since ultimately very little happened to improve conditions for MR children without the punch of the mobilized parents. The papers of individuals involved with the movement—such as Elizabeth Boggs or Congressman John Fogarty (the latter in the Fogarty Archives, Providence College, Providence, Rhode Island)—represent an important resource. (I consulted Boggs's papers at her home in New Jersey. Since her death they have remained in limbo.) The Arc: A National Organization on Mental Retardation has its archives at the national headquarters in Arlington, Texas. Of printed material, the newspaper *Children Limited,* published by the National Association for Retarded Children (later Citizens) is essential yet difficult to come by. There are also local histories such as Larry A. Jones and Phyllis A. Barnes, *Doing Justice: Fifty Years of Parent Advocacy in Mental Retardation* (Olympia, Wash.: Association for Retarded Citizens of Washington, 1987).

The story of MR remains yet so untold that future researchers will simply have to hack it out of the rock face. With the exception of the works mentioned in the first note for chapter 1, almost no preparatory scholarship exists in this area. The field represents a great and exciting challenge.

Notes

Abbreviations

Individuals

EKS   Eunice Kennedy Shriver
EMK   Edward Moore ("Ted") Kennedy
JFK   John Fitzgerald Kennedy, Sr.
JPK   Joseph Patrick ("Joe") Kennedy, Sr.
RSS   Robert Sargent ("Sarge") Shriver, Jr.

Journals and newspapers

AJMD   *American Journal on Mental Deficiency*
AJMR   *American Journal on Mental Retardation*
CQA   *Congressional Quarterly Almanac*
CQWR   *Congressional Quarterly Weekly Report*
NYT   *New York Times*
WP   *Washington Post*

Organizations

HEW   Department of Health, Education and Welfare
NARC   National Association for Retarded Children (later "Citizens")
PCMR   President's Committee on Mental Retardation
PPMR   President's Panel on Mental Retardation

Archives

Boggs private archive   The papers of Elizabeth M. Boggs were at her home in
   Hampton, New Jersey, at the time that I used them.
Cohen Papers   Wilbur C. Cohen Papers, State Historical Society of Wisconsin,
   Madison, Wisconsin
Fogarty Papers   John E. Fogarty Collection, Archives, Phillips Memorial Library,
   Providence College, Providence, Rhode Island

KF   Joseph P. Kennedy, Jr. Foundation in Washington, D.C.
KL   John F. Kennedy Presidential Library, in Boston

Chapter One

1. Robert B. Edgerton, *The Cloak of Competence: Stigma in the Lives of the Mentally Retarded* (Berkeley: University of California Press, 1967), p. 207. Little has been written on the history of MR. The most useful previous works are Steven Noll, *Feeble-Minded in Our Midst: Institutions for the Mentally Retarded in the South, 1900–1940* (Chapel Hill: University of North Carolina Press, 1995); Harvey G. Simmons, *From Asylum to Welfare* (a history of MR in Ontario, Canada) (Toronto: National Institute on Mental Retardation, 1982); James W. Trent, Jr., *Inventing the Feeble Mind: A History of Mental Retardation in the United States* (Berkeley: University of California Press, 1994); Peter L. Tyor and Leland V. Bell, *Caring for the Retarded in America: A History* (Westport, Conn.: Greenwood Press, 1984); David Wright and Anne Digby, *From Idiocy to Mental Deficiency: Historical Perspectives on People with Learning Disabilities* (London: Routledge, 1996). As indispensable background reading, see Edward Berkowitz, *Disabled Policy: America's Programs for the Handicapped* (New York: Cambridge University Press, 1987); Edward Berkowitz, *America's Welfare State: From Roosevelt to Reagan* (Baltimore: Johns Hopkins University Press, 1991).

2. For an introduction see Mark L. Batshaw and Yvonne M. Perret, eds., *Children with Disabilities: A Medical Primer,* 3d ed. (Baltimore: Brookes, 1992), "Normal and Abnormal Development," pp. 259–89.

3. EKS, "Hope for Retarded Children," *Saturday Evening Post,* Sept. 22, 1962, pp. 71–74, esp. p. 72.

4. Pearl S. Buck, *The Child Who Never Grew* (New York: Day, 1950), p. 27. "I would have welcomed death for my child and would still welcome it." On the bitterness of Pearl Buck's experience with her daughter Carol see Peter Conn, *Pearl S. Buck: A Cultural Biography* (Cambridge, U.K.: Cambridge University Press, 1996), pp. 106–07 and passim.

5. Crozet Duplantier, "My Son Is Retarded," *New Orleans States-Item,* Nov. 19, 1963.

6. John N. and Nellie Enders Carver, *The Family of the Retarded Child* (Syracuse: Syracuse University Division of Special Education, 1972), p. 37. The doctor was not named, but on the basis of internal evidence it must have been Powers.

7. Ibid., p. 44.

8. Buck, *Child Who Never Grew,* p. 19.

9. Ibid., p. 8.

10. Wolf Wolfensberger, address to the Kentucky chapter of The Arc, Louisville, Apr. 24, 1993. This day-long talk was adumbrated by Wolfensberger's article, "Reflections on a Lifetime in Human Services and Mental Retardation," *Mental Retardation* 29 (1991), pp. 1–15. A videotape of the address is available from the Kentucky chapter of The Arc.

11. James R. Dudley, *Living with Stigma: The Plight of the People Who We Label Mentally Retarded* (Springfield, Ill.: Charles C. Thomas, 1983), p. 7.

12. Fogarty papers, FL-87-1-6, folder 4. Mr. G. to John E. Fogarty, July 2, 1961.

13. Carver, *Family of the Retarded Child*, p. 77.

14. EKS, "Address to the National Society for Handicapped Children," Mansion House, London, England, July 15, 1964, p. 1.

15. NARC, "Decade of Decision: An Evaluation Report . . . for the 1960 White House Conference on Children and Youth," Oct. 1959, p. 15. I am grateful to Elizabeth Boggs for showing me a copy of this document.

16. Dale Evans Rogers, *Angel Unaware* (n.p.: Revell, 1953), p. 20. The baby died of mumps encephalitis at the age of two. In the book, the child itself "tells" the story as though looking down from heaven.

17. Charlotte Green Schwartz, "Strategies and Tactics of Mothers of Mentally Retarded Children for Dealing with the Medical Care System," in Norman R. Bernstein, ed., *Diminished People: Problems and Care of the Mentally Retarded* (Boston: Little Brown, 1970), pp. 73–105, quote p. 93.

18. Janet M. Bennett, "Company, Halt!" in Ann P. Turnbull and H. Rutherford Turnbull, eds., *Parents Speak Out: Growing with a Handicapped Child* (Columbus, Ohio: Merrill, 1979), pp. 151f, quote pp. 158–59. Although the anecdote is undated, the author's use of "mongoloid" situates it sometime before the 1960s, when the term went out of style.

19. [Marian Wright Edelman, ed.], Children's Defense Fund, *Children Out of School in America* (Washington, D.C.: CDF, Oct. 1974), p. 93.

20. "Significant number" is based on Elizabeth Boggs's calculations, communicated in an internal document to Gunnar Dybwad, executive director of NARC, July 23, 1957. Boggs private archive.

21. "For Segregating Idiots: Expert Urges Prompt Committal to Institution," *NYT*, May 31, 1947, p. 13.

22. Dale Evans Rogers, *Angel Unaware*, p. 19.

23. John P. Frank, *My Son's Story* (New York: Knopf, 1952), p. 92.

24. J. B. Murray and Emily Murray, *And Say What He Is: The Life of a Special Child* (Cambridge, Mass.: MIT Press, 1975), pp. 22, 56, 61.

25. Gunnar Dybwad, interview of Aug. 16, 1993.

26. RSS, interview of Feb. 19, 1992.

27. Robert Cooke, present at Shriver interview of Feb. 19, 1992.

28. Private communication of Cooke to author, Oct. 18, 1994.

29. Frank, *My Son's Story*, pp. 68–69.

30. George S. Stevenson, "Where and Whither in Mental Deficiency," *AJMD* 52 (1947), pp. 43–47, quote p. 45.

31. Josiah Macy, Jr. Foundation, *New Directions for Mentally Retarded Children* (New York: Macy Foundation, 1956), p. 126.

32. Stanley S. Herr, *Rights and Advocacy for Retarded People* (Lexington, Mass.: Lexington Books, 1983), p. 59.

33. Murray, *And Say What He Is*, p. 23.

34. "A Snapshot of Elizabeth Boggs," *Families* (The New Jersey Developmental Disabilities Council), 2(2) (Spring 1993), pp. 2–14, quotes p. 4.

35. Buck, *Child Who Never Grew*, p. 46.

36. W. Newland Reilly, "Let the Parent Live Again," *AJMD* 46 (1941), pp. 409–13, quote p. 409.

37. Burton Blatt, *In and Out of Mental Retardation* (Baltimore: University Park Press, 1981), p. 173.

38. KF, Mayor D. to EMK, Apr. 12, 1973. The senator forwarded the letter to the Kennedy Foundation, which in turn sent it on to Carl Haywood of Peabody College in Nashville with a request for help.

39. Carver, *Family of the Retarded Child,* pp. 113–14.

40. Quoted from the German original in Wolf Wolfensberger, "The Origin and Nature of Our Institutional Models," in Robert B. Kugel and Wolf Wolfensberger, eds., *Changing Patterns in Residential Services for the Mentally Retarded* (Washington, D.C.: President's Committee on Mental Retardation, Jan. 1969), pp. 59–172, quote p. 71. The English translation is much skimpier. See Theodore G. Tappert and Helmut T. Lehmann, eds., *Luther's Work,* vol. 54, *Table Talk,* (Philadelphia: Fortress Press, 1967), pp. 396–97.

41. Dorothea L. Dix, "Memorial to the Legislature of Massachusetts" (1843), reprinted in David J. Rothman, ed., *On Behalf of the Insane Poor: Selected Reports* (New York: Arno, 1971), pp. 3–32, quotes pp. 4–6.

42. Charles Dickens, *Little Dorrit,* Harvey P. Sucksmith, ed. (Oxford, U.K.: Clarendon Press, 1979), pp. 95–96. Reprint. First published 1855–57.

43. Henry H. Goddard, "Causes of Backwardness and Mental Deficiency in Children and How to Prevent Them," *Proceedings of the National Education Association,* San Francisco, Calif., July 1911, pp. 1039–46, quote p. 1040.

44. Elizabeth M. Boggs, "Behavioral Fisics," in *Changing Government Policies for the Mentally Disabled,* edited by Joseph J. Bevilacqua (Cambridge, Mass.: Ballinger, 1981), p. 40. Boggs added a third reason: that they have more trouble coping and getting positive reinforcement from others.

45. Among the several historical accounts of these events, the most detailed is Peter L. Tyor, "Segregation or Surgery: The Mentally Retarded in America, 1850–1920" (Northwestern University, Ph.D. dissertation, 1972, History, modern; available through University Microfilms, Ann Arbor, Mich.), pp. 30–38. See also Tyor and Bell, *Caring for the Retarded in America: A History.*

46. For details of these institutions see Henry M. Hurd, ed., *The Institutional Care of the Insane in the United States and Canada,* 4 vols. (Baltimore: Johns Hopkins Press, 1916), vol. 2, 127–28; vol. 3, pp. 350–51, 504–10. On Barre see Tyor, "Mentally Retarded in America," p. 37, on Germantown, pp. 38–40.

47. Ivor Kraft, "Edouard Seguin and 19th Century Moral Treatment of Idiots," *Bulletin of the History of Medicine* 35 (1961), pp. 393–413, quote p. 396.

48. On Seguin's life see Murray K. Simpson, "The Moral Government of Idiots: Moral Treatment in the Work of Seguin," *History of Psychiatry* 10 (1999), pp. 227–43.

49. See Tyor, "Mentally Retarded in America," pp. 44–47.

50. Simmons, *From Asylum to Welfare,* p. 45.

51. Hurd, *Institutional Care of the Insane,* vol. 3, p. 506.

52. Ibid., vol. 3, p. 250.

53. Tyor provides the most detailed account of this evolution in "Mentally Retarded in America," pp. 68–77 and passim. Wolfensberger also quotes from a wide array of primary sources in *Changing Patterns*.

54. Hurd, *Institutional Care of the Insane*, vol. 2, p. 888

55. Ibid., vol. 3, p. 258.

56. Tyor, "Mentally Retarded in America," p. 128.

57. On these developments, see Ian Robert Dowbiggin, *Keeping America Sane: Psychiatry and Eugenics in the United States and Canada, 1880–1940* (Ithaca: Cornell University Press, 1997); Mark H. Haller, *Eugenics: Hereditarian Attitudes in American Thought* (New Brunswick: Rutgers University Press, 1963); Daniel J. Kevles, *In the Name of Eugenics: Genetics and the Uses of Human Heredity* (Berkeley: University of California Press, 1985); and Angus McClaren, *Our Own Master Race: Eugenics in Canada, 1885–1945* (Toronto: McClelland & Stewart, 1990).

58. On Morel see Gregory Zilboorg, *A History of Medical Psychology* (New York: Norton, 1941), pp. 400–4. On the eugenics movement, see Pauline Mazumdar, *Eugenics, Human Genetics and Human Failings: The Eugenics Society, Its Sources and Its Critics in Britain* (London: Routledge, 1992).

59. Cited in Wolfensberger, *Changing Patterns*, p. 101.

60. See Fernald's entry in Howard A. Kelly and Walter L. Burrage, *Dictionary of American Medical Biography* (New York: Norton, 1928), p. 405.

61. Walter E. Fernald, "The Burden of Feeble-Mindedness," *Journal of Psycho-Asthenics* 17 (1912), pp. 85–111, quote p. 93.

62. On this period see John P. Radford, "Sterilization versus Segregation: Control of the 'Feebleminded,' 1900–1938," *Social Science Medicine* 33 (1991), 449–58.

63. See Herr, *Rights Retarded People*, pp. 23–24.

64. Helen MacMurchy, *The Almosts: A Study of the Feeble-Minded* (Boston: Houghton Mifflin, 1920), pp. 177–78.

65. See, e.g., Anne Moore, *The Feeble Minded in New York: A Report Prepared for the Public Education Association of New York* (New York: State Charities Aid Association, June 1911), pp. 7, 11 and passim.

66. Henry Herbert Goddard, *The Kallikak Family: A Study in the Heredity of Feeble-Mindedness* (New York: Macmillan, 1913), pp. vii—ix.

67. The statement is Elizabeth Kite's, quoted in James Leiby, *Charity and Correction in New Jersey: A History of State Welfare Institutions* (New Brunswick: Rutgers University Press, 1967), p. 240.

68. See Eugene E. Doll, "Deborah Kallikak: 1889–1978, A Memorial," *Mental Retardation* 21 (1983), pp. 30–32.

69. Goddard, *Kallikak Family*, p. 12.

70. In *Buck v. Bell*, 1927. Quoted in R. C. Scheerenberger, *A History of Mental Retardation: A Quarter Century of Promise* (Baltimore: Brookes, 1987), p. 194.

71. Stanley Powell Davies, *Social Control of the Mentally Deficient* (New York: Crowell, 1930), pp. 169, 179.

72. Ernest L. Roselle, "Connecticut's New Institution for Mental Defectives Dedicated," *AJMD* 45 (1940), pp. 464–71, quote p. 467.

73. A. J. M. H. Verkerk et al., "Identification of a gene (FMR-1) Containing a CGG Repeat Coincident with a Breakpoint Cluster Region Exhibiting Length Variation in Fragile X Syndrome," *Cell* 65 (1991), pp. 905–14; Samantha J. L. Knight et al., "Molecular Analysis of the Fragile X Syndrome," *Disease Markers* 10 (1992), pp. 1–5.

74. Cited in Wolfensberger, *Changing Patterns*, p. 126.

75. Charles Bernstein, in discussion of Gertrude Jacob, "Systematic Physical Training for the Mentally Deficient," *Journal of Psycho-Asthenics* 9 (1905), pp. 98–112, quote p. 110.

76. J. Moorhead Murdock [sic for Murdoch], "State Care for the Feeble-Minded," *Journal of Psycho-Asthenics* 18 (1913), pp. 34–45, quote pp. 34–35.

77. Glenn E. Milligan, "History of the American Association on Mental Deficiency," *AJMD* 66 (1961), pp. 357–69, data p. 364.

78. NARC, "Decade of Decision," p. 18.

79. Geraldo Rivera, *Willowbrook: A Report on How It Is and Why It Doesn't Have To Be That Way* (New York: Random House, 1972), p. 3.

80. Muscatatuck State School in the early 1950s must truly have been a horror story. See *Children Limited*, Sept. 1955, p. 15, contrasting the supposedly reformed version with the previous one.

81. "Legislators Weep on Institution Tour," *Children Limited*, Oct. 1959, pp. 1, 12.

82. Wolfensberger, address to the Kentucky chapter of The Arc, Apr. 24, 1993.

83. David Ferleger and Penelope A. Boyd, "Anti-Institutionalization: The Promise of the *Pennhurst* Case," in Robert J. Flynn and Kathleen E. Nitsch, eds., *Normalization, Social Integration, and Community Services* (Austin, Tex.: Pro-Ed., 1980), pp. 141–66, quote p. 149.

84. KL. This anecdote was told by Stafford Warren, Oral History (1966), John F. Kennedy Library Oral History Program, p. 32.

85. Buck, *Child Who Never Grew*, p. 55.

86. KF, "Transcript of Proceedings, the Joseph P. Kennedy Foundation, Planning Committee Meeting," Feb. 25, 1971, pp. 31–32.

87. Wolfensberger, address to the Kentucky chapter of The Arc, Apr. 24, 1993.

88. NARC, ed., *The Record: Newsletter Concerning Residential Care for Retarded Children and Adults* (Fall 1961), note, p. 6.

89. Craig MacAndrew and Robert Edgerton, "The Everyday Life of Institutionalized 'Idiots,'" *Human Organization* 23 (1964), pp. 312–18, quote pp. 313–14.

90. Ibid., p. 315.

91. See Tyor, "Mentally Retarded in America," p. 172. William W. Keen, professor of surgery in the Jefferson Medical College, Philadelphia, occasionally did leukotomies on retarded children who had epilepsy, in addition to the series of craniotomies he conducted on retarded children with microcephaly. William W. Keen, "Linear Craniotomy for the Relief of Idiotic Conditions," *Proceedings of the Association of Medical Officers of American Institutions for Idiotic and Feeble-Minded Persons* (1892), pp. 344–53.

92. Ferleger in Flynn, *Normalization*, p. 146.

93. Blatt, *In and Out of Mental Retardation*, pp. 174, 180.

94. Robert E. Cooke speech, "Clinical Research on Children," Fogarty Center, NIH, March 1978, p. 14.

95. Howard Rowland, "Friendship Patterns in the State Mental Hospital: A Sociological Approach," *Psychiatry* 2 (1939), pp. 367–73, quote p. 370.

96. Martin Russ, *Half Moon Haven* (New York: Rinehart, 1959), p. 18. Wolfensberger, "Reflections on a Lifetime" (1991), believes that the institution might be Letchworth Village (p. 3).

97. Russ, *Half Moon Haven*, pp. 27, 42–43.

98. Wolfensberger, address to the Kentucky chapter of The Arc, Apr. 24, 1993.

99. Wolfensberger, private communication to the author.

100. Wallace, in discussion of Fernald, *Journal of Psycho-Asthenics* (1912), p. 106.

101. From file entitled "Toronto Psychiatric Hospital: Outpatient Cases," at the archives of the Queen Street Mental Health Centre in Toronto.

102. Stevenson, *AJMD* (1947), pp. 45–46.

103. *Miami Herald*, Apr. 29, 1974, pp. 1B, 4B.

104. Quoted in Mora Skelton, "The Mental Retardation Clinic," in Edward Shorter, ed., *TPH: History and Memories of the Toronto Psychiatric Hospital* (Toronto: Wall and Emerson, 1996), p. 301.

105. Robert F. De Vellis, "Learned Helplessness in Institutions," *Mental Retardation* 15 (1977), pp. 10–13.

106. Quoted in Herr, *Rights and Advocacy*, p. 108.

107. Patricia A. Baird et al., "Causes of Death to Age 30 in Down Syndrome," *American Journal of Human Genetics* 43 (1988), pp. 239–48.

108. See, e.g., *Report of the Pennhurst State School, 1924–1926* (Pennhurst, Penn.: Pennhurst State School, n.d.), pp. 42–43.

109. Personal communication, Cooke to author, Oct. 18, 1994.

110. J. E. Wallace Wallin, "New Frontiers in the Social Perspective of the Mentally Retarded," *Training School Bulletin* 59 (1962), pp. 89–104, data p. 102.

111. Wolf Wolfensberger, "Reflections on Reading Old Annual Government Reports on the Lunatic and Idiot Asylums of the Province of Ontario," *Canada's Mental Health* 22 (1974), pp. 21–24, detail p. 21.

112. Ferleger, in Flynn, *Normalization*, p. 146.

113. Robert A. Burt, "The Ideal of Community in the Work of the President's Commission," *Cardozo Law Review* 6 (1984), pp. 267–86, quote p. 279.

114. Buck, *Child Who Never Grew*, p. 24.

115. Tyor, "Mentally Retarded in America," p. 154.

116. See ibid., p. 89; Eugene E. Doll, "Before the Big Time: Early History of the Training School at Vineland, 1888 to 1949," *AJMR* 93 (1988), pp. 1–15.

117. E. E. Doll, *AJMR* (1988), p. 5.

118. Goddard refers to this in his paper, "Four Hundred Feeble-Minded Children Classified by the Binet Method," *Journal of Psycho-Asthenics* 15 (1910), pp. 17–30.

119. E. E. Doll, *AJMR* (1988), pp. 11–13.

120. On Wallin's life see J. E. Wallace Wallin, *Notables Advances in the Understanding and Treatment of Mentally Handicapped Children* (Rock Island, Ill.: Augustana College, 1957; Occasional Papers, no. 1), pp. 7–11.

121. Elizabeth Boggs, "Remarks on Receiving the Wallin Award," *Exceptional Children*, 54 (Sept. 1987), pp. 86–88, quote p. 87.

122. J. E. Wallace Wallin, "Who Is Feeble-minded?" *Journal of the American Institute of Criminal Law and Criminology* 6 (1916), pp. 706–17.

123. Fred Kuhlmann, "One Hundred Years of Special Care and Training," *AJMD* 45 (1940), pp. 8–24, quote p. 16.

124. President's Committee on Mental Retardation, *MR 76. Mental Retardation: Past and Present* (Washington, D.C.: PCMR, Jan. 1977), p. 19.

125. Edward R. Johnstone, "Report of the Committee on Mental Deficiency of the White House Conference," *Journal of Psycho-Asthenics* 36 (1931), pp. 339–50, see esp. pp. 344–45 on "therapeutic prevention," one part of which was "special classes."

126. Boggs, "Remarks on Receiving the Wallin Award" (1987), p. 87.

127. Elizabeth Boggs, "Federal Legislation," in *Mental Retardation and Developmental Disabilities: An Annual Review*, edited by Joseph Wortis, vol. 3 (New York: Grune and Stratton, 1971), pp. 103–27, see p. 104.

128. *Hearing before the Committee on Labor and Public Welfare, United States Senate*, Apr. 4, 1957 (Washington, D.C.: GPO, 1957), p. 58.

129. Ibid., pp. 12–13.

130. Ibid., p. 7.

131. Ibid., table 4, p. 54. Data for 1952–1953.

132. The story circulated among contemporaries was that the midwife deliberately held Rosemary's head back until Dr. Good's arrival to permit the doctor to earn his full fee. Laurence Leamer, *The Kennedy Women: The Saga of an American Family* (New York: Villard, 1994), p. 137. The tale is unlikely on physiological grounds alone and certainly would not have represented standard practice at the time.

133. KF, EKS memo to the grandchildren, Oct. 4, 1985. "One of the grandchildren has, in the past, asked me whether there were any genetic problems in the family regarding mental retardation. They were asking specifically about Rosemary, because their doctor had asked them. So you all understand—there is no genetic problem." EKS had stated in her 1962 *Saturday Evening Post* article, "Hope for Retarded Children," that Rosemary had had "a normal delivery" (p. 71).

134. Her birth certificate, on file with the Town Clerk's Office of Brookline, lists her name as "Rose Marie Kennedy."

135. Rose Fitzgerald Kennedy, *Times to Remember* (New York: Bantam, 1974), quote from p. 161.

136. KF, EKS document "Out of Shadows" (1962). This was an early draft of EKS's *Saturday Evening Post* article, ghostwritten by Donald Stedman, the executive director of the KF, and by Donald Oberdorfer, a journalist for the *Washington Post* (Stedman, interview of Mar. 16, 1993). The authors must have interviewed EKS for

the factual information. Much longer and more informative than the ultimately published version, this draft contained numerous details that either EKS and RSS or the magazine's editors later cut. The comment about "empty head," as is the case with most other details cited in this section, was not published.

137. Doris Kearns Goodwin, *The Fitzgeralds and the Kennedys* (New York: Simon and Schuster, 1987), p. 360.

138. KF, EKS, "Out of Shadows," p. 2.

139. Ibid., pp. 2–4.

140. Ibid., pp. 5–6. None of these details were included in the published version.

141. Doris Kearns Goodwin reports how pleased everyone was when Rosemary was presented along with the others at court and her retardation went unnoticed. *Fitzgeralds and Kennedys*, p. 543.

142. Peter Collier and David Horowitz, *The Kennedys: An American Drama* (New York: Summit, 1984), p. 115.

143. Lem Billings, quoted in Kearns Goodwin, *Fitzgeralds and Kennedys*, p. 640.

144. Leamer, *Kennedy Women*, pp. 318–19.

145. EKS, *Saturday Evening Post* article, pp. 71–72.

146. KF, EKS, "Out of Shadows," p. 1. The news that the family had contemplated institutionalization since 1933 was deleted from publication.

147. EKS, essay on her father, in Edward M. Kennedy, ed., *The Fruitful Bough: A Tribute to Joseph P. Kennedy* (n.p., [1965]), pp. 217–24, quote p. 221. Eunice's account directly contradicts that of Ronald Kessler, who generally makes Joe the villain—and who suggests (improbably) that Rosemary's true diagnosis was not MR but depression. See Kessler, *The Sins of the Father: Joseph P. Kennedy and the Dynasty He Founded* (New York: Warner, 1996), pp. 238–55.

148. Collier and Horowitz, *The Kennedys*, assert that she had the operation at St. Elizabeth's Hospital in Washington, D.C. (p. 116); see also Kearns Goodwin, *Fitzgeralds and Kennedys*, pp. 640–42. Kessler says that the neurosurgeon was James Watts, and that Watts had confided these details to him in a deathbed interview (p. 243). Jack Pressman, the premier student of the history of lobotomy in the United States, doubts on the basis of studying Watts's case records that he ever operated on Rosemary. Personal communication.

149. See Leamer, *Kennedy Women*, pp. 318–22.

150. Cooke expressed this opinion to me in his letter of Oct. 18, 1994, in which he also stated, "The culprit, if any existed, was the neurosurgeon who did the lobotomy without adequate regard for the potentially disastrous outcome or the proven indications for such a procedure."

151. Kearns Goodwin, *Fitzgeralds and Kennedys*, p. 643.

152. Leamer, *Kennedy Women*, p. 842. According to the story "Ground Broken for Kennedy Center for Retarded," *NYT*, May 2, 1966, p. 47, Rosemary had been "in a Roman Catholic school for the retarded, St. Coletta's in Jefferson, Wis., for the last 21 years."

153. KF, EKS, "Out of Shadows," p. 6.

154. KF, EKS to Tom Walsh, June 19, 1975.

155. Buck, *Child Who Never Grew,* pp. 24–25.

156. Harold H. Martin, "The Amazing Kennedys," *Saturday Evening Post,* Sept. 7, 1957, p. 44.

157. James MacGregor Burns, *John Kennedy: A Political Profile* (New York: Harcourt Brace, 1959), pp. 23, 129.

158. *NYT,* Oct. 12, 1961, p. 1.

159. KF, Mrs. XX to JPK, Dec. 19, 1951, mentioned she had heard him discussing a Kennedy family problem with MR on the radio. Other individuals at her son's "Home" (institution) were also in the know.

160. EKS, *Saturday Evening Post,* p. 72.

Chapter Two

1. *NYT,* June 12, 1977, sec. 3, pp. 1, 3.

2. *Time,* July 30, 1945, p. 84. *Business Week,* July 28, 1945, pp. 52, 55, quote p. 55.

3. The purchase price of $13 million, considerably less than the $17 million rumored in the press, was stated in a letter of November 29, 1945, to the U.S. Treasury Department, applying for tax-exempt status. For financial details see Robert P. Vanderpoel, *Chicago Herald American,* Nov. 14, 1945. Vanderpoel was the financial editor and a personal friend of Joe Kennedy. Robert A. Liston places the purchase of the Mart in the context of Joe Kennedy's general business dealings: *Sargent Shriver: A Candid Portrait* (New York: Farrar, Straus, 1964), pp. 50–51. On shifting the marketing strategy from government agencies to private companies, see the article by Wally Ollman, the Merchandise Mart's general manager, in Edward M. Kennedy, ed., *The Fruitful Bough: A Tribute to Joseph P. Kennedy* (n.p., 1965), pp. 45–46. For details on financing, see Richard J. Whalen, *The Founding Father: The Story of Joseph P. Kennedy* (New York: New American Library, 1964), p. 379. Whalen points out that before Joseph Kennedy purchased the Mart, he discovered the federal tenants would be leaving (pp. 379–80).

4. The Certificate of Incorporation of the Mercié Foundation was filed on May 14, 1945, with what is now the Department of Consumer and Regulatory Affairs, Business Regulation Administration, Corporations Division, of the District of Columbia. The certificate gave the foundation's address as Room 559, Munsey Bldg., 1329 E. Street, N.W., in Washington. That was also the address of the Corporation Trust Company, which was closely connected to the Kennedy empire. The foundation's officers at the time were Milton E. Hartley, Ernest O. Paland, and Edward S. Conger. On May 18, 1945, in the Appointment of Agent to Accept Service of Process, Edward O'Leary became president and P. E. Murphy secretary of the Mercié Foundation. For the application for tax-exempt status see KL, MS 79–2, box 4. Paul E. Murphy to Joseph Neunan, commissioner of the Internal Revenue Service, November 29, 1945.

5. On Oct. 29, 1945, a Certificate of Amendment of Certificate of Incorporation was filed with the D.C. Corporations Division requesting that the name of the Mercié Foundation be changed to the "Joseph P. Kennedy, Jr. Foundation"; it was signed by Thomas Delehanty, Vice President, and Paul E. Murphy, Sec-

retary. An additional Consent to Amendment of Certificate of Incorporation of Oct. 29 was signed by Delehanty, Murphy, Edward E. Moore, and John F. Kennedy.

6. These arrangements are spelled out in JPK to Commissioner Neunan, Nov. 29, 1945, and in Murphy to Neunan, also Nov. 29, 1945. Murphy's letter stated, "The Foundation now proposes to purchase a 25 per cent undivided interest in the Merchandise Mart building, located in Chicago, Ill., and will receive 25 per cent of the net profit from the operation of this building. . . ." Joe Kennedy's letter spelled out the division of the profits among Joe, Rose, and the trusts and foundation.

7. See the news story "Views of the Kennedy House: Poignant Past, Busy Present," *New York Times,* Apr. 10, 1991, p. A16. "The house is owned by the Joseph P. Kennedy Foundation, rather than by any individual, and cannot be inherited or sold. . . ."

8. Certificate of Amendment of Certificate of Incorporation of the Joseph P. Kennedy, Jr. Foundation, filed Mar. 11, 1946. Corporations Division, Washington, D.C.

9. Application for Certificate of Authority of Foreign Corporation, filed with the Illinois Secretary of State, Mar. 29, 1946, Office of the Secretary of State, Springfield, Ill., and James A. Fayne. O'Leary went on to become president of the Schenley Import Company.

10. Annual Report under the General Not for Profit Corporation Act, Illinois Secretary of State, dated Mar. 24, 1947. This discussion is based on the Kennedy Foundation's annual reports filed with the Illinois Secretary of State, where the foundation was chartered in order to conduct business in that state. The nonfamily trustees, or "directors," in the 1950s were John J. Ford, a Bostonian who had managed JPK's New England movie theaters; Edward E. Moore, the financier's confidential secretary; and Paul Murphy, who also was secretary-treasurer.

11. In 1952 Eunice's name reappeared for one year only as "Vice-President," along with that of Robert Kennedy. The next mention of Eunice in these records occurred in 1960 when she was listed as a "director" (trustee), along with John F. Kennedy and Patricia K. Lawford; this was the first time Pat's name appeared. James A. Fayne and John J. Ford, holdovers from the past, were the other two directors in 1960.

12. They would sign letters of "waiver," legally excusing themselves from attending annual meetings that never occurred. See, e.g., KL, JPK Gen. Corr. 1947–48, box 9, William Peyton Marin to Paul Murphy, Oct. 23, 1947: "Will you kindly have the waived [*sic*] signed by Messrs. Moore, Fayne, Ford, John Kennedy, and yourself."

13. Personal communication, Cooke to author, Oct. 18, 1994.

14. See Nigel Hamilton, *JFK: Reckless Youth* (New York: Random House, 1992); Ronald Kessler, *The Sins of the Father: Joseph P. Kennedy and the Dynasty He Founded* (New York: Warner, 1996); Ralph G. Martin, *Seeds of Destruction: Joe Kennedy and His Sons* (New York: Putnam, 1995); and, for a more balanced and sympathetic

treatment, Doris Kearns Goodwin, *The Fitzgeralds and the Kennedys: An American Saga* (New York: Simon and Schuster, 1987).

15. In Kennedy, *Fruitful Bough* (1965), p. 53.

16. Jacqueline Bouvier Kennedy in ibid., p. 232.

17. Ethel C. Turner in ibid., p. 22.

18. See Waldemar A. Nielsen, *The Golden Donors: A New Anatomy of the Great Foundations* (New York: Dutton, 1985), pp. 4–5, 13–14.

19. For statistics on American foundations in 1953, see Wilmer Schields Rich, *American Foundations and Their Fields,* 7th ed. (New York: American Foundations Information Service, 1955), p. xiv; data on the Kennedy Foundation, p. 403.

20. Mr. John Hein of Boston, in Kennedy, *Fruitful Bough* (1965), p. 148.

21. KF, Robert Montague to EKS, Apr. 5, 1984. Montague learned this in a conversation with JPK's assistant Thomas Walsh.

22. KL, MS 79–2, box 3, JPK to Robert Martin Spellman, Mar. 16, 1956.

23. This group of letters mailed out Dec. 24, 1946, is in KL, JPK Family Correspondence, box 33.

24. KL, MS 79–2, box 3, list of "Miscellaneous donations" to non-Catholic charities, attached to JPK letter to Evelyn Lincoln, Dec. 1, 1958.

25. See "Miscellaneous donations," ibid., and Kennedy, *Fruitful Bough* (1965), p. 187.

26. *NYT,* Aug. 24, 1960, p. 20; Kennedy, *Fruitful Bough* (1965), pp. 160–61. Twenty-one of the cadets applied, and thirteen actually attended Notre Dame.

27. KL, JPK, Alpha file 1951, box 38, JFK to M. G. Woodward, March 13, 1951.

28. KL, Mrs. JPK Papers, box 7/8, RSS to JPK, Mar. 6, 1958. "About a month ago Jack asked me what was happening about the grant to the Negro college in New Orleans." Mr. Lester Sullivan, archivist of Xavier University, has indicated in a personal communication that there is no evidence in university records of such a grant having been made.

29. This account is based on the interview of Thomas Mboya done at an unknown date for the John F. Kennedy Library Oral History Program, pp. 1–3, and on the *NYT,* Aug. 22, 1960, pp. 1, 15.

30. See, e.g., KL, MS 79–2, box 3, JPK to Rev. John Wright, Sept. 18, 1951, in which Joe Kennedy bitterly criticizes the archbishop for a number of real or imagined sleights, including Cushing's failure to "say a few words at John F's [Fitzgerald's] funeral Mass" and for reprinting in the magazine of the archdiocese, the *Pilot,* newspaper editorials that had been critical of Joe Kennedy.

31. Fogarty papers, Cushing to McCormack, Mar. 22, 1955. (McCormack forwarded the letter to Congressman John Fogarty.)

32. See Fogarty Papers, e.g., Cushing to Fogarty, Dec. 11, 1957. "The picture that I promised to send you and Arthur [Trudeau] is going to you under separate cover. Please accept this little souvenir [unknown] as a Christmas gift."

33. It was Fogarty's opinion that Joe Kennedy's interest in mental retardation dated back to conversations with Cushing after World War II. "Cardinal Cushing had been interested for many years in the problems of children and youth, and

mental retardation in children was his major concern in the medical field. He advised the President's father that no foundation existed to support research in mental retardation and very little money was available for treatment and care." *Congressional Record,* House, 87th Congress, 2nd session, Mar. 16—Apr. 2, 1962, 108 (pt. 4), p. 4785.

34. James C. G. Conniff, "Take My Mind, My Memory . . . ," *Columbia* 35 (Jan. 1955), pp. 15–18, facts p. 18. Other information has been provided by St. Coletta's of Massachusetts, Inc.

35. John Henry Cutler, *Cardinal Cushing of Boston* (New York: Hawthorn, 1970), pp. 213–14.

36. The date 1946 was mentioned in a press release draft written by Al DeCrane at the Merchandise Mart. See KL, MS 79–2, box 3, DeCrane to JPK, Jan. 6, 1956. The hospital was operated under the auspices of Archbishop Cushing.

37. Thomas Broderick, Oral History (1964), Kennedy Library Oral History Program, pp. 24–25.

38. Richard Cardinal Cushing, undated Oral History, Kennedy Library Oral History Program, p. 1.

39. KL, MS 79–2, box 1. Cushing to EKS, Nov. 18, 1957.

40. KL, JFK Pre-presidential Papers, box 543, Cushing to RSS, Aug. 15, 1959. "All of us are of the opinion that we can do much better 'on our own.' We have a combination of the spiritual and the professional. We want to maintain it." Ironically, Harvard had no interest in such a collaboration either, on the grounds that the Kennedy hospital in Brighton was academically too weak. KF, McGeorge Bundy to RSS, Mar. 7, 1959: "The caliber of the professional staff is not such that any member of it could now be recommended for a staff appointment at the Harvard Medical School. . . ."

41. KL, JPK papers 77–23, box 35, JPK to Rev. Maurice S. Sheehy, Jan. 12, 1954.

42. See KL, JPK 77–23, box 35, Sister Mary Inez to Joe and Rose Kennedy, Feb. 27, 1952.

43. KL, JPK 77–23, box 35, John F. Royal to JPK, Feb. 25, 1952.

44. As Elizabeth Boggs said in an interview on Feb. 24, 1993, "We tried desperately hard during the '50s to get [the Kennedys] on board with us, and the Massachusetts Association [for Retarded Children] tried to work through Cardinal Cushing and we got a completely dead response."

45. KF, "Historical Summary," attached to memo from EKS to the Kennedy family of Apr. 9, 1984. In 1957, contributions to MR amounted to $91,000 of the total grants of $528,000 made that year by the foundation.

46. KL, JPK, box 35. See, e.g., Rose Kennedy to Baroness Elizabeth Guttenberg, May 12, 1956. KL, JPK, box 35, Joseph Kennedy to Sister Mary Paula, Apr. 1, 1957. Various stock phrases were used to reject applicants. In 1953 Jack Kennedy did in fact say, "We are limited to the construction of homes for mentally deficient children." KL, JFK Pre-presidential Papers, box 481, JFK to Hugh Packard, June 19, 1953.

47. KL, JPK, box 38, Fayne to RSS, Jan. 29, 1952.

48. KL, JPK, box 35, JPK to Robert H. Hallowell, Jr., of the United Negro College Fund: "May I ask you to make this gift from 'A Friend.'"

49. Eunice Shriver, in Kennedy, *Fruitful Bough* (1965), p. 222.

50. KF, EKS to the family, Apr. 9, 1984.

51. The story is told in "Lt. Joseph P. Kennedy Institute: The History," unpublished pamphlet (1981), quotes from pp. 9–18.

52. KL, JPK 77–23, box 50. Mrs. XX to JPK, Dec. 19, 1951. Punctuation has been slightly modified.

53. KL, JPK 77–23, box 35, JPK to Maurice Sheehy, Jan. 12, 1954.

54. These events are alluded to in KL, MS 79–2, box 3, JPK to Rusk, Dec. 14, 1955.

55. KL, JPK 79–2, box 3, JPK to Howard Rusk, Dec. 14, 1955.

56. See Cushing's enthusiastic letter to Sargent Shriver, KF, Sept. 29, 1957: "I think we may be on the way to reaching the causes and cures for some of these problems of 'exceptional childhood.'"

57. KL, 79–2, Mrs. JPK papers, box 1, Cushing to JPK, Dec. 15, 1955.

58. *NYT,* Feb. 10, 1956, p. 46.

59. Documentary evidence on this ad hoc committee is fragmentary. This account is based on Francis Braceland's letter to JPK of Feb. 16, 1959: "After the last meeting I was to last summer I remember that Doctor Rusk submitted a series of possible projects. I take it from your note that perhaps the Foundation has decided to interest itself mostly in mental retardation" (KL, MS 79–2, box 3). See also Howard Rusk's autobiography, *A World to Care For* (New York: Random House, 1972), pp. 247–48. Rusk incorrectly identifies the year as "1959."

60. KL, MS 79–2, box 1, JPK to Cushing, May 1, 1958.

61. KL, MS 79–2, Mrs. JPK Papers, box 1, Cushing to Rev. William T. Molloy, May 14, 1958.

62. KL, JFK Pre-presidential Papers, box 543, JPK to Mother Stella Maris, Sept. 18, 1958.

63. James W. Hilty, *Robert Kennedy: Brother Protector* (Philadelphia: Temple University Press, 1997), p. 507 n. 6. Also, personal communication from Dr. Hilty.

Chapter Three

1. For a readable and well-researched account of Eunice Kennedy Shriver's personal life see Laurence Leamer, *The Kennedy Women: The Saga of an American Family* (New York: Villard, 1994), esp. pp. 145–46 ff.

2. This analysis is Doris Kearns Goodwin's, *The Fitzgeralds and the Kennedys* (New York: Simon and Schuster, 1987), p. 363.

3. Ibid., p. 363.

4. These details on Eunice Kennedy's education and health are taken from her curriculum vitae, on file at the KF, and from Robert A. Liston, *Sargent Shriver: A Candid Portrait* (New York: Farrar, Straus, 1964), p. 60 (ulcer); Nora Ephron, "Woman in the News: Eunice Kennedy Shriver," *New York Post,* Nov. 19, 1966 (illness at Manhattanville); Rose Kennedy, Oral History (1968) in Kennedy

Library Oral History Collection, pp. 1–2 (on going to California for her health); RSS to a physician at Guy's Hospital in England, Mar. 25, 1981 (on overwork and collapse); "The 'Lucky Life' of Sargent Shriver," *Chicago Tribune*, July 30, 1987, p. 1 (Addison's disease, colitis).

5. Her curriculum vitae has her erroneously graduating in "1943." I am grateful to Ms. Billie Bousman of the Stanford University Libraries for clarifying the date. While at Stanford, Eunice Kennedy listed her home address as "Palm Beach."

6. "One Kennedy Not Interested in Pay—Wants to See Young America Play," *WP*, Feb. 4, 1947.

7. Ibid.

8. These details from *WP*, Jan. 17, 1947, and "Conference Report: National Conference for the Prevention and Control of Juvenile Delinquency," *Recreation*, 40 (Jan. 1947), pp. 552–53. Also articles in *Parents' Magazine*, Mar. 1947, p. 14; Aug. 1948, p. 77. On her father's influence, see Herbert S. Parmet, *Jack: The Struggles of John F. Kennedy* (New York: Dial, 1980), p. 165.

9. KL, John Dowd to JPK, Jan. 18, 1947. KL, JPK 77–23, box 35.

10. KL, JPK to RSS, Mar. 3, 1947. KL, JPK 77–23, box 35.

11. Polly Devlin, "Eunice Kennedy Shriver, the Spark," *Vogue*, March 1, 1968, p. 160.

12. "Shriver's Family," *WP*, Sept. 16, 1972, p. D15.

13. Harold Martin, "The Amazing Kennedys," *Saturday Evening Post*, Sept. 7, 1957, p. 46. This article had Jean, not Eunice, helping Joe Kennedy to dispense the largesse of the Foundation.

14. Devlin, *Vogue* (1968), p. 160.

15. Eleanor Lambert, "Mrs. Shriver Is Mover and Shaker," *WP*, Nov. 18, 1966.

16. Rose Fitzgerald Kennedy, *Times to Remember* (New York: Bantam, 1974), pp. 142–43.

17. Liston, *Sargent Shriver* (1964), p. 59.

18. Christopher Lydon, "Eunice Kennedy Shriver, Campaigner," *NYT*, Jan. 31, 1976, p. 11.

19. *People*, Aug. 27, 1979, p. 26.

20. Quoted in ibid., p. 26.

21. "The Kennedy Who Could Be President," *Ladies' Home Journal*, Mar. 1976, p. 116.

22. Quoted in Goodwin, *Fitzgeralds and Kennedys* (1987), p. 366.

23. "One Kennedy Not Interested in Pay—Wants to See Young America Play," *WP*, Feb. 4, 1947.

24. "The Kennedy Who Could Be President," *Ladies' Home Journal*, Mar. 1976, p. 156.

25. "Shriver's Other Running Mate," *Time*, Aug. 21, 1972, p. 15.

26. "The Kennedy Who Could Be President," *Ladies' Homes Journal*, Mar. 1976, p. 117.

27. John Throne, interview of Mar. 12, 1993.

28. *US News and World Report*, Aug. 21, 1972, p. 17.

29. See, e.g., KF, Throne to EKS and RSS, Mar. 9, 1966, regarding "Religious training research plans." In a memo to the file at KF of Sept. 24, 1980, EKS wrote, " . . . In the early days, after President Kennedy started NICHD and I had served on the Board, I was appalled that religious values were never discussed. I talked to Dr. Shannon. He spoke to a small group about this but nothing ever had become of it."

30. Richard Ragsdale, interview of Nov. 4, 1992.

31. Peter Jenkins, "Candidate Sargent Shriver," *NYT Magazine,* Oct. 15, 1972, p. 100.

32. Some reports in 1981 had Bobby Shriver as part of an "intercontinental pair" with Princess Caroline of Monaco. *People,* June 22, 1981, p. 53.

33. On her coldness to Jack, see Nigel Hamilton, *JFK: Reckless Youth* (New York: Random House, 1993), pp. 112–13, 420, and 690. As a corrective to Hamilton's overdrawn portrait, see Kearns Goodwin, *Fitzgeralds and Kennedys* (1987), pp. 308, 314–15.

34. Jerome Lawrence and Robert E. Lee, "Matriarch: The Many Lives of Rose Fitzgerald Kennedy," ms. of August 1982 in KF, pp. 5, 10, 86.

35. Quoted in "Rose Kennedy at 76," in *America,* Nov. 18, 1967, p. 595.

36. KL, JPK 77–23, box 36, Rose to EKS, May 19, 1959.

37. KL, JPK 77–23, box 35, Rose to EKS, Feb. 14, 1957.

38. Barbara Grizzuti Harrison points out that not just Eunice was the recipient of such notes. "When [Rose Kennedy's] children were grown, she saw nothing untoward in sending them notes about the advisability of buying apples when they were on sale, or instructing Ethel about the inadvisability of letting her children leave their bicycles outdoors overnight." "Rose Kennedy's Triumph Over Tragedy," *McCall's,* Aug. 1984, pp. 109, 147–48, quote p. 148.

39. Eunice Shriver essay, in Edward Kennedy, ed., *The Fruitful Bough: A Tribute to Joseph P. Kennedy* (n.p., 1965), p. 217.

40. Quoted in Rose Kennedy, *Times to Remember* (1974), p. 83.

41. KL, 79–2, box 8, Rose to EKS, May 20, 1958.

42. Peter Collier and David Horowitz, *The Kennedys: An American Drama* (New York: Summit, 1984), p. 159.

43. See, e.g., David Condon's interview with Eunice Shriver, *Chicago Sunday Tribune Magazine,* March 12, 1961, p. 8: "The President's sister, like any other understanding housewife, courteously overlooked the mud and snow tracks left on her beige carpet. . . ."

44. "Last Will and Testament of Joseph P. Kennedy," Dec. 30, 1955, on file with the Clerk of the Circuit Court, Probate and Guardianship Division, West Palm Beach, Florida.

45. KF, Undated memo from "Lucy" to EKS, sometime in September, 1982.

46. Kennedy, *Fruitful Bough* (1965), p. 203. Emphasis added. In this volume Bobby Kennedy also dilated upon how much Joe Kennedy did to help his sons (pp. 213–14).

47. KL, 79–2, box 8, EKS to JPK, undated, evidently sometime in 1959 or early 1960.

48. Rita Dallas and Jeanira Ratcliffe, *The Kennedy Case* (New York: Putnam's, 1973), p. 232.

49. See, e.g., KL, JPK, 77–23, box 35, RSS to JPK, Dec. 25, 1953. "What she has done for all those nuns in Chicago is only half-indicated by all the wonderful messages they wrote her on Christmas cards. . . ." See also KL, 79–2, box 3, RSS to JPK, Sept. 15, 1950.

50. KL, JPK, 79–2, box 3, RSS to JPK, Feb. 8, 1950.

51. Harris Wofford, *Of Kennedys and Kings: Making Sense of the Sixties* (New York: Farrar Straus Giroux, 1980), p. 46.

52. Liston, *Sargent Shriver* (1964), pp. 11–22. *Time,* July 5, 1963, p. 20.

53. Peter Braestrup, "Peace Corpsman No. 1—A Progress Report," *NYT Magazine,* Dec. 17, 1961, p. 14.

54. *Time,* Aug. 14, 1972, p. 14.

55. *Time,* July 5, 1963, p. 21. Information on summer work from the "attachment" (a curriculum vitae that itself had been misplaced), on file at KF.

56. Quoted in *NYT Magazine,* July 5, 1963, p. 4.

57. Braestrup, "Peace Corpsman No. 1."

58. RSS's wartime record has been pieced together from Liston, *Sargent Shriver* (1964), pp. 37–44; *NYT Magazine,* Dec. 17, 1961, p. 65; and curriculum vitaes on file in KF.

59. "'Lucky Life' of Sargent Shriver," *Chicago Tribune,* July 30, 1987, pp. 1, 6.

60. KL, 79–2, box 4, JPK to Murphy, Jan. 15, 1946.

61. Braestrup, "Peace Corpsman No. 1."

62. KL, JPK "Personal Correspondence," box 35, RSS to JPK, Nov. 22, 1946.

63. A. H. Raskin, "Generalissimo of the War on Poverty," *NYT Magazine,* Nov. 22, 1964, p. 92.

64. KL, 79–2, box 3, RSS to JPK sometime in 1956, regarding an operation Joe Kennedy had just undergone: "I remember you frequently in my prayers."

65. KL, 79–2, box 3, RSS to JPK and Rose Kennedy, circa Dec. 25, 1950.

66. "The Kennedy Who Could Be President," *Ladies' Home Journal,* Mar. 1976, p. 156. Collier and Horowitz have Eunice Kennedy meeting Sargent Shriver "at dinner at the St. Regis with Peter Hoguet, a friend of both" (Collier and Horowitz, *The Kennedys,* p. 159). Yet the details that Hoguet supplied of Shriver's departure from *Newsweek* were erroneous, and possibly Hoguet's story of their initial meeting is less dependable than the account the Shrivers spontaneously gave to the *Ladies' Home Journal.*

67. Liston, *Sargent Shriver* (1964), p. 172.

68. Mentioned in a draft curriculum vitae on file at the KF, this fact was stricken from the final version.

69. Anthony Lewis, "Shriver Moves Into the Front Rank," *NYT Magazine,* Mar. 15, 1964, p. 45.

70. In Liston's judgment, the courtship was "pretty one-sided" at first. Shriver said, "Eunice wasn't the sort of girl you could sweep off her feet." *Sargent Shriver* (1964), p. 54.

71. Among her previous beaux was Senator Joseph McCarthy, evidently introduced to Eunice by her brother Bobby, who worked for McCarthy's Permanent
Investigations Subcommittee in 1952–53 as assistant counsel. See James W. Hilty,
Robert Kennedy: Brother Protector (Philadelphia: Temple University Press, 1997), pp.
62–63.

72. Nora Ephron, "Woman in the News: Eunice Kennedy Shriver," *New York
Post,* Nov. 19, 1966.

73. Liston, *Sargent Shriver* (1964), p. 53.

74. Quoted in David E. Koskoff, *Joseph P. Kennedy: A Life and Times* (Englewood
Cliffs: Prentice-Hall, 1974), p. 388.

75. Liston, *Sargent Shriver,* p. 59.

76. Wofford, *Kennedys and Kings* (1980), p. 96.

77. See, e.g., Yves R. Simon, *The Community of the Free,* English trans. by Willard
R. Trask (New York: Henry Holt, 1947), p. ix and passim.

78. Sargent Shriver, "The Moral Basis of the War on Poverty," *Christian Century,*
Dec. 14, 1966, p. 1533.

79. Donald Stedman, interview of Mar. 16, 1993.

80. KF, RSS to Patricia Lawford, Dec. 4, 1973. Copies also went to other family
members and friends.

81. RSS, "Our Purpose . . . is to help people everywhere strive toward human
dignity and physical health and political self-government." *Saturday Review,* June
17, 1961, pp. 19–20, quote p. 19.

82. An example from the files of the KF: While RSS was doodling on the
margin of notes made by a staffer for a meeting of the KF science advisers on
Oct. 26, 1983, under a section entitled "Basic Questions," the staffer had written,
"What do we believe in?" RSS added, "What do we do about what we believe in?"
Further down the page he queried in his tidy hand, "Will it be helpful to get our
values in order? This is the question we should ask about every proposal we are
asked to finance."

83. Quoted in *NYT Magazine,* Mar. 15, 1964, p. 45.

84. Wofford, *Kennedys and Kings* (1980), p. 281.

85. Michael Novak, "Campaigning with Shriver," *Commonweal,* Feb. 14, 1975,
p. 383.

86. The documents clearly contradict Eunice Shriver's later account of these
events, in which her father was said to charge her with responsibility for getting the
scientific program going. On the dating of this new assignment, JPK told Thomas
V. Moore on June 2, 1958, "Since I have been doing most of the planning in
connection with the Foundation, along with all of the other responsibilities, I
feel that I have arrived at the age when I do not have the time or the inclination
to work out details of plans that seem to be at all complicated. I am going to
leave that to the younger generation" (KL, MS 79-2, box 3). This is the first such
reference I have seen. On the responsibility having been placed specifically on
Sargent Shriver's shoulders, RSS told his father-in-law on June 14, 1960, "When
you instructed me to develop a program of medical research for the Foundation,
it was my understanding that you wanted a research program focused on mental

retardation rather than on cerebral palsy [etc.] . . . ." (KL, 79–2, box 3). Yet it was clearly in the financier's mind that both his daughter and son-in-law would be active in the new program. As he told one correspondent, "I would suggest that Dr. Stafford get in touch with Mr. Sargent Shriver at the Merchandise Mart in Chicago because he and his wife, my daughter Eunice, are exploring all of the possibilities on our mental retardation program" (KL, 79–2, box 3, JPK to William J. McDonald, Sept. 8, 1959).

87. Jerome Schulman, interview of May 12, 1993.

88. Manuscript version of Eunice Shriver's paper for the *Fruitful Bough*, p. 9, on file at KF. Sargent Shriver edited this manuscript to make clear that "mental health" meant mental illness. None of the material quoted above appeared in the published version.

89. Ibid., p. 10. The published version is somewhat different: "We held a meeting in New York at which several doctors and psychiatrists made proposals. I disagreed with them. I felt that the Foundation should be staffed with people previously interested in mental retardation, with a good record of experience in the field. . . ." Eunice continued: "When we were going back to the hotel, he [JPK] said to me, 'You don't know what you want to do with the Foundation and I don't either.' I said, 'Will you give me and Sarge six weeks and we'll get back to you with a plan.' He said, 'OK—but if you haven't anything in the next six weeks I'm going ahead with the plan of today.'" There is no evidence of such a six-week tour having taken place. Kennedy, ed., *Fruitful Bough* (1965), p. 222.

90. On these Chicago experiences see KF, EKS, "Out of Shadows," draft article for the *Saturday Evening Post*, 1962, p. 32. These details were never published. (EKS's article was published as "Hope for Retarded Children," *Saturday Evening Post*, Sept. 22, 1962, pp. 71–75.)

91. Jerome Schulman, interview of May 12, 1993.

92. Richard Masland, interview of May 14, 1993.

93. I have not seen the letter itself. This summary of it is taken from Richard Masland, Oral History (1968), John F. Kennedy Library Oral History Program, pp. 1–2. Robert Cooke, in his own Oral History for the Kennedy Library said it was Joe Kennedy who approached Masland. Although Masland's own recollections in 1993 of these events were dim, it was his impression that Eunice Shriver had contacted him. Cooke emphasized, however, that Masland had been influential in switching the foundation onto the scientific track. Cooke, Oral History (1968), John F. Kennedy Library Oral History Program, p. 32. Eunice Shriver's later account of these events was quite garbled, "I remember going out to dinner one night and thinking to myself, 'Where do you go with no resources?' as my father asked me to develop a focus for the Foundation." So, she said, she bought a copy of Richard Masland's *Mental Subnormality*, got on the train to New York "and went up to see him." Eunice Shriver, speech on "History of Special Olympics" delivered at the annual conference of the Georgia Special Olympics, Oct. 16, 1987, p. 3.

94. Herbert Grossman, interview of Apr. 21, 1993.

95. Quoted in Robert O. Pasnau and Henry H. Work, "George Tarjan, M.D., 1912–1991," *American Journal of Psychiatry*, 150 (1993), pp. 691–94, quote p. 693.

96. KF, Schulman to RSS, Nov. 24, 1958.

97. See the "Proposed Outline for an Agreement between the Kennedy Foundation and Harvard University," attached to memo from RSS to Masland, Schulman, and Tarjan, Nov. 25, 1958. Also McGeorge Bundy to JPK, Feb. 5, 1958; JPK to Bundy, Feb. 11, 1958; and Bundy to JPK, May 16, 1958 (all in KL, 79–2, box 1).

98. Koskoff, *Joseph P. Kennedy* (1974), p. 384. James Hilty, personal communication.

99. KF, Jerome Schulman to RSS, Nov. 20, 1958. "Unless adequate safeguards are provided, the Kennedy Foundation, in supporting a large project of this sort, could find itself expending large sums of money on work that is either currently going on, or that would have gone on in any event, with or without the grant."

100. KF, Masland to RSS, Mar. 16, 1959.

101. In the 1970s the foundation sponsored a bioethics program at Harvard. And in 1982 Rose Kennedy endowed a professorship at the Harvard Medical School for research on MR and child neurology. *NYT*, July 18, 1982, p. 14. Yet these initiatives did not add up to a program in MR.

102. Raymond Adams, interview of May 21, 1993.

103. See, e.g., RSS to JFK, July 29, 1959, where JPK has ordered RSS to "explain to Jack and Bobby the Massachusetts General Hospital deal." KL, JFK Prepresidential Papers, box 551.

104. See KF, RSS to Pat Lawford, Oct. 16, 1978.

105. KF, Schulman to RSS, Dec. 15, 1959.

106. Raymond Adams, interview of May 21, 1993.

107. KL, 79–2, box 4, JPK to Rusk, Apr. 23, 1959.

108. Jerome Schulman, interview of May 12, 1993.

109. See RSS to JPK, May 20, 1959. KL, 79–2, box 3.

110. Nate Gross's column, *Chicago American*, Feb. 25, 1959, p. 35.

111. Robert Haslam, interview of Oct. 21, 1992.

112. Cooke speech, "Clinical Research on Children," given in March 1978 at the Fogarty Center of NIH.

113. *Children Limited*, Oct. 1959, note, p. 14.

114. In his Oral History for the Kennedy Library (p. 1), Cooke places this initial contact in 1958. On the basis of the correspondence, however, it is likely that it occurred in the summer of 1959. See KF, Masland to RSS, Aug. 19, 1959. "Dr. Cooke is working toward an October deadline. I am sure that he will come up with a very thoughtfully developed proposal."

115. KF, RSS to JPK, Nov. 10, 1959.

116. KF, RSS to Cooke, Nov. 23, 1959.

117. KF, Cooke to EKS, Sept. 23, 1960.

118. Cooke tells some of this story in his article, "The Origin of the National Institute of Child Health and Human Development," *Pediatrics* 92 (1993), pp. 868–71.

119. Robert B. Kugel and Ann Shearer, eds., *Changing Patterns in Residential Services for the Mentally Retarded*, rev. ed. (Washington, D.C.: PCMR, 1976), pp. 217, 222. This article was not present in the first edition, published in 1969.

120. Eunice Shriver, "The Sun Has Burst Through," *Parade Magazine*, Feb. 2, 1964, pp. 6–7.

121. Sargent Shriver, interview of Feb. 19, 1992.

122. KF, Sleeper to Peter Bowman, Apr. 14, 1959.

123. KF, RSS to Peter Bowman, Apr. 22, 1959.

124. KF, RSS to JPK, Aug. 12, 1959.

125. KL, 79–2, box 3. RSS to Bowman, Apr. 22, 1959.

126. Jerome Schulman, interview of May 12, 1993.

127. KF, RSS to JPK, Nov. 10, 1959.

Chapter Four

1. According to a story in *Life* in Dec. 1963 by Theodore White, Jackie Kennedy erected one of Jack's favorite lines from the musical "Camelot" into the symbol of her husband's administration: "Don't let it be forgot, that once there was a spot, for one brief shining moment that was known as Camelot." Reprinted in Philip B. Kunhardt, Jr., *LIFE in Camelot: The Kennedy Years* (Boston: Little, Brown, 1988), pp. 314–15. David Wolper incorporated these lyrics in his 1964 film tribute to JFK shown to the Democratic National Convention.

2. KF, "RSS speech at Chicago, Apr. 8, 1964," p. 1.

3. Details from Liston, *Sargent Shriver* (1964), pp. 98, 181; "Shriver Quits," *Chicago Tribune*, Oct. 11, 1960, p. 1.

4. On these events see Wofford, *Kennedy and Kings*, pp. 68–71.

5. See, e.g., the White House press release of Nov. 10, 1961, on the President's Panel for Mental Retardation.

6. The words are Edward Berkowitz's, to whom I am indebted for showing me the chapter on the Kennedy years from his manuscript biography of Wilbur Cohen published as *Mr. Social Security: the Life of Wilbur J. Cohen* (Lawrence: University Press of Kansas, 1995).

7. Eunice Shriver, Oral History (1968), John F. Kennedy Library Oral History Program, pp. 3–4. All other oral histories cited in this chapter are from this collection.

8. The other members were Dean A. Clark, dean of the School of Public Health of the University of Pittsburgh; Herman Somers, a professor of political science at Haverford College; and Elizabeth Wickenden, a professor of urban studies at City University of New York.

9. See *New Frontiers of the Kennedy Administration: the Texts of the Task Force Reports Prepared for the President* (Washington, D.C.: Public Affairs Press, 1961), pp. 53–64, on "Social Welfare Frontiers"; the creation of a "National Institute of Child Health" was requested, pp. 61–62. See also Robert Cooke, Oral History (1968), p. 2, and Cooke "The Origin of the National Institute of Child Health and Human Development," *Pediatrics* 92 (1993), pp. 868–71.

10. Robert Cooke, interview of Feb. 19, 1992.

11. Ibid.

12. According to Michael Begab, at the time a specialist for social services in mental retardation at the Children's Bureau of HEW, the White House had

originally proposed an institute for MR research. NIH was said to have rejected the proposal as "too narrow." Begab, Oral History (1968), p. 23.

13. See the profile of Feldman in *Business Week*, July 13, 1963, p. 50.

14. Stafford Warren, Oral History (1966), p. 37.

15. Based on Cooke's interview with the author and his Oral History of March 29, 1968, deposited in the John F. Kennedy Library, pp. 5–6.

16. *CQWR* 18 (Mar. 2, 1962), p. 349.

17. On Eunice Shriver's lobbying: Robert Cooke, interview of Feb. 19, 1992. On Sargent Shriver and Robert Kennedy as lobbyists for NICHD: Donald Stedman, interview of Mar. 16, 1993.

18. On Hill, see Stephen P. Strickland, *Politics, Science, and Dread Disease: A Short History of United States Medical Research Policy* (Cambridge, Mass.: Harvard University Press, 1972), pp. 93–94 and passim. See also Milton Viorst, "The Political Good Fortune of Medical Research," *Science* 144 (Apr. 17, 1964), p. 270.

19. Fogarty introduced it in the House as HR 13840; George McGovern backed it in the Senate. Eisenhower signed it on Sept. 6, 1958. See *CQWR* 16 (Sept. 12, 1958), p. 1214. It became PL 85–926, authorizing the first federal program to train teachers for mentally retarded children. See also David Braddock, *Federal Policy toward Mental Retardation and Developmental Disabilities* (Baltimore: Brookes, 1987), p. 17. On Fogarty's interest in MR, see Elizabeth M. Boggs, "Federal Legislation" in *Mental Retardation and Developmental Disabilities: An Annual Review*, edited by Joseph Wortis, vol. 3 (New York: Grune and Stratton, 1971), pp. 108–10. Boggs explained Fogarty's relationship with Arthur Trudeau in an interview with me on Feb. 24, 1993.

20. When the Kennedy Administration introduced in the Senate a bill for the National Institute of Child Health in 1961 (S 2269), any appropriation was deliberately omitted from the bill so that it would not have to pass through Fogarty's appropriations subcommittee in the House. See Boggs private archive, Gunnar Dybwad to Vincent Fitzpatrick, July 20, 1961.

21. On Cooke's astute lobbying see Boggs private archive, Boggs to Powers, May 11, 1961. Cooke had asked Boggs to help get Fogarty onside.

22. *CQWR* 18 (Aug. 31, 1962), p. 1444.

23. See ibid., for Oct. 5 and Oct. 27, 1962.

24. Robert Cooke, Oral History (1968), p. 45. See also Edward Zigler, "National Crisis in Mental Retardation Research," *American Journal of Mental Deficiency* 83 (1978), p. 4.

25. Robert Cooke, Oral History (1968), p. 37.

26. See *NYT*, Aug. 8, 1963, p. 1; Aug. 10, p. 1.

27. Eunice Shriver (1968), Oral History, p. 27.

28. Robert Cooke, Oral History (1968), p. 8.

29. Edward Kennedy, *Fruitful Bough*, Eunice Shriver's essay, p. 223. The final report was published as Joint Commission on Mental Illness and Health, *Action for Mental Health: Final Report of the Joint Commission of Mental Illness and Health, 1961* (New York: Basic Books, 1961). There were preliminary newspaper accounts

in 1960 of its findings. See *NYT*, June 1, 1960, p. 43, "One in Four Tells of Emotional Ills."

30. Edward Kennedy, *Fruitful Bough*, p. 223.

31. John Throne, interview of Mar. 12, 1993.

32. Donald Stedman, interview of Mar. 16, 1993.

33. Elizabeth Boggs, interview of Feb. 24, 1993. On the Senate hearings see *Mentally Retarded Children: Hearing before the Committee on Labor and Public Welfare, United States Senate. . . . April 4, 1957* (Washington, D.C.: GPO, 1957); in fact, Jack Kennedy did not attend the public session (p. 1). Boggs came down from New Jersey but was not given an opportunity to testify (p. 34).

34. Boggs private archive, Myer Feldman to Elizabeth Boggs, Feb. 10, 1960. "Senator Kennedy has asked me to write you concerning the study of needed federal legislation. . . ."

35. See the various oral histories whose authors believed JFK had a heartfelt commitment to MR, e.g., Leonard Mayo, p. 49; John Macy, p. 75; and David Ray, p. 15.

36. Leonard Mayo put this historical comparison to JFK during a reception in the White House Rose Garden. The President responded, "Exactly, exactly." Leonard Mayo, Oral History (1968), p. 3.

37. Robert Cooke, Oral History (1968), p. 8.

38. Kennedy, *Fruitful Bough*, p. 223.

39. See the undated "Memorandum of Conference between Mr. and Mrs. Shriver and Myer Feldman," August or September 1961, KL, Myer Feldman, box 13. See also Victor Weingarten's detailed memo of Dec. 4, 1961, KL, Myer Feldman, box 13. The friends were Charles ("Chuck") Spaulding, a New York investment banker, and Len Billingsley.

40. Weingarten to Mayo, Dec. 4, 1961, KL, Myer Feldman, box 13.

41. In his oral history for the Kennedy Library, Masland claimed it was he who recommended Mayo (p. 2). Eunice Shriver, in her oral history, claimed that she had first asked Howard Rusk, and that Rusk had recommended Mayo (p. 5). Cooke, in his oral history, said that Mayo was selected because he (Cooke) and the Shrivers already knew Mayo through the Crippled Children's Association (p. 9).

42. Elizabeth Boggs, interview of July 15, 1993.

43. Eunice Shriver, Oral History (1968), p. 6.

44. Leonard Mayo, Oral History (1968), pp. 4–5.

45. Elizabeth Boggs, interview of May 1, 1993.

46. White House press release, Oct. 11, 1961, p. 1.

47. For an account of these events see Dorothy Garst Murray, "The Burning Power of Love: The Story of the National Association for Retarded Children, 1950–1970," undated MS, p. VI-3. I am grateful to Mrs. Murray for letting me see a copy of the manuscript. See also President's Committee on Mental Retardation (PCMR), *MR 76. Mental Retardation: Past and Present* (Washington, D.C.: GPO, Jan. 1977), pp. 52–53.

48. *NYT* report, Oct. 12, 1961, p. 1.

49. KL, Papers of Family (POF), box 32. Rosemary Dybwad to Eunice Shriver, Mar. 22, 1962.

50. *NYT,* Oct. 19, 1961, p. 24.

51. KF, press release of Nov. 10, 1961.

52. Robert Cooke, Oral History (1968), p. 19.

53. See, e.g., KL, Myer Feldman, box 13, Mayo to EKS, Jan. 18, 1962, giving her the results of the first two weeks in January.

54. Robert Cooke, Oral History (1968), p. 12.

55. David Bazelon, Oral History (1969), p. 12.

56. Leonard Mayo, Oral History (1968), p. 28.

57. The version presented to JFK that morning was really a rough draft. After the Bureau of the Budget had worked it over, deleting some recommendations and adding others, it was finally published in February 1963, The President's Panel on Mental Retardation, *Report to the President: A Proposed Program for National Action to Combat Mental Retardation* (Washington, D.C.: GPO, October 1962 [*sic*]). See Boggs on the delay, in Wortis, vol. 3, p. 115. The Library of Congress gives the publication date as 1963. *National Union Catalog: 1956–1967,* v. 116, p. 547. For a succinct outline of the panel's recommendations, see Edward Berkowitz, "The Politics of Mental Retardation during the Kennedy Administration," *Social Science Quarterly* 61 (1980), pp. 135–36. For a more extended discussion, see PCMR, *MR 76. Mental Retardation: Past and Present,* pp. 14–15. The President's Panel on Mental Retardation (PPMR) also presented its chief recommendations in a "Chart Book" filled with graphics. PPMR, *Mental Retardation: A National Plan for a National Problem* (Washington, D.C.: GPO, Aug. 1963). Because of errors in some of the material, the Chart Book was never widely distributed.

58. Edward Davens, Oral History (1968), pp. 32–33.

59. Ibid., p. 33

60. Eunice Shriver, Oral History (1968), p. 12.

61. See, e.g., KL, Myer Feldman, box 13, memo from Mayo to Feldman, Dec. 12, 1961.

62. Nicholas Hobbs, Oral History (1968), p. 22.

63. Leonard Mayo, Oral History (1968), p. 13.

64. Eunice Shriver, "Remarks Before the National Association for Mental Health," Mar. 5, 1962. Reprinted in *Congressional Record,* 1962, pp. 4785–87.

65. Edwin Bayley, Oral History (1968), pp. 111–12. The story actually ran on p. 24, "President Spurs Retarded Study," *NYT,* Oct. 19, 1961.

66. Eunice Shriver, Oral History (1968), p. 12.

67. Cited in Martha Lentz Walker, *Beyond Bureaucracy: Mary Elizabeth Switzer and Rehabilitation* (Lanham, Md.: University Press of America, 1985), p. 35.

68. David Braddock, "Federal Assistance for Mental Retardation and Developmental Disabilities I: A Review Through 1961," *Mental Retardation* 24 (1986), p. 177; *NYT,* Oct. 28, 1962, p. 82.

69. David Braddock, *Federal Policy Toward Mental Retardation,* table 8, p. 52. See also Howard Rusk, "Help for Mentally Ill [*sic*]," *NYT,* Oct. 28, 1962, p. 82.

70. John Gardner, "Remarks," Stanford University, Feb. 25, 1984. See also Edward Berkowitz, "Mary E. Switzer: The Entrepreneur within the Federal Bureaucracy," *American Journal of Economics and Sociology* 39 (1980), pp. 79–81.

71. See KF, Gunnar Dybwad to Cooke, Dec. 12, 1970.

72. *CQA*, "Vocational Rehabilitation," 10 (1954), pp. 213–15. See also Boggs, in Wortis, vol 3, p. 106. Walker, *Switzer*, pp. 149–52.

73. Walker, *Switzer*, pp. 178, 186, 215.

74. PPMR, *Report* (1962), pp. 115–17; see also Berkowitz, "Mary E. Switzer: The Entrepreneur within the Federal Bureaucracy," *American Journal of Economics and Sociology* (1979).

75. For details see Braddock, *MR* (1986), pp. 176–78. PCMR, *MR 76. Mental Retardation: Past and Present*, pp. 87–88.

76. See Martha Eliot's "Foreword," in *New Directions for Mentally Retarded Children, Report of a Conference on New Directions in Community Planning for Mentally Retarded Children, Convened by the Josiah Macy, Jr. Foundation at the Request of the Interdepartmental Committee on Children and Youth and Held at Princeton, New Jersey, February 26–29, 1956* (New York: Macy Foundation, 1956), pp. vii—ix. This subcommittee was usually referred to as HEW's Committee on Mental Retardation. On this committee's history see PCMR, *MR 76. Mental Retardation: Past and Present*, p. 102.

77. Michael Begab, Oral History (1968), p. 1.

78. Braddock, *MR* (1986), p. 180.

79. On the history of the Office of Education see PCMR, *MR 76. Mental Retardation: Past and Present*, pp. 85–87.

80. See *CQWR* 16 (Aug. 22, Sept. 12, 1958), pp. 1110, 1214. See also Boggs in Wortis, vol. 3, pp. 106–9, and Elizabeth Boggs, Oral History (1986), Boggs private archive, vol. 3, pp. 19–20.

81. Nicholas Hobbs, Oral History (1968), p. 19.

82. See Paul Starr, *The Social Transformation of American Medicine* (New York: Basic Books, 1982), pp. 348–51; David Braddock, *Federal Policy Toward Mental Retardation*, pp. 156–58.

83. Macy Foundation, *New Directions for Mentally Retarded Children*, p. 34.

84. See Boggs in Wortis, vol. 3, p. 105.

85. Eunice Shriver, Oral History (1968), p. 25.

86. See the memo from the Acting Director of the Bureau of the Budget to Feldman, Oct. 20, 1962. KL, Myer Feldman, box 13.

87. Eunice Shriver, Oral History (1968), p. 25.

88. KL, Myer Feldman, box 13, Tarjan to Feldman, Oct. 23, 1962.

89. *NYT Biographical Service* 12 (July, 1981), p. 1012.

90. "Kennedy Picks Aide," *NYT*, Dec. 24, 1962, p. 1.

91. Stafford Warren, Oral History (1966), p. 33.

92. Ibid., p. 25.

93. Ibid., p. 24. In 1963, Ted Kennedy was president, Thomas Walsh treasurer. See "Annual Report," filed Jan. 22, 1963, with the Illinois Secretary of State.

94. Patrick Doyle, Oral History (1968), p. 34.

95. Ibid., p. 5.

96. Ibid., pp. 34–35.

97. See, e.g., Warren's memo to the Shrivers and Feldman, Aug. 23, 1963, KL, Myer Feldman, box 13. "PR office activity this week included. . . ."

98. See, e.g., "Minutes, Advisory Committee on Mental Retardation," Aug. 21, 1963. KL, Myer Feldman, box 13.

99. Stafford Warren, Oral History (1966), p. 10. "If he [Cooke] disliked them, he wouldn't work with them or consider them in any way."

100. David Ray, interview of June 12, 1993.

101. Ibid.

102. Ibid. See also Stafford Warren, Oral History (1966), p. 25.

103. See David Ray, Oral History (1968), p. 10; Elizabeth Boggs, "Federal Legislation, 1966–1971," in *Mental Retardation: An Annual Review,* edited by Joseph Wortis, vol. 4 (1971), p. 166.

104. Stafford Warren, Oral History (1966), p. 36.

105. Patrick Doyle, Oral History (1968), pp. 5–6, 35.

106. Ibid., p. 36.

107. David Ray, interview of June 12, 1993.

108. Eunice Shriver, Oral History (1968), p. 25.

109. Berkowitz, Cohen MS, p. 9.

110. On the indifference of the secretaries see Luther Stringham, Oral History (1968), p. 27.

111. Berkowitz, Cohen MS, p. 64.

112. On the SCMR see Michael Begab, Oral History (1968), p. 11; Luther Stringham, Oral History (1968), pp. 2–8; PCMR, *MR 76. Mental Retardation: Past and Present,* p. 102; Braddock, *MR* (1986), p. 179. On Cohen's office see Berkowitz, Cohen MS, p. 7.

113. David Bazelon, Oral History (1969), p. 18.

114. Robert Cooke, Oral History (1968), pp. 24–25.

115. Ibid., p. 22.

116. Eunice Shriver, Oral History, p. 13.

117. KF, Cohen to EKS, Feb. 11, 1963.

118. Eunice Shriver, Oral History (1968), p. 21.

119. John Throne, interview of Mar. 12, 1993.

120. Patrick Doyle, Oral History (1968), p. 22.

121. KL, Myer Feldman, box 13, Gunnar Dybwad to EKS, June 20, 1963.

122. KL, Myer Feldman, box 13, RSS to Feldman, June 24, 1963.

123. KL, Myer Feldman, box 13, Cohen to Feldman, Aug. 13, 1963. Dybwad refused the post. KL, box 13, Cohen to Stringham, Aug. 21, 1963.

124. KL, Myer Feldman, box 13. Cohen to Feldman, undated memo, evidently September 1962. "Arrangements also have been made to retain a portion of the space presently assigned to the Panel so that it will continue to be available to Mrs. Shriver, Mrs. [Ruth] Gray and Mrs. [Isadora] Moore." Gray and Moore were secretaries.

125. Eunice Shriver, Oral History (1968), p. 16.

126. KF, Cooke to EKS, Mar. 30, 1961. In this letter Cooke did not use the phrase "university-affiliated facilities," but the germ of the idea was present. The panel's own proposal of "research centers on mental retardation" was much less consumer-oriented than Cooke's idea. See PPMR, *Report,* (1962), pp. 24–27.

127. Cooke speech, "Recognition Day Luncheon, Council of Auxiliaries of the State Department of Mental Hygiene," Baltimore, Nov. 15, 1962.

128. House of Representatives, 88th Congress, 1st Session, Document no. 58, "Message from the President of the United States Relative to Mental Illness and Mental Retardation," Feb. 5, 1963.

129. Eunice Shriver, Oral History (1968), p. 17.

130. For the text of JFK's "Message on Mental Illness and Retardation," see *CQWR* 21 (Feb. 8, 1963), pp. 170–74.

131. See *CQWR* (1963) for Mar. 15, pp. 323–324; May 31, p. 829; Aug. 23, pp. 1470–71; Sept. 13, p. 1559; Oct. 25, p. 1844. Title I was called "The Mental Retardation Facilities Construction Act"; Title II, "The Community Mental Health Centers Act"; Title III simply provided for the training of "teachers for mentally retarded and handicapped children." The actual numbers of UAF's and MRRC's were not spelled out in the Act; figures given in the text are for 1969. On mental-health aspects of this legislation see Gerald N. Grob, *From Asylum to Community: Mental Health Policy in Modern America* (Princeton: Princeton University Press, 1991), pp. 277–34.

132. See *CQWR* 21 (Aug. 23, 1963), pp. 1470–71.

133. See David Braddock, "Federal Assistance for Mental Retardation and Developmental Disabilities II: The Modern Era," *Mental Retardation* 24 (1986), pp. 209–218, esp. p. 209. See also Boggs in Wortis, vol. 3, pp. 118–20.

134. See *CQWR* Aug. 16, 1963, p. 1449; Aug. 30, p. 1499; Oct. 4, p. 1706; Oct. 18, p. 1803.

135. Stafford Warren, Oral History (1966), p. 28.

136. Wofford, *Kennedy and Kings,* p. 266.

137. Ibid., p. 267.

138. "On Trial," *Look,* Nov. 7, 1961, p. 34.

139. *NYT Magazine,* Dec. 17, 1961, p. 14.

140. *NYT Magazine,* Mar. 15, 1964, p. 21.

141. Eunice Shriver, Oral History (1968), pp. 23–24.

142. On the controversy about whether the New Frontier represented a legislative success, see the review of the scholarly literature (and the positive assessment) in Irving Bernstein, *Promises Kept: John F. Kennedy's New Frontier* (New York: Oxford University Press, 1991), pp. 3–7. Bernstein does not mention the tremendously successful MR legislation.

143. Robert Cooke, Oral History (1968), p. 35.

144. Fogarty papers, SpF 65, folder 764; see the "Review of the West Warwick-Coventry Camping Proposal" by Francis Kelley, attached to Kelley to Fogarty, Apr. 30, 1963.

145. David Ray, Oral History (1968), p. 11.

146. Ibid., p. 25.

147. Stafford Warren, Oral History (1966), pp. 17–18.

148. Fogarty archive, FL 88–1-88, F.7. HR 7033. Cooke to Fogarty, Mar. 27, 1963. See also Cooke to Fogarty, May 2, 1963, and EKS to Fogarty, Aug. 2, 1963. ("Two weeks ago when we were talking. . . .")

149. Robert Cooke, Oral History (1968), p. 41.

150. Eunice said the conference was Mayo's idea. Eunice Shriver, Oral History (1968), p. 26.

151. Ibid., p. 26.

152. Warren sent to Sarge a copy of a memo of July 8, 1963, that he had sent to HEW, asking for their cooperation. He penciled on it, "Dear Sarg [sic]: This request has been turned down twice and I am referred back to Mike Feldman again. . . . We are ready to roll now and should have a clear way [?] to do so. Anything you can do to convince Mike will be appreciated." KL, Myer Feldman, box 13.

153. Stafford Warren, Oral History (1966), p. 21.

154. Ibid., pp. 21–22.

155. Michael Begab, Oral History (1968), p. 14.

156. Stafford Warren, Oral History (1966), p. 22.

157. Michael Begab, Oral History (1968), p. 15.

158. See KF, "Program. White House Conference on Mental Retardation, September 18, 19, and 20, 1963, Airlie House, Warrenton, Virginia."

159. David Ray, Oral History (1968), p. 29.

160. *NYT,* "Kennedy Foundation to Honor 6," Nov. 15, 1963, p. 31.

Chapter Five

1. Frank J. Hayden, *Physical Fitness for the Mentally Retarded* (Toronto: Rotary Physical Education Research Committee, 1964), p. 3.

2. Wolf Wolfensberger, "A Brief Overview of the Principle of Normalization," in *Normalization, Social Integration, and Community Services,* edited by Robert J. Flynn and Kathleen E. Nitsch (Austin: Pro-Ed, 1980), pp. 7–29, quote p. 26.

3. E. Paul Benoit, "The Play Problem of Retarded Children: A Frank Discussion with Parents," *AJMD* 60 (1955), pp. 41–55, quote pp. 43–44.

4. Ibid., p. 43.

5. Joan Ramm, "Seaside," *Challenge: Recreation and Fitness for the Mentally Retarded* (an AAHPER newsletter, hereafter cited as *Challenge*), Sept. 1966, pp. 1, 8, quote p. 1.

6. Benoit, *AJMD* (1955), p. 46.

7. Quoting Jack Hammond, director of the Willowbrook State School on Staten Island, of which Gouverneur was a branch. "Gouverneur Care Defended," *New York Post,* Sept. 10, 1965.

8. Wolf Wolfensberger, address to the Kentucky chapter of The Arc, Apr. 24, 1993.

9. NARC, ed., *The Record: Newsletter Concerning Residential Care for Retarded Children and Adults,* (Fall) 1962, p. 5. The incident occurred at the Manitoba School, Portage-la-Prairie. Emphasis in original.

10. Wolf Wolfensberger, address to the Kentucky chapter of The Arc, Apr. 24, 1993.

11. KF, cited in a report by Frank Hayden of Jan. 14, 1969, to the trustees of the Kennedy Foundation. The term "average" means reaching the 50th percentile of the nonretarded.

12. Hayden, *Physical Fitness for the Mentally Retarded*, p. 3.

13. Rarick reported his findings to the KF in 1967. They are summarized in Eileen McCaffery Lapriola, "The Joseph P. Kennedy, Jr. Foundation and Its Role in Physical Education and Recreation for the Mentally Retarded" (University of Maryland, Department of Physical Education, M.A. thesis, 1972), pp. 156–57.

14. KF, memo to the file from Beverly Rowan, Oct. 9, 1974.

15. Aileen Vines and Eleanor Coleman, "Physical Education Classes for Mentally Retarded," *Challenge,* Dec. 1965, pp. 4–5, quote p. 5.

16. KF, EKS, "Recollections on the Start and Development of Recreation and Special Olympics," Jan. 1981, p. 2.

17. "Stevenson Quips," *NYT,* Dec. 7, 1962, p. 1.

18. KF, EKS speech at "Annual Awards Dinner of Comeback, Inc.," New York, Mar. 5, 1966, p. 5.

19. KF, EKS, "Recollections on Special Olympics," pp. 2–4.

20. Donald Stedman, interview of Mar. 16, 1993.

21. Eiler died in 1992. This information was obtained from an interview with his widow, Lee Eiler, Aug. 27, 1993.

22. The number 26 comes from Lapriola, "Joseph P. Kennedy, Jr. Foundation," p. 4; Lapriola gives the founding date of the camp as 1961.

23. KF, EKS "Recollections," p. 6.

24. KF, EKS, "Out of Shadows" (1962), pp. 14–15. This was a draft of her article for the *Saturday Evening Post.* These details were not included in the published version.

25. EKS, "Hope for Retarded Children," *Saturday Evening Post,* Sept. 22, 1962, pp. 71–74, quote p. 73.

26. "Rose Kennedy Pleads for Retarded," *NYT,* June 16, 1964, p. 21.

27. RSS, interview of Feb. 19, 1992.

28. Donald Stedman, interview of Mar. 16, 1993.

29. See, e.g., "Potomac Journal," *WP,* Aug. 14, 1975, Va. 1.

30. KF, EKS, "Address . . . before the National Society for Handicapped Children, Mansion House, London, England," July 15, 1964, p. 3.

31. EKS, "Observation of Campers, 1962–1964," quoted in Lapriola, "Joseph P. Kennedy, Jr. Foundation," p. 29.

32. Lapriola, "Joseph P. Kennedy, Jr. Foundation," p. 25; EKS, "Recollections," pp. 7–8.

33. Ann Hart, interview of Mar. 6, 1993.

34. EKS, "Hope for Retarded Children," p. 72.

35. KF, EKS, "Speech before the President's Committee on Employment of the Handicapped," May 9, 1963, p. 12.

36. Boggs private archive, Boggs to Lund, Aug. 1, 1957. She later published with David Ginglend, *Day Camping for the Mentally Retarded* (New York: NARC, 1962). In 1931–1932, the Provincial Training School in Red Deer, Alberta, organized a week-long overnight camp for its retarded trainees. Yet this example seems not to have been followed. See Provincial Training School, *Annual Report, 1931*, p. 109.

37. These details are mentioned in Boggs private archive, Boggs to Alton Lund, Aug. 1, 1957. Lund was a member of the NARC executive committee. For the figure "150" see NARC, "Decade of Decision" (1959), p. 14, a document prepared for the 1960 White House Conference on Children and Youth, a copy of which is also in Boggs private archive.

38. See KL, MS 79–2, box 3, Rev. R. O. Boner to JPK, Apr. 2, 1958; for an example of an early non-Catholic overnight camp see Roland Larson, "The Mentally Retarded at Camp," *Recreation*, Mar. 1957, pp. 77–78. Silver Lake Camp for the Mentally Retarded near Minneapolis opened in the mid-1950s.

39. Boggs private archive, NARC, "Seventh Annual Meeting, Oct. 25–27, 1956 —Convention Report: Moving Forward," pp. 12–13.

40. Ann Hart, interview of Mar. 6, 1993.

41. Lapriola, "Joseph P. Kennedy, Jr. Foundation," p. 30.

42. John Throne, interview of Mar. 12, 1993.

43. KF, EKS, "Recollections," p. 8.

44. Most of this information about Freeberg's life is based on an interview of Aug. 5, 1993, with his son Glen Freeberg.

45. John Throne, interview of Mar. 12, 1993.

46. Ann Burke, interview of July 17, 1993.

47. KF, EKS, "Recollections," p. 9.

48. This account is based on KF, Freeberg to EKS, June 19, 1979; Freeberg, "The Need for Recreation Programs for the Retarded," *Illinois Parks*, Jan.—Feb. 1964, pp. 3–4; Lapriola, "Joseph P. Kennedy, Jr. Foundation," pp. 11–12.

49. KL, Feldman papers, box 13, EKS to Feldman, Apr. 23, 1963.

50. Lapriola, "Joseph P. Kennedy, Jr. Foundation," pp. 16, 22.

51. See Harold D. Meyer and Charles K. Brightbill, "Important Historical Events in the Recreation Movement in the United States," in *Recreation: Pertinent Readings*, edited by Jay B. Nash (Dubuque: Brown, 1965), pp. 23–24. Donald C. Weiskopf, *Recreation and Leisure: Improving the Quality of Life*, 2d ed. (Boston: Allyn and Bacon, 1982), pp. 85–107.

52. Bertha Schlotter and Margaret Svendsen, *An Experiment in Recreation with the Mentally Retarded* (Chicago, n.d. ["1932" handwritten on title page]), pp. 3, 7.

53. State Colony, Woodbine, New Jersey, "Final Report: Hospital Improvement Program Grant no. 5, R20 MR02019. Therapeutic Recreation for the Profoundly Retarded (Sept. 1968)," pp. 65, 67, 75. I am grateful to Woodbine State Colony for making a copy of this report available to me.

54. KF, EKS, "Recollections," pp. 10–11.

55. AAHPERD archives in Reston, Va., Jackson Anderson, "A Review of the Project," attached to a report of Apr. 13, 1965, pp. 1–2.

56. AAHPERD archives, Board of Directors Meeting, Official Minutes, Nov. 1–4, 1964, p. 49.

57. AAHPERD archives, "A Proposal for the Establishment of a Project on Recreation and Fitness for the Mentally Retarded, Submitted by the American Association for Health, Physical Education, and Recreation to the Joseph P. Kennedy, Jr. Foundation, April, 1965."

58. See A. Gertrude Jacob, "Systematic Physical Training for the Mentally Deficient," *Journal of Psycho-Asthenics* 9 (1905), pp. 98–112. The Seguin school had its children spend "days of untiring effort" on the rings, rope and high jump. "The results since we formed our heavy work classes have been most encouraging. The fleshy have reduced their flesh. . . ." (p. 101).

59. *Challenge*, Nov. 1966, note, p. 1.

60. Ibid., note, p. 6.

61. According to an AAHPER survey, summarized in KF, Julian Stein memo to EKS, Sept. 29, 1967, p. 3.

62. John Friedrich, "Teaching Sports Skills to the Mentally Retarded," in "Proceedings: Workshop on Physical Education and Recreation for the Mentally Retarded, University of North Carolina, Chapel Hill, Apr. 1–2, 1966," pp. 18–22. MS in AAHPER Archive.

63. From this period see Julian U. Stein, "Adapted Physical Education for the Educable Mentally Handicapped," *Journal of Health, Physical Education and Recreation,* Dec. 1962, offprint.

64. Julian Stein, interview of Mar. 1, 1993.

65. Dolores Geddes, "Modified Circuit Training," *Challenge,* Sept. 1966, p. 4.

66. James Lounsberry, "Weight Training for the Mentally Retarded at the Primary Level," *Challenge,* May 1967, pp. 1, 4.

67. AAPHERD archives, "Official Minutes, Board of Directors Fall Meeting, Nov. 9–12, 1969," p. 1. The directors stated that official policy "prevents endorsement of competition for children beyond the local level."

68. Frank Hayden, interview of July 13, 1993.

69. "They Develop through Golf," *Challenge,* Sept. 1968, p. 4. Frank Hayden, interview of July 13, 1993. Stein: "Frank Hayden got very upset with me." (Julian Stein, interview of Mar. 1, 1993).

70. Donald Stedman, interview of Mar. 16, 1993.

71. KF, EKS to Philip E. Ryan, Jan. 7, 1964.

72. KF, "John F. Kennedy Birthday Committee," p. 7.

73. KF, Young to Collins, Jan. 7, 1964.

74. KF, RSS to Jackson Anderson, June 15, 1965.

75. Lapriola, "Joseph P. Kennedy, Jr. Foundation," pp. 44–45, citing Oliver's "Comments on Camps Visited—With Some Suggestions," Oct. 5, 1965.

76. KF, "Lt. J. P. Kennedy Institute: The History," pp. 52–53.

77. In 1966 AAHPER distributed copies free of charge, paid for by the KF, to school staff throughout the country who were responsible for physical education for the mentally retarded. See Holland to directors, Apr. 15, 1966. (This letter seen in KF.)

78. AAHPER archives, Rarick to Freeburg, Sept. 22, 1964. Rarick had known Freeburg since serving as a visiting professor at Southern Illinois University in 1957–1958.

79. Throne thinks it likely that Freeberg called Hayden to the Shrivers' attention (interview of Mar. 12, 1993). EKS, on the other hand, says that RSS learned of Hayden's work from "a clipping." (EKS, "Recollections," p. 12.)

80. Frank Hayden, interview of Oct. 8, 1992.

81. KF, Foster to JPK, Aug. 27, 1963.

82. Frank Hayden, interview of Oct. 8, 1992. Hayden was reluctant to show me a copy of the paper. He gave this version of events to a previous researcher as well. See Janice M. Deakin, "A Study of the Special Olympics Movement in the United States and Canada," B.A. honors thesis, Department of Physical and Health Education, Queen's University, Kingston, Ontario, March 1980, pp. 4–5.

83. Frank Hayden, interview of Oct. 8, 1992.

84. Robert Holland, interview of Dec. 7, 1992.

85. John Throne, interview of March 12, 1993.

86. Frank Hayden, interview of Oct. 8, 1992.

87. Beverly Campbell, interview of July 13, 1993. There was some tension between Hayden and Campbell, and Campbell bridled to learn that Hayden had referred to her as his "secretary." David Ray agreed that the Special Olympics was basically Eunice Shriver's idea; interview of June 12, 1993.

88. EKS, "Recreation for the Mentally Retarded," *Journal of Health, Physical Education and Recreation* 36 (May 1965), pp. 16–18, 55, quote p. 18.

89. KF, EKS speech, "National Conference on Recreation and Fitness for the Mentally Retarded," given to NEA, Nov. 2, 1966, p. 11. Penciled notes indicate that the speech was written by Milton Gwirtzman, a close family friend, and revised by William Rapp, a fitness consultant for the Kennedy Foundation.

90. Mentioned in Lapriola, "Joseph P. Kennedy, Jr. Foundation," p. 115.

91. See, e.g., John A. Lippold, "A Successful Recreation Program for the Retarded," *Illinois Parks,* Jan.—Feb. 1964, pp. 1–2.

92. KF, EKS, "Recollection on Sports Program," draft of Oct. 23, 1979, p. 7. For details of the grant see Lapriola, "Joseph P. Kennedy, Jr. Foundation," pp. 58–62.

93. KF, EKS, "Continuation of Notes re Recreation Program," Jan. 1981, p. 2.

94. This account is based on KF, Freeberg to EKS, June 19, 1979. Executive director Robert Montague attached a memo to the letter saying, "Mrs. Shriver: This supports your recollection of the origin of Special Olympics."

95. McGlone/Burke's initial feeler to Freeberg did not mention a special athletic event at all but simply requested Freeberg's advice about overcoming staff and money shortages in order "to expand our Special Recreation Program into several more of our Park facilities." McGlone/Burke to Freeberg, Nov. 29, 1967. Copy courtesy of Anne McGlone/Burke. (Hereafter cited as Anne Burke.)

96. This account is based on Anne Burke, interview of July 17, 1993. In Hayden's recollection, Freeberg and Anne Burke made the initial contact with

the KF by phoning Hayden and not EKS. Frank Hayden, interview of July 13, 1993.

97. Anne Burke and William H. Freeberg to the KF, Jan. 26, 1968. Copy courtesy of Anne Burke.

98. "Press Conference on Chicago Special Olympics, statement by Mrs. Eunice Kennedy Shriver," Mar. 29, 1968. Copy courtesy of Anne Burke.

99. See Lapriola, "Joseph P. Kennedy, Jr. Foundation," p. 376.

100. Frank Hayden, interview of Oct. 8, 1992.

101. Anne Burke, interview of July 17, 1993. The Burke-Freeberg proposal, however, did provide for "100 yard dash, relay race, high jump" and so forth. These events were to take place from 10 a.m. until 1 p.m.; "finals" would occur from 2 to 4 p.m. See their proposal of Jan. 26, 1968, attachment III.

102. KF, EKS, "Continuation of Notes re Recreation Program," p. 3.

103. Frank Hayden, interview of Oct. 8, 1992.

104. Anne Burke, interview of July 17, 1993.

105. See Burke to Freeberg, undated; Burke to Freeberg, Feb. 23, 1968. Courtesy of Anne Burke.

106. KF, EKS, "Continuation of Notes re Recreation Program," p. 3.

107. Frank Hayden, interview of Oct. 8, 1992.

108. Anne Burke, interview of July 17, 1993.

109. Frank Hayden, interview of Oct. 8, 1992.

110. Frank Hayden, interview of July 13, 1993. "Herb was the speech writer, but what he put in it he got from me. . . . I arrived in Chicago earlier that week, Monday or something, and had spoken to her on the phone maybe Tuesday or Wednesday and explained to her on the phone this idea, that it was not a one-shot event. . . . [I told her] that she would be explaining it at the press conference on Saturday morning."

111. Beverly Campbell, interview of July 13, 1993.

112. KF, EKS, "Continuation of Notes re Recreation Program," p. 4.

113. Beverly Campbell, interview of July 13, 1993.

114. "Eunice Kennedy Shriver Statement, July 20, 1968," copy courtesy of Anne Burke.

115. Anne Burke, interview of July 17, 1993. The outrage of the Park District officers was reflected in some of their subsequent correspondence with the KF. See, e.g., Shannon to EKS, May 6, 1969. "It is difficult to reconcile the thoughts expressed in your letter [EKS to Shannon April 25, 1969], when we at the Park District conceived the idea some time ago." Copy courtesy of Anne Burke.

116. Hayden, "Sometimes They Stumbled," *Challenge,* Nov. 1968, pp. 1, 4, quote p. 1.

117. Ibid., pp. 1, 2.

118. Quoted in *Sports Illustrated,* Aug. 17, 1987, p. 48.

119. Frank Hayden, interview of Oct. 8, 1992.

120. Beverly Campbell, interview of July 13, 1993.

121. KF, EKS to Arthur Lazarus, Jan. 29, 1986.

122. Kramer, who died of prostatic cancer in April 1992, left a record of his thoughts about terminal illness, coauthored with his wife Kay. *Conversations at Midnight: Coming to Terms with Dying and Death* (New York: Morrow, 1993). The book gives a sense of his mind and character.

123. Anonymity of person providing description requested.

124. RSS, interview of Feb. 19, 1992.

125. Donald Stedman, interview of Mar. 16, 1993.

126. KF, undated note from Anthony to Bobby Shriver, evidently when Anthony was in his early teens and Bobby, who was eleven years older, in his early twenties (c. 1977).

127. Donald Stedman, interview of Mar. 16, 1993.

128. EKS, "The Games Where Olympic Spirit Is All That Counts," *NYT*, Aug. 14, 1983.

129. KF, EKS, "Remarks, Association of Physical Fitness Centers Award, Las Vegas, Nevada," June 4, 1980, p. 7.

130. "The Kennedy Who Could Be President," *Ladies' Home Journal*, Mar. 1976, pp. 116–17, 156, 158, 160, quote p. 117. Emphasis in original.

131. James N. Oliver, "The Effect of Physical Conditioning Exercises and Activities on the Mental Characteristics of Educationally Sub-Normal Boys," *British Journal of Educational Psychology* 28 (1958), pp. 155–65.

132. W. Owens Corder, "Effects of Physical Education on the Intellectual, Physical, and Social Development of Educable Mentally Retarded Boys," *Exceptional Children* 32 (1966), pp. 357–63.

133. KF, EKS, "Address, National Conference on Recreation and Fitness for the Mentally Retarded," Nov. 2, 1966, pp. 2–3.

134. KF, EKS, "Address to Annual Meeting of Phi Epsilon Kappa," St. Louis, Mar. 28, 1968, pp. 9–10.

135. KF, EKS to Bob Montague and Herb Kramer, Aug. 13, 1980.

136. KF, EKS, "Remarks, Special Olympics Chapter Directors Conference, Smugglers' Notch, Vermont," Aug. 18, 1980, p. 2.

137. Ibid., p. 6.

138. Ibid., p. 11.

139. Frank Hayden, interview of Oct. 8, 1992. The following events, unless otherwise indicated, were related in this interview.

140. KF, "A Report to the Trustees from Frank J. Hayden . . . Activities in Physical Education and Recreation," attached to Trustees Report, Jan. 14, 1969.

141. On the threatened black boycott see *NYT*, Mar. 30, 1968, p. 42; Apr. 12, p. 28; June 23, sec. 5, p. 1; Aug. 1, p. 35; Sept. 1, sec. 5, p. 1. Rafer Johnson had publicly opposed the boycott; see *NYT Magazine*, May 12, 1968, p. 42.

142. Lapriola, "Joseph P. Kennedy, Jr. Foundation," p. 385.

Chapter Six

1. Donald Stedman, interview of Mar. 16, 1993.

2. Ibid.

3. "Many Old Friends Gather," *NYT*, June 8, 1968, p. 11.

4. KL, JPK box 35, personal correspondence 1945—, "H." JPK to Mrs. William Randolph Hearst, Jr., Feb. 20, 1952.

5. KL, MS 79–2, box 3. JPK to RSS, Apr. 6, 1950.

6. KL, MS 79–2, box 3. RSS to JPK, Aug. 27, 1950.

7. "Talk of the Town," *New Yorker,* Feb. 24, 1962, pp. 26–27, quote p. 27.

8. Edwin Bayley, Oral History (1968), John F. Kennedy Library Oral History Collection, pp. 94–95.

9. Bayley, ibid., quoting RSS verbatim, p. 93.

10. According to his brother-in-law RSS. KF, RSS handwritten note on a memo to him from his secretary, dated July 9, 1990. RSS wrote, "[A separate place for the press to be given lunch was] not necessary but would be deeply appreciated and create good will . . . maybe avoid some disgruntled 'ink-stained wretch' from blasting 'Those millionaire Kennedys who won't even give a sandwich to hard-working members of 4th Estate . . .' If Teddy were asked I think he'd say yes pay for them . . it's [etc.]" Ellipses in original.

11. KF, Fred McDonald to Robert Kennedy, Apr. 26, 1966.

12. KF, McDonald to Stephen Smith, Mar. 7, 1966.

13. KF, Patricia K. Lawford to Smith, Feb. 15, 1980.

14. KF, EKS to Bobby Shriver, June 9, 1980. I have not been able to locate the article in question. EKS said it had been ghostwritten for the most part by Herb Kramer.

15. KF, MS "John F. Kennedy Birthday Committee," undated; the names of the participants were not recorded. Quotes pp. 5, 8.

16. On RSS initiating the Advertising Council campaign, see Murray, "NARC," p. x—20.

17. KF, T. S. Repplier to LeRoy Collins, Jan. 8, 1964.

18. KF, Collins to RSS, Jan. 14, 1964. By January 7 at the latest the Shrivers had reached the decision to link JFK's birthday celebration specifically to MR. See Charles Young, of the New York ad agency Young and Rubicam, to Collins, Jan. 7, 1964.

19. KF, Ray to Collins, Jan. 6, 1964.

20. KF, Annual Trustees Report for 1968, Jan. 14, 1969. Of the $250,000, the KF contributed $149,000.

21. Boggs private archive, Luther Stringham, Report of the Executive Director of NARC, Oct. 2, 1965.

22. KF, RSS to Randolph A. Hearst, Jan. 27, 1965.

23. KF, Gene Yarnell to RSS, May 26, 1965.

24. KF, MS "History of the Joseph P. Kennedy, Jr. Foundation" (1984), p. 15.

25. KF, Ray to the Shrivers, Feb. 3, 1965.

26. RFK-biographer James Hilty made this point to me in a personal communication.

27. David Ray, interview of June 12, 1993.

28. Cohen papers, box 122, folder 10, Cohen to Feldman, Oct. 11, 1963.

29. KF, Cohen to RSS, Jan. 21, 1965.

30. Cohen papers, box 122, folder 10, Cohen to Warren, Jan. 3, 1964.

31. Cohen papers, box 122, folder 10, Cohen to John Gardner (HEW Secretary), Jan. 15, 1965.

32. Stafford Warren, Oral History (1966), John F. Kennedy Library Oral History Program, pp. 38–39.

33. KF, Cooke to RSS, Mar. 5, 1965.

34. Cohen papers, box 122, folder 10, Crozet Duplantier to Julius Cahn (an aide in the Vice President's office), June 7, 1965.

35. This meeting was alluded to in Duplantier to Cahn, June 7, 1965.

36. Cohen mentioned this new arrangement in a talk of May 19, 1965, Cohen papers, box 122, folder 12.

37. *NYT,* May 30, 1965, p. 25.

38. Cohen papers, box 122, folder 10. Cohen to the Secretary, June 2, 1965.

39. Cohen papers, box 122, folder 10, Moyers to John Macy, June 21, 1965.

40. Cohen papers, box 122, folder 10, Babington to Cohen, June 28, 1965.

41. Wallace Babington, interview of Aug. 18, 1993.

42. Cohen papers, box 122, folder 10, Babington to Cohen, May 6, 1965.

43. Fogarty papers, SF series, box 38, folder 409, RSS to Fogarty, May 17, 1966. Since EKS and Bob Cooke were both members, RSS must have been referring to some other list. Twenty-one of the members were appointed by "the President." Six served ex officio.

44. See, e.g., Patrick Doyle, Oral History (1968), John F. Kennedy Library Oral History Program, pp. 5, 9.

45. See KF, Beverly Rowan to EKS, report of Sept. 24, 1974.

46. KF, Montague to RSS, Jan. 3, 1978.

47. Boggs, "Medicaid Coverage of Residential Services," in *An Analysis of Medicaid's Intermediate Care Facility for the Mentally Retarded (ICF—MR) Program,* edited by K. Charles Lakin et al. (Minneapolis: University of Minnesota Center for Residential and Community Services, Sept. 1985), pp. I-1–31, quote p. I-4.

48. PCMR's official history comes, of course, to quite different conclusions and presents virtually none of the information above. See PCMR, *MR 76. Mental Retardation: Past and Present* (Washington, D.C.: GPO, Jan. 1977), pp. 127–33.

49. In 1977 a study of the Comptroller General indicted PCMR's "inability to mobilize and coordinate other agencies' efforts. . . ." *Report to the Congress by the Comptroller General of the United States. Returning the Mentally Disabled to the Community: Government Needs To Do More* (Washington, D.C.: GPO, pub. no. HRD-76–152, Jan. 1977), p. 34.

50. Nan Robertson, "A Diligent Senator: Edward Moore Kennedy," *NYT,* July 26, 1969, p. 11.

51. Quoted in an editorial, *NYT,* Nov. 6, 1987, p. 38.

52. In 1974 a feminist newspaper, *The Woman Activist,* gave his voting record a perfect 100 score of approval. See *NYT,* Jan. 20, 1974, p. 47. On the list of approval of the Americans for Democratic Action, EMK ranked first in the Senate, with 92 points out of 100. See *NYT,* Jan. 12, 1976. In 1973, e.g., Eastland asked EMK if the Kennedy Foundation could support a program for mentally retarded children at the Little Red Schoolhouse in Greenwood, Mississippi. KF, Eastland to EMK, May 8, 1973.

53. Burton Hersh, *The Education of Edward Kennedy: A Family Biography* (New York: Morrow, 1972), p. xi.

54. Morton Kondracke, "The Marathon Commences," *New Republic,* July 18, 1981, p. 25; the quote is Kondracke's, not Kennedy's.

55. George Will column, *Newsweek,* Mar. 16, 1987, p. 82.

56. *U.S. News & World Report,* Apr. 4, 1988, p. 20.

57. *NYT,* Oct. 26, 1971, p. 23.

58. KF, EKS to EMK, Jan. 14, 1977.

59. *Time,* Dec. 30, 1985, p. 12.

60. *Report to the Congress by the Comptroller General,* p. 52.

61. KF, Bowes to EKS, Apr. 27, 1966. The above facts were also derived from a copy of Dr. Bowes's curriculum vitae dated 1961, and from KF, Bowes to Mrs. Herman Jones, Aug. 19, 1968.

62. KF, Fred McDonald, executive director of the KF, to Bowes, Feb. 8, 1968.

63. He introduced S 3045 on Feb. 27, 1968, "A bill . . . to assure the continuation of various immunization programs. . . ." Copy attached to KF Trustees Report 1968.

64. KF, EMK to Lister Hill, c. July 11, 1968.

65. EMK, "The 'Shots' That Can Save a Million Lives," *Ladies' Home Journal,* Sept. 1969, pp. 62–63. The article does not mention Bowes. So extensively did Herb Kramer and the senator's own people edit Bowes's draft that Diane Sheahan, a secretary at the KF, feared Bowes would "hardly recognize it now." She sent him the revised text. KF, Sheahan to Bowes, June 19, 1969.

66. KF, McDonald to the Shrivers, July 7, 1966; the clippings were attached to the letter from Diane Sheahan to Walsh, Sept. 20, 1966.

67. See KF, John Throne to EMK, July 16, 1965; *Boston Globe,* Nov. 19, 1965; Throne to EKS, May 23, 1966, "MR Contributions of Two Senators."

68. *WP,* June 12, 1974, p. C2.

69. "100 Aides Help Senator to React Quickly to Events," *NYT,* May 6, 1979, p. 17. On the organization of this large staff see Richard E. Cohen, "The Kennedy Staff—Putting the Senator Ahead," *National Journal,* Dec. 3, 1977, pp. 1880–82. On the occasional effacing of the line, see "Senate Abuse of Payroll Rule Alleged, *NYT,* Feb. 16, 1975, p. 41.

70. Elizabeth Boggs, interview of July 15, 1993.

71. KF, Rowan to Cooke, Aug. 1, 1975.

72. In 1970, Diane Sheahan reminded him of the words he had used in 1968, regarding RFK's campaign. KF, Sheahan to Knight, Mar. 9, 1970.

73. KF, Knight to EMK, Jan. 10, 1968. EMK downgraded his commitment to accepting an award rather than giving a speech. See *Children Limited,* June, 1968, p. 2.

74. See, e.g., EKS to Sheldon Schneider, executive director of the Range Center in Chisholm, Minn., Oct. 22, 1973. EMK donated $5,000 in speaking fees he had garnered over the previous few months to the Range Center for a sheltered workshop.

75. KF, EKS to EMK, Dec. 13, 1977.

76. KF, EKS to Bob Kenny and Bob Howard; George Zitnay (the executive director of the foundation), Mar. 24, 1987.

77. KF, EKS to EMK, Oct. 12, 1978.

78. KF, undated note to Judy Toth, attached to a list of several hundred names.

79. Paraphrased by reporter Lucinda Franks, *NYT*, Dec. 31, 1975, p. 4.

80. The quote is from Peter Jenkins, "Candidate Sargent Shriver," *NYT Magazine*, Oct. 15, 1972, p. 100.

81. Jenkins's paraphrase in ibid., p. 100.

82. Robert A. Liston, *Sargent Shriver: A Candid Portrait* (New York: Farrar, Straus, 1964), pp. 154–55.

83. Frank Hayden, interview of Oct. 8, 1992.

84. The story quotes an unnamed source, *Time*, Aug. 14, 1972, p. 15.

85. "Sargent Shriver," *Ladies' Home Journal*, Apr. 1970, p. 154.

86. KF, RSS to Cohen, June 8, 1978.

87. KF, undated briefing book for "Sargent Shriver meeting," evidently Mar. 1981.

88. KF, Robert Cooke, memo to file, May 10, 1974.

89. KF, EKS to staff, Feb. 1, 1989.

90. KF, undated "Resumé Robert M. Montague, Jr. (Brigadier General, USA, Retired)."

91. For example, in 1966 the Vocational Rehabilitation Administration nearly terminated its support for the MR camping program because the Kennedy Foundation had missed a deadline. Only a personal appeal from EKS to Mary Switzer saved the program. See Eileen McCaffery Lapriola, "The Joseph P. Kennedy, Jr. Foundation and Its Role in Physical Education and Recreation for the Mentally Retarded" (M.A. thesis, University of Maryland, 1972), pp. 12–14.

92. Maris A. Vinovskis, "An 'Epidemic' of Adolescent Pregnancy? Some Historical Considerations," *Journal of Family History* 6 (1981), pp. 205–30; see also p. 216. Vinovskis was a staffer on the House Select Committee on Population in 1978.

93. KF, Montague to RSS, May 8, 1979.

94. See, e.g., KF, June 1, 1978, Cooke to Montague, requesting appointments on Capitol Hill for the following week "in the early afternoon for Mrs. Shriver and me."

95. KF, Cooke to RSS, July 31, 1980.

96. KF, Cooke to Kelley, July 26, 1968.

97. In Boggs's words. Elizabeth Boggs, interview of July 15, 1993.

98. See NARC, "Voices in Chorus" (1965), p. 17; Boggs private archive, "Report of governmental affairs committee to NARC," Jan. 22, 1966; PCMR, *MR 76. Mental Retardation: Past and Present*, p. 55.

99. Elizabeth Boggs, interview of July 15, 1993.

100. According to Boggs, the notion of developmental disabilities dated from the "introduction of the Adult Disabled Child Benefits Program under Social Security in 1957. This entitled adults to receive benefits on the basis of their

parents' record of working rather than their own. A majority of the adults who qualified under that legislation had MR rather than physical disabilities." Elizabeth Boggs, Oral History (1986), vol. 4, p. 7.

101. Elizabeth Boggs, "Federal Legislation 1966–1971," in *Mental Retardation: An Annual Review,* vol. 4, edited by Joseph Wortis (New York: Grune and Stratton, 1971), pp. 165–206, data on p. 187.

102. Ibid., p. 186.

103. For an overview see E. Clark Ross, "Development of Constituencies and Their Organizations," in *Changing Government Policies for the Mentally Disabled,* edited by Joseph J. Bevilacqua (Cambridge, Mass.: Ballinger, 1981), pp. 101–57, esp. pp. 111–15. Just as Pearl Buck's *The Child Who Never Grew* or Dale Evans's *Angel Unaware* were the charter documents of the MR movement, Mary Louise Hart Burton's *Your Child or Mine: The Story of the Cerebral-Palsied Child* (New York: Coward-McCann, 1949) was the foundation stone of the CP movement.

104. Bevilacqua, *Changing Government Policies,* p. 149; also, private communication from Boggs.

105. Boggs private archive, Boggs to Sampson, June 7, 1952.

106. See PCMR, *MR 76. Mental Retardation: Past and Present,* pp. 69–72.

107. Boggs private archive. See William Geer to Patria Winalski at HEW, Nov. 19, 1964.

108. Schnibbe coolly wrote to Mike Feldman, as funding for the Kennedy MR legislation seemed about to be gutted in committee, "Mike, I'm in touch with the State Directors and their Governors on this. If there's any help you need from your end let me know." KL, Feldman papers, box 13, note attached to Cohen to Feldman, July 22, 1963.

109. On these organizational arrangements see Boggs, *Mental Retardation,* vol. 4, p. 186.

110. KL, Michael Begab, Oral History (1968), p. 19.

111. Elizabeth Boggs, Oral History (1986), vol. 4, p. 16.

112. Ibid., pp. 18–19. An added incentive in adopting "DD" was that it let the parents' groups escape the clutch of the psychiatrists, especially the "dynamic" kind. MR, it could be argued, was a social "developmental" problem, not a medical one, and a medical model for its management was inappropriate. Pp. 5–9.

113. In 1966 NARC had hired Gettings as governmental affairs analyst; in 1968 he went to PCMR. See Ross, "Development of Constituencies," p. 149.

114. The following account is based on Boggs, *Mental Retardation,* vol. 4, pp. 187–200, and on Elizabeth Boggs, Oral History (1986), vol. 5, pp. 23–42.

115. Elizabeth Boggs, interview of July 15, 1993.

116. Ibid.

117. Ibid.

118. Elizabeth Boggs, Oral History (1986), vol. 5, pp. 3–10.

119. *84 Stat. U.S.C., 91st Congress, 2nd Session, 1970–71* (Washington, D.C.: GPO, 1971), pp. 1316–27 for text of PL 91–517, definition of DD on p. 1325.

120. Boggs interview in *Families* (Spring) 1993, p. 13.

121. KF, Press release from the office of EMK, Oct. 14, 1970, "Remarks. . . . Dedication of Eunice Kennedy Shriver Center," p. 2.

122. On these legislative details see *CQA* 1970, pp. 595–97, 1174. The bill, S 2846, became PL 91–517.

123. Boggs, *Mental Retardation,* vol. 4, p. 188.

124. These figures from David Braddock, "Federal Assistance for Mental Retardation and Developmental Disabilities II: The Modern Era," *Mental Retardation* 24 (1986), pp. 209–18, data p. 216.

125. On the history of federal programs and federal spending see David Braddock's indispensable *Federal Policy toward Mental Retardation and Developmental Disabilities* (Baltimore: Brookes, 1987). For trends in services, income maintenance, research, etc., over the years 1950–1985, see p. 178.

126. Office of EMK, "Remarks. . . . Tenth Anniversary Dinner, Disability Rights Education and Defense Fund, San Francisco, Nov. 3, 1989," p. 3.

Chapter Seven

1. KF, Dick Sargent to EKS, May 10, 1978.

2. Sally Quinn, "Olympic-Sized Problems," *WP,* Mar. 8, 1975, D1.

3. "East Meets West," *WP,* Mar. 10, 1975, B1.

4. KF, EKS to David Hartman, Dec. 11, 1980.

5. Rose Kennedy, *Times to Remember* (New York: Bantam, 1974), pp. 198–202, quote p. 198.

6. KF, p. 13 of the undated manuscript of EKS's contribution to *The Fruitful Bough: A Tribute to Joseph P. Kennedy,* edited by Edward M. Kennedy (n.p., 1965). This information was not included in the published version.

7. KL, MS 79–2, box 8, JPK to EKS, Apr. 4, 1960.

8. Fogarty papers, SpF 65, folder 765, staff memo to Fogarty of July 3, 1961.

9. KF, XXX to RSS, May 31, 1979.

10. Jeannette Smyth, "Coast to Coast Contrast," *WP,* Mar. 10, 1975, B1.

11. KF, RSS to the Celebrity X's, June 22, 1987.

12. KF, RSS to Henry Fonda, June 23, 1980.

13. "The Founding Mother," *WP,* July 21, 1980, pp. B1.

14. KF, EKS to Ross, Dec. 19, 1988; EKS to Bobby Shriver, Dec. 21, 1988.

15. KF, Bobby Shriver to EKS, undated memo, with cover slip dated "7 May" (1984).

16. KF, see EKS to JFK Jr. thanking him for his role, Apr. 15, 1987.

17. In 1992 A&M Records released "A Very Special Christmas 2," co-produced by the Iovines and Bobby Shriver.

18. Details on the album's history from *NYT,* Dec. 13, 1987, p. 108.

19. *Billboard,* April 2, 1988, p. 4.

20. KF, Bobby Shriver to members of the family, Nov. 29, 1988.

21. Special Olympics, "Board of Directors Handbook and Profiles," 1993, p. 23.

22. KF, RSS to Neil Diamond, Dec. 17, 1982.

23. AAHPERD archives, Joey Giardello, statement at press conference on National Fitness Program for the Mentally Retarded, June 17, 1965.

24. Eileen McCaffery Lapriola, "The Joseph P. Kennedy, Jr. Foundation and Its Role in Physical Education and Recreation for the Mentally Retarded," University of Maryland, M.A. thesis, 1972, p. 255.

25. "Presidential Kin and Friends Lead Crowd to 'Mad World' Premiere," *NYT*, Nov. 18, 1963, p. 36.

26. *WP*, Dec. 11, 1974.

27. *WP*, Mar. 8, 1975, p. D1.

28. See KF, Montague to EKS, Dec. 13, 1988, complaining of Kennedy family members' interference with the "Presidential Premiere" of the movie "Twins."

29. *WP*, Mar. 10, 1975, p. B1.

30. "East Meets West," ibid., p. B1.

31. *Women's Wear Daily*, Mar. 11, 1975. See also *New York* magazine, Mar. 24, 1975, pp. 36f.

32. *WP*, Mar. 10, 1975, p. B1.

33. *NYT*, Dec. 12, 1978, p. 10

34. *Newsweek*, May 31, 1982, p. 64. See also Vincent Canby's review, *NYT*, June 11, 1982, p. C14.

35. KF, Bobby Shriver to EKS, Apr. 19, 1984.

36. KF, EKS to Spielberg, Aug. 10, 1982.

37. KF, Bobby Shriver to Spielberg, Nov. 8, 1982.

38. KF, Montague to "the record," Dec. 19, 1983.

39. KF, Bobby Shriver to EKS, Apr. 1, 1984.

40. KF, Bobby Shriver to EKS, Apr. 19, 1984.

41. Ibid.

42. KF, agenda for meeting, July 30, 1984

43. KF, see EKS to Stuart Upson, Chairman of Dancer, Fitzgerald and Sample, Aug. 3, 1984.

44. Dougherty, "Advertising," *NYT*, May 23, 1985.

45. KF, EKS to Joe Pytka, Oct. 8, 1985.

46. KF, EKS to Spielberg, May 19, 1986.

47. KF, EKS to Spielberg, Aug. 6, 1986; Susan Trembly, an official of Spielberg's production company Amblin Entertainment, to EKS, Sept. 15, 1986.

48. KF, EKS to Robert Blattner, the president of MCA Home Video, Apr. 25, 1989.

49. KF, EKS to Robert Lester, Board of Directors, New Hampshire Special Olympics International (SOI), June 18, 1986.

50. KF, Bankhead to EKS, Apr. 28, 1989.

51. KF, EKS, "Random Thoughts re South Carolina Special Olympics Games," May 16, 1978, pp. 1–2.

52. KF, EKS speech for chapter directors' conference, Aug. 18, 1980, p. 4.

53. KF, EKS memo to Montague and Kramer, Aug. 13, 1980, on the inadequacies of an earlier draft of the speech.

54. KF, EKS speech, Aug. 18, 1980, p. 4.

55. KF, Montague to Bankhead, Aug. 16, 1982. Montague was evidently conveying EKS's instructions.

56. KF, EKS memo to file, July 7, 1988.

57. Ibid.

58. KF, Holly's mother to SOI, Apr. 21, 1989.

59. *Baltimore Sun,* June 8, 1989.

60. Kramer was interviewed by a university student, Janice M. Deakin, for her undergraduate thesis, "A Study of the Special Olympics Movement in the United States and Canada," B.A. thesis, Department of Physical and Health Education, Queen's University, Kingston, Ontario, March, 1980, pp. 29–30.

61. KF, "Jan" to Bobby Shriver, Apr. 30, 1979.

62. KF, EKS to Maria Shriver, Sept. 27, 1988.

63. Mentioned in EKS speech to Association of Physical Fitness Centers meeting, Las Vegas, June 4, 1980, p. 8.

64. KF, EKS to Jacqueline Onassis, Aug. 22, 1986.

65. Jim Murray, sports column, *Los Angeles Times,* Aug. 18, 1972. "Tears were running down my face so hard . . . ," mentioned in George Will column, *WP,* Aug. 13, 1975, p. A13.

66. G. Lawrence Rarick, "Adult Reactions to the Special Olympics," in *Psychological Perspectives in Youth Sports,* edited by Frank L. Smoll and Ronald E. Smith (New York: Wiley, 1978), pp. 229–47, data p. 239.

67. Tovah Klein et al., "Special Olympics: An Evaluation by Professionals and Parents," *Mental Retardation* 31 (1993), pp. 15–23, data p. 19.

68. KF, Mrs. M. to the Shrivers, Feb. 19, 1988.

69. James Haskins, *A New Kind of Joy: The Story of Special Olympics* (New York: Doubleday, 1976), pp. 29–30.

70. KF, EKS to "chapter executives/board chairmen," May 25, 1989.

71. "The Graduation of Christi Todd," *Down Syndrome News,* Oct. 1990, p. 109.

Chapter Eight

1. Anonymous source.

2. John Throne, interview of Mar. 12, 1993.

3. KF, EKS to Anthony Shriver, June 19, 1980.

4. KF, EKS to Anthony Shriver, June 23, 1980.

5. *Baltimore Sun,* June 8, 1989.

6. KF, EKS telegram to Bobby Shriver, Mar. 3, 1980.

7. KF, EKS to RSS et al., Sept. 22, 1983.

8. See, e.g., EKS's apologetic memo of Feb. 27, 1978 to RSS, Cooke, and Montague on the subject of EMK's growing concerns about the Kennedy Institute of Ethics.

9. KF, Jean Smith to RSS, Nov. 24, 1981. Of $478,000 in the foundation's budget for bioethics programs in 1979, $375,000 went to the Kennedy Institute of Ethics at Georgetown. Trustees Meeting 1979, subsection "1979 programs."

10. KF, EKS to RSS et al., Sept. 28, 1983.

11. KF, RSS to Cooke, Dec. 17, 1980. After pointing out that the Kennedy Foundation trustees (the family) had never questioned any of Eunice's decisions with respect to programs, salaries, or expenditures, RSS said, "I doubt that statement could be made with respect to any other foundation executive in America."

12. The agenda of the special meeting of the four siblings on April 9, 1984, mentions, among other possible alternatives to continuing the foundation's support of mental retardation, "restoration of historic Cape Cod house." KF, agenda dated Apr. 9, 1984.

13. KF, EKS to RSS et al., Sept. 22, 1983.

14. KF, Bobby Shriver to EKS et al., Oct. 4, 1983.

15. Ibid.

16. The will, dated Dec. 30, 1955, is on file at the Circuit Court of West Palm Beach.

17. KF, EKS to "The Trustees," Dec. 28, 1983.

18. KF, from EMK, Patricia K. Lawford, and Jean K. Smith to "the Trustees," Jan. 25, 1984. At this point the only other trustee was EKS, James Fayne having died in 1972.

19. Ibid.

20. Nigel Hamilton, *JFK: Reckless Youth* (New York: Random House, 1992).

21. In fairness to Eunice, it must be said that Very Special Arts rebuffed the author's efforts to gather information on its work.

22. KF, "Proposed Agenda, Special Meeting of the Trustees," Apr. 9, 1984.

23. KF, memo of Jan. 25, 1984.

24. See *Newsweek*, May 7, 1984, pp. 50–57, for an example of the widespread coverage David Kennedy's death received.

25. KF, EKS to RSS et al., Sept. 28, 1983.

26. KF, EKS, "Remarks," Special Olympics Chapter Directors Conference, Smugglers' Notch, Vermont, Aug. 18, 1980, p. 12.

Index